Earle V. Pierce #5738

ROBERT G. LEE

A Chosen Vessel

by
E. SCHUYLER ENGLISH, Litt. D.

"If our hearts are not 25,000 miles in circumference, they are too small. If our arms do not embrace the whole world, they are too short," said Dr. Lee. It is that breadth of spirit which Dr. English has caught in this pen-portrait of the under-privileged share-cropper lad who became a pulpiteer famous the world around.

Letters written by Dr. Lee and to him, telegrams, gleanings from the Lee "scrap-books," hitherto hidden incidents of his family life—these bring this biography close to experience. Producing an aware-ness not only of the man but of his mes-sage, the biographer has wisely included in his account Dr. Lee's peerless sermon "Pay Day—Some Day."

With that steadiness of purpose which distinguishes the Christian biographer, Dr. English declares: "If, upon laying aside this volume, the reader should exclaim, 'What a great man is Lee!' we have utterly failed in our purpose. For the life-story of Robert G. Lee is a record of the greatness of our God and an example of what He can and will do through one who is obedient to His Word, surrendered to Him, and willing and prepared to be an instru-ment to His hand . . . The life-story of Robert G. Lee serves as a challenge." It is in this spirit that Dr. English pays tribute to the man whom God made great.

Enthusiastically Recommended . . .

"This book will do more to quicken the steps of the weary in soul-winning, to stimulate the preaching of the messenger of God in the pulpit, and to encourage faint hearts in de-nouncing sin, holding up a Saviour, and pro-claiming a great Gospel than any other book I have read or heard of in my day and gen-eration."—DR. PORTER M. BAILES, *Pastor of the great First Baptist Church, Tyler, Texas.*

"The perusal of this gripping life-story has stirred my heart to its depths and quickened my admiration, both for the author and his hero."—DR. H. A. Ironside, *former Pastor Moody Memorial Church, Chicago.*

"This book is, like the great preacher him-self, irresistably appealing."—DR W. A. CRIS-WELL, *Pastor of the First Baptist Church, Dallas, Texas.*

"He has exhausted the material for the life of his subject from earliest childhood to his now international fame, and all this he has sympathetically appropriated and interpreted in a book that on every page reveals a transparent, smooth and effective style."—WILBUR M. SMITH, *Professor, Fuller Theological Seminary.*

". . . a full-length portrait drawn with strong and striking lines by one who is, himself, a trained artist in the business of biography."—DR. M. E. DODD, *Pastor First Baptist Church, Shreveport, Louisianna.*

"A tale that grips your heart and your head, puts tears in your eyes and a smile on your lips, and conviction in your soul that God still reigns . . . a gripping and dramatic biography of one of God's great servants."—DR DUKE K. McCALL, *Executive Secretary of the Southern Baptist Convention.*

ROBERT G. LEE

A Chosen Vessel

TITLES BY THE AUTHOR

BIOGRAPHICAL

By Life and By Death (Excerpts and Lessons from the Diary of John C. Stam of China)

H. A. Ironside—Ordained of the Lord

Robert G. Lee—A Chosen Vessel

EXPOSITORY

Studies in the Gospel According to Matthew

The Life and Letters of St. Peter

Studies in the Gospel According to Mark

Studies in the Epistle to the Colossians

APOLOGETICAL

Things Surely To Be Believed

BOOKLETS

This Is the Life

The Shifting of the Scenes

The Two Witnesses

Did Christ Descend into Hades?

Robert Greene Lee

ROBERT G. LEE

A Chosen Vessel

"... for he is a chosen vessel unto Me,
to bear My name before the Gentiles,
and kings, and the children of Israel"

Acts 9:15

by

E. SCHUYLER ENGLISH, LITT.D.

Editor, Our Hope
Author, *H. A. Ironside*, Ordained of the Lord

ZONDERVAN PUBLISHING HOUSE
Grand Rapids 2, Michigan

To

ROBERT G. LEE

PREACHER OF RIGHTEOUSNESS

SHEPHERD OF THE SHEEP

VESSEL UNTO HONOR

"A BELOVED BROTHER AND

FAITHFUL MINISTER IN THE LORD"

THIS BOOK IS DEDICATED

WITH CHRISTIAN AFFECTION

PREFACE

In the American way of life, "from rags to riches" is not an uncommon experience. There are, however, some men whose struggles and triumphs are so notable, so colorful, so romantic that the telling of them presents truth that is stranger than fiction. Abraham Lincoln, in his rise from the log cabin to the White House, was such a man. Robert Greene Lee, the share-cropper boy of South Carolina, who has become the outstanding preacher-orator of the South and the leader of more than 6,000,000 Baptists, is another. There is as much romance in the life-story of Robert G. Lee as will be found in the tales of Jules Verne or Alexandre Dumas.

It is not surprising, therefore, that a publisher should want to issue a Lee biography, for it was inevitable that it should be written. Actually, several persons have, during the past decade, approached Dr. Lee for his permission to produce it. But he could never give his consent to having his life-story written until P. J. and B. D. Zondervan, in two conferences, presented the appeal in such a way as to make Dr. Lee realize that the account of his life, and God's working in it, must surely prove an inspiration to young men and women to give themselves wholly to the Lord and to let no obstacles deter them from serving Him and giving Him their best.

The author is honored to have been appointed by

9

the publishers to prepare this biography. As God chose Robert G. Lee, putting His hand upon the poor farmer of South Carolina and fashioning him, inspite of hardships, lack of encouragement, and handicaps of many kinds, into a vessel unto His own honor, to proclaim Christ to multitudes of high and low estate, so, we trust, God placed His hand upon the author to make that life-story known. As it was in the case of the biographee, who experienced some hesitancy before he could give full consent to having his biography written, so it was that the biographer felt uncertainty, at first, about entering upon an engagement as great and exacting as the writing of the biography must be. However, after conferences with the Zondervan brothers and Dr. Lee, and following months of prayer on the part of all four of us as we sought the Lord's will in the matter, in due course the author, aware of God's evident approval of Dr. Lee's ministry, conscious of the good that this tale might do in the lives of young people, and impressed by a verse of Scripture that he could not get out of his mind, namely, "Withhold not good from them to whom it is due, when it is in the power of thine hand to do it" (Prov. 3: 27), the author felt impelled to undertake the assignment.

From the beginning, Dr. Lee has made it clear that it was not his desire that the story of his life be written in order to extol him, Christ alone being worthy of praise, exaltation, and glory. The very first letter that he wrote to the author, following the decision as to the writing of the book, contains these words: "As God knows my heart and life, I want this biography to be an inspiration to poor boys and girls with little advantage—to plant their feet on higher ground—and so work and live that Christ shall be glorified in them as the sun is glorified in the flowers."

This volume could never have been completed apart from the gracious attitude of the biographee, who, without question or reserve, turned over everything in his files for the author's perusal. From the beginning to the end Dr. Lee has been courtesy, and patience itself, and has been helpful in every possible way. There are others who have had a part in the work, too, not the least of these being the publishers, who have co-operated splendidly and shown the utmost forbearance during unpredictable delays. To all of these friends the author owes deepest gratitude, and he hereby happily acknowledges it.

It is the author's sincere desire and earnest prayer that the true story told in these pages will point its readers, not to a man, but to the Lord Jesus Christ. The servant of the Lord herein portrayed is a godly man, a devoted pastor, and a gifted preacher of the Word, but he himself will be the first to confess that he is a sinner saved by grace and that whatever abilities, favors, and blessings have been his are from above. It is, then, with the hope that Christ will be magnified to every reader of this book, and that His power to work miracles in the lives of His own will be seen, that this biography is presented, in the Name of our Lord Jesus Christ.

E. SCHUYLER ENGLISH

Skytop, Pa.
August, 1949

TABLE OF CONTENTS

PART I
PREACHER-BOY

PREAMBLE 1

CHAPTER I

Birth and childhood—A humble beginning in a log cabin
—Share-cropper's circumstances—The order and full names
of the Lee children—Life in the old Springs' mansion—
Sunday, day of rest, and "extras."

CHAPTER II

Boyhood days—Sporadic grade schooling—Swimming with
Catawba Indians—Other diversions—Plow-boy at nine—
Conversion at twelve.

CHAPTER III

Young manhood and great dreams—Earning money for
Latin lessons—The pine tree, place of prayer—Words and
books—First public speech—Discouragements as to ill-
nesses—Influence of Dr. E. M. Poteat.

CHAPTER IV

Stepping stones to an education—Leaving home—New
Orleans—Evidence of God's watchful care—Panama—Letters
to mother—Life in a strange land.

CHAPTER V

Another sacrifice—Entering Furman Fitting School—Odd
jobs—Introduction to the future Mrs. Lee—Furman
University—School activities—Preaching begins—Winning
the oratorical contest.

CHAPTER VI

Principal of a grade school—Courtship and marriage—Early
ministries—At Tulane University—Disappointment and
discouragement—Back to the High Calling.

Contents

Contents

Contents

CHAPTER XVI

CHAPTER XVII

Struggles and accomplishments at Bellevue—Boom years, but no boom in financial status—Building a new auditorium—Excerpts from old church minutes—"Barking up a tree where there never has been a possum"—The preacher makes many gifts to his beloved church—Most difficult period—Most glorious day—Stubs of a checkbook—Unbelievable love for his people—A larger vision for a larger ministry.

CHAPTER XVIII

A heart and mind that embrace the world—A Presbyterian deacon writes of a Baptist preacher—The radio—An unforgettable scene in a lobby—Answering the call of distress from small churches—Gifts to colleges and seminaries—A bird's-eye view of a busy man's engagement book—"Have you prayed today?"—Honors bestowed—Bearing Christ's Name before rulers—Invitations and calls—Preaching to college students.

CHAPTER IXX

The one-time country boy filling the pulpit of the great —Before the hosts of Southern Baptists—Preaching in Chicago's Coliseum—Elected to the highest honor that Southern Baptists can bestow—Fort Mill, S. C., boasts of her sons—Letters of love and esteem—"A parable in black and white, written in red"—"One man's influence"—Reelected with unsurpassed unanimity—Another myriad of commendatory letters—Dr. John W. Bradbury expresses an opinion—"Highest Hour."

CONCLUSION

What God hath wrought—A challenge to youth—A secret that all can share—Looking forward to the unfinished task—Bula G. visits Memory Lane.

LIST OF ILLUSTRATIONS

List of Illustrations

Part I
PREACHER-BOY

Preamble
—1—
A SHINING SWORD

People who say, "The hotter it is, the better I like it," would have been perfectly happy in Miami on May 18, 1946. It was one of those scorching, humid days that comes to Florida in May, as if to warn all to flee to the north and to the hills, for summer is drawing nigh.

The Southern Baptist Convention of 1946 was moving toward its close. It was Saturday noon. Meetings had been going on all morning in the auditorium that seats about 3,500 people, less than half the number registered at the convention. The atmosphere during the forenoon had been that of a summer camp-meeting. Outside the auditorium, vendors of peanuts and popcorn shouted their wares. "IIot dog" stands peddled their savory, if indigestible, offerings. The lobby of the convention hall issued a constant hum of voices, as small groups met to discuss church interests, or other matters far removed from convention business. Within the auditorium, delegates came and went as they pleased during the morning sessions.

But as the noon hour approached, the seats began to be filled, so that well before the clock struck twelve times, the auditorium was packed to capacity, with even the standing room over-crowded. The lobby was also full, and in a few minutes time, the bleacher seats outside were taken, while hundreds of people sat upon the ground, or leaned against the wall of the building, or just stood. Hardly a delegate of the eight thousand that were registered was absent as promptly at noon, Dr. Pat Neff, ex-Governor of Texas and President of the Convention, introduced the speaker in a most gracious fashion, concluding his presentation with these words: "Many of our preachers have bright swords, and they use them for the Lord. But the sword of Dr. Robert G. Lee is the brightest of them all."

A sudden silence enshrouded the auditorium, the lobby, and the grounds outside. Commotion ceased and stillness reigned, the silence being broken by the sound of one voice only—that of Dr. Lee. It was carried to the outside audience by amplification. The vendors ceased promoting their tidbits. Rustling programs and booklets were laid aside, and the steaming heat was forgotten as the audience, almost in unison, leaned forward eagerly amid the flutter of many fans, so as not to miss a single word. Here was oratory of a high order, but oratory that drew its power from the Spirit of God. Outside, a mother, quieting a restless little boy, was heard to whisper: "Be quiet, child, and listen to Dr. Lee. He is the greatest preacher in the world, and when you are a grown man I want you to be able to say: 'I heard Dr. Robert G. Lee.' "

The subject of the message is not important for the purpose of this narrative. Its theme was the theme of all of Robert Lee's messages: the matchless name, "Jesus." The development of that theme

brought into view the Person and work of the divine
Christ. And its aim was, as is always the case with
Dr. Lee's messages, to bring his hearers to the place
of decision—for the unsaved to receive the Lord
Jesus Christ as Saviour; and for Christians to walk
in obedience to Him.

As the preacher continued his sermon on that hot
May day in Miami, all the changes of emotion were
rung within the vast throng. Pathos, humor, and dead
seriousness were intermingled, but never for a moment was the message of the Lord for those people
lost sight of, nor its ultimate aim—that they should
dedicate themselves to Him. For one hour Dr. Lee
spoke, and as he came to his conclusion, multitudes
of men, as well as women, were using their hand-
kerchiefs to dry tears from their eyes now, rather
than the perspiration from their faces. Finally, the
speaker asked for a show of hands on the part of
all who would pledge themselves anew to a re-
dedication of their lives to the Saviour, with the
determination, in the Spirit's power, "always
[to be] bearing about in the body the dying of the
Lord Jesus, that the life also of Jesus might be made
manifest in our body" (II Cor. 4:10). In so far as
could be determined by those on the platform, nearly every hand in the visible audience was raised. The
sword of Dr. Lee shown brightly in that hour, for
it was wielded in dependence upon the Holy Spirit
and in His power.

This was a high day in the ministry of Robert
G. Lee, but not the only one, nor the highest. And
Dr. Lee is more than an orator, more than a preacher;

he is a pastor, an organizer, and a builder. His name must be coupled with those of Charles Haddon Spurgeon, of London; Russell H. Conwell, of Philadelphia; and George W. Truett, of Dallas, as Baptist pastors who have seen their churches grow, during their own ministry, from comparatively moderate sized memberships to seven or eight thousand.

What is the secret of this numerical success? Above that in importance, what is behind the spiritual success of this man? The record that follows will, we believe, reveal what it is that makes Robert G. Lee eloquent and his ministry for God flourish. More than that, it will demonstrate the power of God through an instrument willing to be used by Him for His glory, through the Lord Jesus Christ.

Chapter I

SO LITTLE OF HEAVEN

Birth and Childhood

On a frosty autumn morning in a three-room log cabin in York County, South Carolina, in the year 1886, the fifth child was born to David Ayers Lee and Sarah Bennett Lee, share-croppers. The date was November eleventh, and the time four o'clock. While Dr. Kell attended to the mother after her fifth journey into the land of motherhood, and urged her to "rest now," old "Mam" Lindy, beloved Negro nurse and midwife, held the little baby boy in her black arms, and almost dancing about in the small room that was warmed and faintly illuminated by a flickering fire, ejaculated: "Praise Gawd! Glory be! The good Lawd done sont a preacher to dis here house. Yas, sah! Yas, ma'am! Dat's what He's done gone and done." Thus was Robert Greene Lee introduced to the world.

It has been said the hardship among white folks of the South has not been seen until one has beheld the circumstances of the share-croppers. Even they are rich, as a class, compared with their kind in South Carolina. The bleak hills and gully lands of York County have naught to give but hard work and a grim "living." And when it is remembered that

25

a share-cropper is a tenant farmer, who leases the ground by tilling the soil and sharing its increase half and half with the owner of the land, it can be understood how scant his earnings must be, and the undisguised poverty of the home, in which Robert Greene Lee first saw the breaking light of a winter's dawn.

A humble beginning is not a detriment to success in the American way of life. Some of the most illustrious figures in the history of this land were nursed as babes and nurtured as children in lowly cabins of the plains, or mountains, or farm lands, and very early learned the discipline of poverty. It is no great handicap to a strong and determined will to have been fostered in an environment of calloused hands and aching backs and heavy feet, where the sun seems always to rise too soon and to set too late, and where, for months on end, the waking hours know little except the splitting of rails, the sawing of wood, the plowing of fields, the pulling of fodder and stumps, the digging of ditches, the harnessing of mules, the cleaning of stables, and the clearing of new ground. It is possible to rise above the confining and discouraging atmosphere of hardships and privation and want of opportunity, but this ascent is reserved for those who are wise, resourceful, strong, and determined.

David Lee, and his wife, Sarah Elizabeth, inherited no material wealth from their parents. Poor of purse, indeed, was this man who took to himself this woman as wife and future mother of his children.

After the couple had taken their wedding vows in
the poorly furnished home of a neighbor, and after
the bridegroom paid the preacher the customary
two dollars, there was only fifty cents left. This was
spent at a little "cross roads" store for a tucking
comb for the bride's hair. In their honeymoon hut
they ate their first breakfast as husband and wife off
the top of a trunk, having no table. Neither did
Dave and Sally Lee have any property to offer their
children in later years, but only "the wisdom that is
from above [which] is first pure, then peaceable,
gentle, and easy to be intreated, full of mercy and
good fruits, without partiality, and without hy-
pocrisy" (Jas. 3:17). And it should be added, in
fidelity to truth, that a portion of that citation might
better be omitted in the case of David Lee, who, to
his children, seemed neither gentle, except on occasion, nor easy to be entreated. He was a hard
taskmaster, and a severe one. His word was law in
the home. Yet these qualities in the father may have
been more responsible than any trait that he possessed, other than his faith in God and love for His
Word, for the development of the characters of his
children.

The three-room cabin, not far from Fort Mill and
located in what is known as the Fork Section, between the Catawba River and Sugar Creek, was
home. About 200 yards away stood the big two-story
house of Mr. Frank Massey, from whom David Lee
rented his place on half-shares. He raised cotton,
wheat, corn, and watermelons, and had a garden.

The half share that Lee marketed, at a time when
cotton was between four and five cents a pound,
brought him an annual income of around $250.00, in
good years. The return from the other crops was
negligible, perhaps $50.00 all told.

Father Lee and Mother Lee, brothers and sisters,*
had a great family affection blended together to make
life tolerably happy, if terribly hard and almost
unbelievably lacking in any sort of luxury. There
were at this time older brothers, Jim, Ben, and
Frank, and a younger one, Tom, three years Bob's
junior; and there was sister Fanny, the second oldest
of the children. Even for the youngest, chores and
errands were abundant and work in the field was
hard. But there were also occasional hours when the
pastimes of youngsters engaged them, as when they
walked to the Catawba River or Sugar Creek or
smaller streams and idled on their banks or refreshed themselves in their waters. At the farm the
scent of honeysuckle hedges wafted to them, and
also the fragrance of magnolia blossoms from across
the way. In the early spring the daffodils pirouetted
in the sun. When the winds blew across the fields,
the pine trees hummed their deep melodies, while on
still days the beautiful songs of the mocking-birds

---

* The order and full names of the Lee children were: James Hampton
Lee, born October 11, 1876; Frances Lavonia Lee, born June 12, 1878;
Benjamin Massey Lee, born November 10, 1880; David Franklin Lee, born
November 24, 1884; Robert Greene Lee, born November 11, 1886;
Thomas Kirkpatrick Lee, born June 18, 1889; and two others, Samuel
Ayers Lee, born October 13, 1893, who was sometimes called "the little
aristocrat" because he first saw the light of day at the palatial Eli
Springs home; and Sarah Ella Fair Lee, known as "Fairy," who was born
on August 10, 1895, at the farm that "Dad" Lee purchased.

brought lightest and sweetest music to vie with the
play of the sunbeams as to which would bestow the
more abundant cheer. And from far across the
Catawba could be heard the shrill whistles of trains
carrying people to distant places still unknown to
Bobby Lee. Even in childhood, however, the longing
to venture out into the world developed within his
breast.

The recollections of the first five years of life are
many, and vividly remembered even now. Days
beginning before the light of the morn. Nights that
started when the sun sank across the fields. Bedtime right after supper so as to be ready to arise
by the light of a kerosene lamp. Father working—
plowing, repairing, hoeing, shoveling, chopping, and
slaughtering. Mother working—cooking, washing, tai-
loring, feeding the chickens, gathering vegetables,
and caring for the babies. Wonderful Sundays—sleeping an hour longer, the buggy ride to church, music,
walks through the woods and on the hills, and
"special" dinners when the preacher and his wife, or
some neighbor, would come over after morning
worship.

One day something happened that made Bobby
Lee imagine, as he lay upon his bed at night gazing
up at the stars through the window, that he was
already in Heaven, or nearly there. For "Dad" Lee
was employed by wealthy Mr. Eli Springs, of
Charlotte, North Carolina, to act as general manager
of the Springs' farm near Fort Mill, at a salary of
$30.00 per month. The house to which the Lee family

moved—only a few miles distant from the log cabin*
—was an old *ante bellum* mansion of majestic colonial
dignity and great architectural beauty. It was built
mostly by supervised slave labor, in 1804, and was
a spacious dwelling place, having eighteen rooms,
with three additional enclosures in the attic. Mr.
Springs reserved two rooms and the library for himself and occasionally visited the farm, but there was
still ample accommodation for the Lee family which
here grew to nine in number, as Sam was born
here.**

Stately white columns acted as sentinels outside,
before the front door; and within, in a great hall, was
a winding staircase that spoke of the prosperous days
and lively gaity of yesteryear, when the South was
rich, imperious, and young. This house of beauty
struck awe into the hearts of children who had been
used only to the bare walls and restricted quarters
of a log cabin. And in the cellar were old rooms, some
said to have been used for the punishment of
recalcitrant slaves, and some to shelter the house
servants. The farm-land stretched east and west for
800 acres that seemed that many miles to the hands
and feet that guided and followed the plows.

At the Springs' house, toil, sometimes bordering
on drudgery, began in earnest for young Robert. It
had been rather fun back at the cabin, where there
was no well in the yard, to help carry the water

---

* The little log cabin still stands in the Fork Section. For awhile it
was used as a "church meeting house." In the very room where
Robert Lee's birth cries were first heard, the tears of new-born souls have
fallen. Three years ago, Lee himself preached in the very room where
he was born.
** Refer to footnote on page 28.

from a spring under a nearby hill. But at the new
farm there was a sort of transition into man's estate.
The task ceased to be a novelty and matured into
tedious labor. From the age of six to eight the lad
carried water in earnest to all the farm hands,
dreading the displeasure of his father at any in-
dication of "lazying around." Sometimes he wished
that they would not drink so much water. Then, other
work fell to his hands also. He helped his mother
around the house. He set rat traps, killed snakes—
and, of course, went swimming. He fed nux vomica
to the chickens to kill the hawks, a procedure that
brother Tom likened to shutting the barn door "after
ye mule was gone." He picked cotton until his fingers
were sore and he thought he could never stand erect
again, and began to learn to do some of the manifold
and endless tasks that fall to the lot of the dirt
farmer—how to follow a furrow, milk a cow, make a
rail fence, dig sassafras sprouts, slaughter a hog, and
ride a stubborn mule. Every day, Sunday always
excepted, began at 4 a.m., when it was so dark the
boys had to dress "by feel." There were no complaints
when bedtime came in that household, so tired
they all were; and it seemed to Bobby that his head
had barely rested on the pillow a minute when he
would be routed out for another day's work.

Many memories of childhood days at the "mansion"
still linger as fresh as if they happened yesterday,
frightening memories and happy ones that bring
tears to the eyes and laughter to the throat alter-
nately. There was the time, when, at seven years of
age, Bob Lee crawled under the barn, erected by

slaves before the Civil War, to gather eggs from a
hen's nest, only to be met by the ominous sound of
two rattlesnakes that had squirmed under the barn
to avoid the broiling summer sun and, incidentally,
to rob the nest of its fruit. Stark fear gripped him
for an instant. Then the lad moved out backwards
much faster than he had crawled in forwards, and
"Ma" sent "Boss," the dog, in to kill the rattlers.

There were the ghost stories that "Mam" Lindy used
to tell him as he snuggled his head against her knee,
tales that struck terror, but delightful terror, into his
heart. And when the old darky would see his eyes
open wide in fear, she would pat his head and hug
him, and say: "Law sakes, honey chile, doan you
know de Lawd Jesus gwinter take care o' you—no
matter how many ghostses dar bese in dis here
worl'?"

And again, the Sundays, days of rest indeed, of
surcease from labor, and to which, a half-century
later now, Dr. Lee attributes his present good health
and strength. It was an oasis in the desert for the
Lee boys. No work that day—no plow should make
a furrow, no scythe should mow a swath, nor should
the sound of an axe ever mar the peace of the day.
The cows had to be milked, "a Christian necessity,"
and the mules might be harnessed and driven to
church, "a Christian imperative." But otherwise, man
and beast rested on the Lord's Day from their labors.

Everyone in the Lee family went to Sunday school
and church, even to the babes in arms, who were
laid upon straw pallets on the church floor where they
might cry, coo, or sleep, according to their moods.

David Ayers Lee

Sarah Elizabeth Bennett Lee

*Where David A. Lee and Sarah E. Bennett Were
Married, December, 1875*

*Birthplace of Robert G. Lee, now a
Mission Sunday School*

*The Farm near Fort Mill, S. C.
Purchased by David A. Lee*

Sunday was a day of extras—for after the cows were milked in the morning and the cattle turned out to pasture, the family sat down to the "extra big" breakfast, composed of biscuit, grits, eggs, perhaps some meat, milk, and molasses. The mules would be bridled, carefully curried and harnessed, and then the children put on their "extra special" clothes, which meant, for a boy, wearing a clean, ironed shirt, and whatever suit he might have at that time, mostly hand-me-downs; and for a girl, a starched calico dress, home-made, of course.

After church and the mid-day dinner, the children were allowed to walk in the woods, to pick flowers, but never to play any games. They might laugh, but not boisterously—unless, of course, they were at a far distance from their elders. One is reminded of the old Scotch minister who was asked, by a member of his congregation, whether it was all right to take a walk on the Lord's Day. "Well," said the preacher, "I ken there be nae harm in taking a walk on the Sabbath, sae long, mind ye, as ye dinna enjoy yersel." The rigid discipline of the Lee household on Sunday seemed equally strict, and perhaps unreasonable, to the children. Yet they welcomed the day as the glory day of the week. Its end would come all too soon. "Dad" would call his family together for Bible reading, and each of the children who was able to read at all must take part in this portion of evening worship. Then the father would lead in prayer, and off to bed they would go, dreading the morning as a slave dreads a whip on his naked back. But they were made thoroughly aware of it long before the darkness began to melt into dawn by a brusque and stentorian voice that might well have raised the dead from their graves, shouting: "Get up, Jim! Get up, Ben! Up, Frank! Up, Bob, Tom! Up, *everybody!* Today's Monday, tomorrow's Tuesday, next day's Wednesday—half the week gone already, and nothin's done."

Chapter II

PEACE IN A FENCE-CORNER

Boyhood and New Birth

Heaven on earth may be a transient experience when it finds its source in material benefits. David Lee grew weary of living in another's home and working another's land. Wanting a farm that was his own, he began to scan the country for a place to dig his roots. He even made a journey to Texas. If he should like "the fur west," he would settle there. But he did not take to Texas and, upon his return to South Carolina, elected to purchase a piece of land owned by Dr. T. L. Kirkpatrick, only a mile and a half from the old log cabin where six of his children had been born.* It was a 188-acre farm of red hills and rocky gullies and swamp lands, so barren, so arid, and so desolate that his family used to tell him that had he searched earnestly for years, he could not have found a poorer place.** It had been cultivated since 1750, and was so badly cared for that

*"Fairy" Lee was born here. See footnote on page 28.
** The cost of the farmstead was $1,880.00, to be paid off in ten years, with interest at 8 per cent. The land was so poor, however, that it was necessary for "Dad" Lee to sell off a section in order to finish paying for the farm. Familiar talk around the house in those days was: "If we had the farm paid for . . ." or, "When we get the farm paid for . . . we shall do so-and-so."

it seemed a hopeless task to begin to turn the soil. But to David Lee it was home, his own home, and that was fulfilment.

Robert Lee, with his brothers and sisters, wept when it came time to leave the old Springs' mansion. Nor was his sorrow, very painfully real to a boy of eight, alleviated, but rather intensified, when he saw the little five-room house and the strange acreage that were to be habitat and sweatshop until he should become of age. He had learned to work, to do hard work, at the Springs' farm, but always, after the day's labor, there was the satisfaction of eating and sleeping and living in what he deemed to be the most beautiful house in the world. There was the lovely, winding stairway that somehow filled the small boy's heart with a pride of ownership, even though it was not his to hold. There were the giant magnolia trees in the yard, whose fragrance was a periodic reminder of the sweetness of this house of many mansions. Bidding farewell to the Eli Springs' homestead meant the closing of a door upon the only tangible beauty and rest this lad had ever known.

Youth is not youth without schooling of one kind or another. Bob Lee's schooling, with that of his brothers, was sporadic at best. In his fifth and sixth years he attended a little one-room school house across the railroad tracks from the Springs' mansion. It was known as "Railroad Bridge School," and it was open in the summer only, for it had no stove or chimney. He still remembers his teachers' names. There were Miss Maggie McNutt and Miss Mollie

Clark, one being a blonde and the other a brunette. There was also a one-armed soldier of the Confederate army, named Davidson, who knew, along with his real ability as a teacher, how to use a switch in spite of his physical limitations.

For the next two years Bob attended school in Flint Hill. It was a walk of about three miles, but he did not mind. On very rainy days "Dad" would drive the children in the buggy, and rarely, in clear weather, if he was not too busy, he would get "Old Bob," the horse, out of the barn and riding him, with the boys sitting behind their father, they would make the three miles in "jig time."

From the day when the Lee family left the Springs' house until Bob was in his twentieth year, he attended only one school, the Massey school, another one-room school house by the side of the road near Fort Mill, where all grades were taught by Miss Suzie White. But this educational training was irregular and extremely sparse and inadequate. Only in "spare time," when it was too rainy to work on the farm, or in "lay-by time," as from the middle of July to the third week in August, were the children permitted to attend school, so that it is no exaggeration to say that the Lee boys' grammar school education consisted of about one day out of ten.

Unlike many of his companions, Bob Lee was never happier than when he was under Miss White's tutelage. School was like a gate out of the unknown, into light, where opportunity was offered to learn wisdom with the wise and benefit from the knowledge accrued by students and teachers over the centuries. Sweeter than any memories of the "old swimmin' hole," to Bob Lee, are the recollections of learning to parse and conjugate, of studying geography, history spelling, reading, writing, and arithmetic. Early in his school days he began to love words and sentences and delighted in tracking down every noun, and verb, and conjunction, and adjective, and adverb as fully as his brothers found their pleasure in hunting rabbits, a sport that Bob also enjoyed, however.

In all of the schools that Robert Lee attended, the Bible was read, revered, and believed. Nor did any teacher ever think of leaving a question mark in the minds of her scholars about any part of the Bible or its authenticity. The "Readers" used in the schools in those days were amply fortified with Bible stories.

There was a lighter side to school days and life in general, of course. When all the boys and girls did well in their lessons, Miss Suzie's reward was to read to them serial stories from *Youth's Companion* or the much beloved books of G. A. Henty. During recess periods, the simple games of the country were engaged in by all—tag, "andy-over," tree baseball (where the batter ran for trees selected as bases, and the fielders tried to hit the tree, or the runner, with the ball before he touched base), and pitching horseshoes. There were rougher games, too, as wrestling, and "hot jacket." The latter was rather severe. Two boys would get keen switches and thrash each other below the hips until one of them had enough. And woe betide the lad who hit above the hips—he was "a skunk," and was discredited by all, male and female!

Youngsters chewed gum in those days, just as they do today, only it was manufactured by nature. The favorite was the sweet gum, but when the sweet-gum trees were "stingy," rosin from pine trees served the purpose. In those times, before people had been educated to fear germs, when teacher and pupils alike would all drink water from the same dipper, it was a mark of conquest for a boy if he could persuade a girl to let him chew her gum in recess. One of Bob Lee's greatest attainments, he thought, was the time he prevailed upon the "prettiest girl in school" to let him chew her gum. This triumph, and the fact that, though tall for his age and rather thin, Bob was victorious in most of his "rastlin' matches," compensated to an extent for the shame that he and his brothers and sisters felt when they opened their lunches at "big recess," because they did not have flour bread as most of the others did, and thus disclosed their pantry lack of flour at home.

Outside of school, too, there were certain pleasures and excursions, as when the Lee boys swam across the river to see the Catawba Indians, about five miles from home. Bob learned to be a fine swimmer from instruction by, and competition with, the Indian boys. They taught him how to catch fish without hook and line—just to feel under the river bank until you touch one, and then rub it gently below the median line.

Around the farm, also, there were some few diversions—teaching tricks to Zack and Zeb, black and white shepherd dogs; scratching the side of a hog to make it lie down; imitating the call of the quail; learning the habits of the wild animals—the skunk, the weasel, the mink, and the possum; discovering the marks and tracks of the blacksnake, the highland moccasin, and the king snake; watching the robins get drunk from eating China berries and wild cherries; and mastering the names of the trees and flowers. What fun it was to teach Zack and Zeb to distinguish between whistle-commands for one task and another, and to obey! One long whistle was an order to the dogs to bring the hogs from the wallow holes to the feeding trough. Three quick, shrill blasts meant that the cows were to be driven from the pasture to the barn. Two notes was the sign that the mule must be put in his stall for the night.

Such memories, all too few, compose the dearness of "the dear, dead days beyond recall." Other days— yes, weeks, months, and years—would not be recalled if they could be; days of drudgery, of sweat, of heavy heart, but days of precious dreams and resolute purpose.

At the age of nine Bob Lee was plow-boy. He went to the fields when the "grown-ups" went, and he did not return until they did. And as the years passed he learned to do everything that must be done on a farm, and did them until he fairly dropped in his tracks. He picked cotton, stooped over beneath the September sun, "until every hour was filled with ten thousand aches and pains." He swung a wheat cradle until he thought his arms would drop from their sockets in his shoulders. He plowed the fields for fifteen hours on June days, until it seemed that the rows were ten miles long, every one. He pushed a cross-cut saw until his hands and arms were as lead. He hoed corn, pulled fodder, dug sassafras, cleaned stables, split rails, milked cows, dug ditches, built fences, slaughtered hogs, gathered blackberries, and battled with chiggers. He could express with deep feeling the verse of doggerel:

> Here's to the chigger
> That ain't any bigger
> Than the point of a small-size pin,
> But the lump that it raises
> Itches like blazes,
> And that's where the scratchin' comes in.

At the age of twelve, this tender-hearted boy who would weep over a broken bird's nest, who yet would watch, with a small boy's delight, a king snake whip a highland moccasin to death, received Christ as his Saviour. Let him tell the story:

One Sunday morning, when I was a boy, the preacher preached a sermon which I think now must have been on the subject, "The Gates of Heaven." In the sermon he asked: "If the gates of Heaven were opened, would you enter?" The question startled me. I knew that if the gates of Heaven were opened that day I could not enter, because I could not claim to be a Christian boy.

That night the preacher's text was, "What Then Shall I Do with Jesus Who Is Called the Christ?" He said very simply and earnestly that to accept Christ as Saviour meant Heaven, that to reject Him as Saviour meant hell.

I went home that night with the most wretched feeling. I could not sleep. I got up in the night, slipped out of the window that opened on the back porch, and went down to the moonlit watermelon patch. It was a beautiful clear night, and I thought of the Heaven beyond the stars and of the hell somewhere in the vast region below.

At the breakfast table next morning, my mother said: "Son, you look like you didn't sleep much last night."

"No, ma'am," I said. "I didn't."

"What is the matter?"

"I feel awful sinful," I admitted.

I had to plow that day. My misery grew until finally I drove out to the end of a long row and dropped the plow down by the side of Barney, my old white mule. I got down in the fence corner, the corner of an old rail fence, and told God that I felt awfully bad—awfully sinful—and that I wanted to be saved.

"If one must accept Jesus to be saved," I prayed, "then I accept Him."

There in a fence corner the Lord saved me. That night—the text of the preacher's sermon I do not now remember—I walked down the church aisle and let it be known that the Lord had saved me.

I do remember the hymn they sang:

> "Out of my bondage, sorrow, and night;
> Jesus, I come! Jesus, I come!
> Into Thy freedom, gladness, and light;
> Jesus, I come to Thee."

The peace that came to me in the fence corner is in my heart until this day.

The first step along the rough road that would lead to a life of Christian service had been taken. The pathway to the pulpit had been broken.

Chapter III

FOR THIS HOUR OF THIS DAY

YOUNG MANHOOD AND GREAT DREAMS

A few days after Robert Lee's conversion, and after his baptism by Dr. E. S. Reaves, on August 5, 1898, life became but a means to an end—to preach the Gospel of Christ. Within his breast there burned an unquenchable fire—the desire to preach. Within his soul was the conviction that he must preach. Within his mind was the belief that it was for this that he was born and born anew—to be a preacher.

Impelled as the twelve-year-old boy was by the urgency of his calling, he began to dream of it and plan for it. While the average youngster will do anything in the world to avoid studying, Lee studied at every opportunity. While the normal boy would rather mow the lawn than study Latin, and will offer his parents and teachers one excuse after another as to why he should not take up the subject, Robert Lee walked three miles periodically to learn Latin under a Professor Boyd, because this ancient language was not taught in Massey School. Fifty cents a lesson it cost the boy, which he earned trapping rabbits to sell, peddling broom straw, and selling peanuts at five cents a bag. This money went to Hughes and Young, Grocers, who supplied the

43

peanuts and paid Bob Lee twenty-five cents for a Saturday afternoon. Even such half-days were permitted only when the work on the farm was caught up. Prof. Boyd would spend two hours a week delighting his pupil with his conjugating, and, as Dr. Lee says, "putting me in a despairing mood about the subjunctive mood."

Bob had promised his father that he would remain on the farm until he was twenty-one years of age, for the father was not wholly in sympathy with his son's zeal for "being a preacher." And stay Bob did—working ever, shirking never. But never for an instant did his eagerness to learn, so that some day he might preach, leave him. Opportunity for attending school continued to be limited, and by the time he was of age, he had been to high school—eighth grade in those days—only three months and these in the Fort Mill Graded School in his twentieth year. These happy school days, when he went home after school hours and worked until dark and studied until midnight, went all too quickly. But his marks were high and his conduct excellent.

Any odd job that young Lee could get, he took. He became known in Fork Section as "the Comfort Boy," for he took subscriptions for the magazine, *Comfort*. But the way continued hard indeed.

There was nothing to keep him from dreaming dreams, however. For what his life's calling was, was "as clear as a path of tar across a field of snow." Had anyone dared to tell him that God did not want him to preach, he would have replied that his tormentor was out of his mind. His dreams and desires haunted his nights, awoke with him in the morning, and shadowed him throughout all the days. They beset him before and behind. Following the old gray mule, he thought of pursuing the profession of preaching. Holding the plow handles, he dreamed of one day being a preacher, to turn the leaves of the Book instead of the soil. Cutting wheat, pulling fodder, picking cotton, gathering corn, splitting rails, feeding hogs, milking cows, hauling manure, digging ditches, he thought of preaching. Life would have become suddenly empty and meaningless without his dreams and without his plans to make them materialize.

In the pasture near the farm was an old pine tree, and here Robert Lee would repair at some time almost every day, and throwing his arms as far around the tree as they would reach, and with his face against its trunk, would pour out his soul to God, pleading with Him to help him overcome all the obstacles in his path, to educate and fit him so that he could preach. Every prayer he ever offered by that old tree ended with this cry: "O God, make me a preacher."

Meanwhile Bob continued diligently to study and, of course, to work. Whatever books he could lay his hands on, he read. But they were not many. There was the Bible, a book of *Sam Jones' Sermons,* a volume of *Talmadge's Sermons, Biography of Buffalo Bill, Les Miserables,* an encyclopedia, a dictionary, *The Yorkville Inquirer, The Atlanta Constitution, The Fort Mill Times, Youth's Companion,* and *The Baptist Courier.* A mighty thin literary diet, excepting the

Word of God! There was one other book, last but
not least—*The Sky Pilot,* by Ralph Connor. Aside
from the Bible, this volume, given to Bob Lee by
a young lady, a very dear friend, meant more to him
in respect to his becoming a preacher than any other
book, before or since. Even to this day Robert Greene
Lee reads this book twice a year. Twenty years after
he had read it the first time, he traveled more than
one hundred miles to see its author and to grasp his
hand. Dr. Lee says that he will never be able to
express the measure of the influence of *The Sky
Pilot* on his life through all the years, and even now.

The Lee family kept on being poor. The farm
would yield scant crops in spite of the grueling work
of the hands. It all seemed so futile to Robert, when
his heart was elsewhere—as unavailing for him to be
working on a farm as it was for his father to fertilize
that barren, stubborn soil.

The soil was fertilized with guano, a wry-smelling
yellow dust, but it appeared to do little good, and
poverty abode. They used to laugh among themselves
as they would tell of the old Negro who went into
Mr. Massey's store to buy a ton of guano. "What do
you want with that much guano?" Massey asked him.

"To make cotton," replied the colored man.

"What do you want to make cotton for?" Mr.
Massey queried, teasing him.

"To pay for guano."

So Bob Lee worked simply to do more work, it
seemed to him, when the one thing he desired,
craved, pined, longed for, was to study, learn, and
prepare for preaching. Yet the Saviour said that he

that is faithful in the few things will be made ruler over many, and life on his father's farm was a test as to faithfulness for the young man.

Opportunities came for him to speak, even then. His very first message was delivered when he was sixteen years of age. It was spoken before the "Sunbeam Band," a missionary society in the church, for children of five to eight years old. But there was no other missionary organization to which he could belong, so the tall, gangling boy, now a young man, remained in the group. We have before us the original draft of that message, written in ink on two sides of paper (three sheets) that are now yellow with age. The title is: "The Children's Work," and it was given on October 6, 1905. Space does not permit the recording of the message in full, but we cite below a portion of its concluding paragraph:

But if we cannot do some great thing for Jesus, there are lots of little things we can do. Speak kind words to someone each day. That's for Jesus. Do you remember how He healed the broken heart? Do some deed of love, and though it seems insignificant, it will not be forgotten, for that's for Jesus. Could we ever forget how He befriended the needy? Pray for someone, for the mission bands, for God's messengers *everywhere*. Pray that *we* may reach the loftiest heights of human attainment and Christ-like life. That's for Jesus. Do you remember how earnestly He prayed for His followers? Oh, let us *work* and above all let's love, for *love* makes *work* complete. We are here in this world to realize the finest qualities of life possible. To clear our skies of all clouds of ignorance and fear . . . [*writing dimmed by age*] . . . We are here to call forth into our own consciousness that deep and eternal consciousness which is ours in the *perfect ideal* that the mind of God holds for us. "When only the Christ *within* is our Master, then He is the touchstone of all that claims to be truth. Embosomed in God, living and moving and having our being in Him, our feet walk in light, our hearts beat in tune with that *perfect Life* which is the greatness of all worlds and the splendor of eternity." And then it is we join with hearts filled with triumphant gladness in the victor's exultant song:

"In the Cross of Christ I glory
Towering o'er the wrecks of time;
All the light of sacred story
Gathers round its head sublime."

Once the dreamer of "preaching dreams" told some of his friends of his longings and that he hoped, some day, to go to college and that perhaps, in the years ahead, he might be pastor of a big city's church. But most of them walked with unanointed feet within the sanctuary of his ambition, looked with cheap scorn behind the veil of his yearning, and smiled skeptically or pitifully at the boy's aspiration, so that henceforth Bob kept his fond fancies to himself, the most part. His family knew his longings. Only his mother and a few friends were allowed to enter as they would within the chamber of vision, where the fires burned so brightly.

We shall not dwell much longer upon the dread and difficult early years. However, we have run across two letters from Bob's brothers, written a quarter of a century or more after all of them had left the farm, that will establish better than any word we could say, the hardship of those years in the desert place, and the bond of love that held the family together.

Frank was two years Bob's senior, you will recall. He still lives in Fort Mill, and here is a portion of a letter dated January 15, 1947:

Dear Bob:

I dreamed of you again last night and when I awoke all the scenes and happenings of our days together on the old farm came crowding my memory. We had such a sad, terrific struggle paying for that old farm in the days when cotton was 4 and 5 cts. Those days were so inexpressibly gloomy and hard to bear.

Do you remember one day when working in the field that joined the old Massey place, dear angel mother walked all the way to us to bring us buttermilk? And another time she did the same to bring us a few wild strawberries. Don't know how we could have survived all the sorrows, horrors, and unspeakable hardships had it not been for our pastors, Mr. Finch, Dr. Reaves, and others visiting us occasionally.

Dad was good at times, when we did more work than he thought we could, but he was also unreasonable. One day while we were at dinner eating corn bread and bean "pot likker" I remember you told him you intended to study for the ministry.

I can't forget either your plowing up that entire farm with a two-horse plow with old Ben and Barney, in order that I might go to school in Fort Mill a few weeks. I shall never forget how you looked plowing barefooted, wearing that old, long, black swallow-tailed coat Jim sent you.

You know, the third day I had been to school Dad met me and said I wasn't doing any good—that I looked just like I did when I started!

I was so utterly frightened when you got fastened in the plow line one day when you were breaking that mean, wild young mule "Dan" that Dad got from the gypsies. Surely looked bad for you, but God saved you so you could preach. Seems as if we had to do everything the hard way but we always knew Mother loved us.

There's so many dear, dead days since we were boys
together, and I could never get through talking about
them if you were only here. I want to thank you again
for giving me your hand when the hill was steep.

Now I will put old dreams away. It is done—the old
farm bell is still and there is lamplight on a haunting face.

With undying love
Your brother,
FRANK

Ben left the farm when he was twenty-one and
went west. Bob was only fifteen at the time. Writing
years later of some of his visits to the old farm, he
said, in part:

Dear Bob:

    . . . When I would come home I was with you heart
and soul and the times we said good-bye were terrible.
I shall never forget the *one* time in particular when I
was going back to Arizona and I walked over back of the
house in the old sandy field where the little house was.
And there you were—driving the "drag harrow" over
the old poor land with the two ghostly gray mules. And
your *face*—I shall always remember—was sad and sweet
and streaked with dust, and terribly earnest. I carried
that picture all over the west and all over the world
wherever I have been since. A sort of inspiration.

    You *did* have a lot of grief and trouble in your drive
and determination to "go up" somehow. You never would
accept anything that tried to block you, and I know some
that it is better not to mention . . .

    Do you remember the time I cut my foot with the axe
when Frank and I were chopping wood? Ma took three
stitches in it with white thread and I went to plowing
again in two days. Now it takes three doctors and two
nurses to handle a case like that! . . . Such a change!

    Rainy day today, and I wish you were here.

Yours,
BEN

But back to Bob. The years between fifteen and twenty-one are long. The young man went on plowing and sometimes the fields seemed as big as the Sahara, and the furrows as long as the great rivers of the earth. But always the vision of his destiny clung close to him. Nor did he forget that he who would preach abroad must preach first at home. A Sunday school superintendent of Fort Mill once offered a two foot by three and one-half foot picture of Bible scenes to every boy who would bring another boy to the Sunday school. Young Lee heard about it and went to town on Saturday afternoon, spending the night at his married sister's (Fanny's) home. Then he went to work on the "boy power" of the town, and on Sunday morning he led between forty and fifty boys to Sunday school. The superintendent did not have enough pictures to meet his pledge—but he did supply them later.

There came a time when Bob, having gotten soaking wet while working, was taken with a severe cold and a cough that lasted for about six months, shaking and tearing his body continually. It would worry his mother so that she frequently cried about it. The doctor told him that he would never have a voice for preaching after that, and "Dad" discouraged him from pursuing his purpose. But the young man's faith would not yield to these pessimistic prophecies. Down to the old pine tree he went, and there he prayed it through, until the Lord gave him peace of mind and heart. Like Gideon of old, Bob Lee asked for a sign, pleading with the Lord to show him what was in store for him in this way: if the

Lord wanted him to be a preacher, would He grant
that his cough would leave him, and that a short
story he was writing would be sold? In a few days
his bronchial trouble ceased, and shortly the county
paper, *The Yorkville Inquirer,* accepted the story
for which they paid him ten dollars.

In his fifteenth year, there came to Fort Mill to
speak at the church, Dr. E. M. Poteat, the President
of Furman University. More than forty years have
passed since that day, but Robert Lee clearly recol-
lects how Dr. Poteat looked, what he wore, and more,
what he said. He was greatly impressed by the dignity of the man, dressed in striped trousers with a
black, long-tailed coat. Dr. Poteat had on a black
and white tie, with a pink pearl stick-pin, and he
wore half-moon glasses. As he addressed the Baptist
Association, looking directly at Lee, Dr. Poteat
said: "If Galileo knew the earth went around the
sun, this country boy has a right to know it, too."
Bob left the meeting in tears, and told his mother
afterward: "Ma, I want to learn something so I can
be a preacher."

This man who, Dr. Lee says, influenced him as
to his speaking in public more than any man he ever
knew, came back to Fort Mill a year or so later.
Wanting to have a point of contact with such a great
man of God, Bob approached him at a picnic supper with one of Mrs. Lee's cherry pies, and offered
it to him. Dr. Poteat was eating a piece of goat at
the moment, and jokingly, with laughter, asked: "Are
you trying to get my goat?"

Now Bob Lee had never heard the expression, "get

my goat," before this. And he was a very timid person. He felt embarrassed, and in his confusion turned away from Dr. Poteat. But the good doctor discerned that he had confused the young man, and later sought him out, and asked him, "Why don't you come to Furman College?" Bob said he did not know enough, and then and there Dr. Poteat told him of the Furman Fitting School, and extracted a promise from Lee that he would give grave consideration to coming.

And still the trying years dragged on and on. And still Bob Lee hoped and trusted in God. Dressed in his inevitable hickory shirt and jeans, sweating and weary, he followed the plow, wishing the days were shorter and the nights longer, that the old mule was less stubborn, droughts less frequent, and the hard earth more fertile. Ahead of him, as he followed row upon row across the field, he could see —only a few miles distant as the crow flies— the towers of Winthrop College in Rock Hill, South Carolina. Between the ears of the old white mule he would look at those towers, and would ask God to enable him to get an education, so that he could preach. Across winter snows he would gaze at the same towers, and plead with God: "O God, help me *some day* to attend a place like that, and prepare me to preach." He went to bed praying for this. He awoke in the night to pray for this. He arose in the morning, and again he prayed this. And down by the old pine tree, he cried to God with strong crying to help him become a preacher.

God heard Bob Lee's prayers, and He answered them.

It was many years later that this former farm boy was honored by being invited to give the baccalaureate address at Winthrop College. Rising to his feet, he begged that he might be allowed a few minutes to indulge in personal reminiscences. For a minute or two he told his audience of his boyhood dreams and longings, and then he said: "And now, at this college, inside this building on which I often lovingly and prayerfully looked as a barefoot boy, plowing behind a contrary mule, I am to preach to you. Had I time to talk one thousand hours I could not express the goodness of God to me—God, who took me from the plow handles and put me on this platform; God who led me from the furrow of often fruitless fields to preach in many places the Gospel of His Grace. For this, and this day, and this hour of this day as I speak for the Lord to you graduates, there is a peculiar gratitude in my heart. As I speak to you the soft murmur of the Catawba is in my ears, and the raucous call of the crows, and somehow I see, as when I was a boy, the towers of Winthrop, across the fields of white cotton, and against the blue sky above. God be thanked for every experience and every opportunity to proclaim the matchless Name of Jesus."

Chapter IV

SOMETHING VENTURED AND
SOMETHING GAINED

STEPPING STONES TO AN EDUCATION

Bob Lee was twenty-one in 1907. He had promised his father that he would work on the farm until he became of age. Now the promise was fulfilled. He must get an education so that he could preach, for to this young man to preach was to live, and to live was to preach.

Learning that the Government was hiring men for work on the Panama Canal, Bob made application for employment and was accepted. He had no money with which to get to Panama, but he had courage and a good reputation. Thus he was able to borrow $250.00 at the local bank, without a note, and not long thereafter, dressed in a new brown suit, and wearing new black, button shoes and a derby, Lee set forth on a great adventure. He had never traveled more than 200 miles on a train before, but here he was on his way to New Orleans, a brand new trunk in the baggage car and an equally resplendent suitcase by his side.

The adventuresome spirit that most young men possess was in Bob Lee's breast also. But far and beyond the desire to see the world was the passion

that never left him by day or in the wakeful hours
of the night—to preach the Gospel of Christ. It was
a thrilling experience to see New Orleans for the
first time and to recognize places that were pictured
in the old *Maury Geography* that had been used
in the country school. But it was more exciting to
realize that he was walking the pathway that was
to lead to an education for becoming a preacher.

More than fascination and elation coursed through
young Lee's veins, however. Confusion and frustra-
tion, and a sense of unutterable loneliness, swept over
this country boy in the big city for the first time.
Urban din pressed upon him—jostling cabs, shrill
police whistles, the hoarse wails of the ferryboats, and
the rising and falling hum of people talking, talking,
talking. Strange faces were everywhere around him,
but there was no smile of friendliness from any of
them. Rather, he was snarled at by a policeman of
whom he inquired directions, and cursed at by a
cab-driver who had almost run him down.

The traveler found his way at last to the United
Fruit Company. He purchased a steamer ticket to
Panama, which nearly took his last cent. But what
did that matter? He had accommodation, including
meals, to his place of destination, and there was
work awaiting him there. With what consternation
he heard the bald-headed, bespectacled, clerk tell him
that the ship that he had expected to embark upon,
had already sailed—Lee's train was five hours late
in arriving in New Orleans—and that the next sailing
would be a week hence, is still so vividly recalled by
Robert Lee that a chill goes down his spine at the

thought of it! He had less than a dollar in his pocket, no bed, and no food.

Saturday evening was beginning to fall. The strange scents of the city—odors of sea relics, dry rot, beer-soaked sawdust; the worldly sounds of cursings, raucous laughter, foreign words mixed with his native tongue; and the glaring lights of the city streets, seemed so unreal to young Lee that it was as if he walked in a dream whose pattern was vague and transient. He stood at a street corner, uncertain where to turn, and a police officer, whose face was kinder than his gruff voice, asked: "Say, boy, where's your habitat?" Confused and miserable, Bob replied: "I left it home."

Lee was standing at the corner of Canal and Baronne Streets. Hundreds were passing him in this direction or that. They would sleep in comfortable beds tonight, he thought, but not he. They would be eating in a short while, but not he. And he began to walk along Canal Street, from the 700 block until he reached the 1000 block, where he saw a sign in the window of a house: "Room and Home Cooking." Well, nothing ventured, nothing gained, he surmised, and finding the door in a small corridor away from the street, he knocked. He had to repeat the rapping several times before the door opened. The little lady who appeared, slim, precise, and quick of eye and movement, asked him: "Why don't you push the bell-button?" At Fort Mill they did not have electric door bells, but he said nothing about that.

"I want somewhere to sleep," he told the lady, "and something to eat. I don't have any money to pay

you. I'm on my way to Panama—see, here is my
ticket." Then he related his plight and said: "If you'll
take me in, I'll get a job and pay you before my
steamer sails next Saturday."

Something of the desperate earnestness of the
dispirited young man must have touched her kindly
heart. The frown that had first appeared gave way to
at least the suggestion of a smile. "You are from
the country, aren't you?" she asked.

"Yes, ma'am, I am."

"Is your mother living?" she inquired further.

"Yes, ma'am."

"Are you a good boy—a Christian?"

"Yes, ma'am," Lee said once again.

"I'll take you then," she told him with some reluctance, he thought, but they were sweet words
to his ears.

The landlady led him up two flights of stairs to a
tiny room on the third floor. In it were a single iron
bed and a marble-top wash stand, with bowl and
pitcher. One small window seemed to squint down
upon the lighted street, a window draped with some
flowery, but dirty and dingy material. And on the
wash stand was a partially used cake of Cashmere
Bouquet soap. That was the kind of soap that Bob's
mother put in "the prophet's room" at home. The
Lee family washed their hands with Octagon soap,
or home-made lye soap, and never anything as
fancy and costly as Cashmere Bouquet. A cake of
this fragrant soap, used by the preacher upon occasion when he visited, would last a year in the Lee
home! One look at the soap on the wash stand of

that tiny room, one whiff of its familiar perfume, and the pent-up homesickness that the boy had checked during the last few hours almost brought him to open and unashamed tears in the presence of his benefactor; but not quite.

"I hope you'll get along all right," said the kind-hearted lady, and she closed the door and went downstairs. Supperless, but not prayerless, the young adventurer went to bed and, after he became used to the diligent gnawing of a rat in the wall, to sleep.

The next day was Sunday. Bob Lee had three meals at the boarding house that day. Nor did he forget to go to church, although he still recalls that there were only a few in attendance, and neither the preacher nor the people in the pews seemed very enthusiastic about any part of the service.

Before the breakfast hour on Monday, Lee was awake, accustomed as he was to early morning activity. He went down the stairs and was about to go out when the landlady called to him: "Here is a key to your room. Go back and lock your door. You're not on a farm here." He ran up the forty-seven steps to the third floor, locked his door, and came down again, arriving at the wharf on the river within ten minutes from the moment that he had first left his room. He inquired where he might get a job, and a man replied: "Some banana ships came in last night . . . You get twenty-five cents an hour as long as you can hold out to carry 'em."

Twenty-five cents an hour! And Bob had "held out" cutting wheat and plowing corn and picking cotton for from fourteen to sixteen hours a day.

Fourteen hours a day here would bring him $3.50. With such thoughts in his mind, Lee got the job. He had had no breakfast, but the boss told him that he could eat all the ripe bananas he wanted. He will not tell how many he ate, lest his veracity should be doubted, he says. At any rate, he found that carrying bananas for fourteen hours was less taxing than the work that had been his daily stint back on the farm. So from Monday through Friday Lee labored at the wharf, carrying bananas and rolling barrels of molasses.

The paymaster for the United Fruit Company issued the weekly wages in those days at a corner saloon. Standing in line on Saturday morning to await his turn, Bob remarked to the man in front of him that he had promised his mother he would never enter a saloon. "And I don't quite see how," he added, "I'm going to keep my promise and get my pay."

The man to whom Lee talked offered immediately to get the young man's pay for him, and Bob Lee, ignorant of the ways of the world, innocent and trustful, was very grateful for this kind assistance. And so he dropped out of line to await the return of this obliging "friend." But the man who was now next in line had overheard the conversation. He was suspicious of the intentions of Lee's new acquaintance, and watched him. He observed that, after obtaining his own pay and Lee's also, this man was going to sneak out through the rear door of the saloon and slip away unnoticed. So he seized him by the collar and brought him forcibly to the door by which they had entered, where Bob was standing, and the lad received his hard-earned pay, $21.80. Through the watchfulness of this genuine friend, God cared for the earnest lad who was to be a keen instrument in His service in the years to come.

The kindly landlady of Canal St. charged him only $7.00 for the week's room rental and his meals, and the young adventurer boarded ship, Panama bound, at noon on Saturday, wiser than when he had arrived in New Orleans, and with $14.80 in his purse.

Bob had written to his mother every day, and as the ship sailed down the Mississippi River, he wrote her again, giving the letter to the pilot when he left the ship. For regular letters that he had received from his sister, Frances, and other loving letters that came from his mother, had been a source of great encouragement. Without them, he says, sometimes his loneliness would have been almost unbearable.

Bob's ship docked in Colon, Canal Zone, in the evening. He immediately entrained for Empire, where he was supposed to have a job, and the first thing that he did was to go to the Post Office, hoping for letters from home. There was one from his brother Tom, who was attending a business college. Bob sent Tom $10.00 to help with his expenses there.

But again young Lee met with a shocking disappointment. Five hundred canal workers had just been laid off by the Government, and the job that he thought was awaiting him vanished in thin air. Baffled and disillusioned, he hardly knew what to do. Fortunately, he did know the value of prayer and the power of God, and he took his troubles to the right Person, to the Lord.

The nest-egg of $14.80 had dwindled now to less than four dollars. Bob rented a cheap room and bought a loaf of bread and a jar of cherry jam. For three days he hunted for work, his only food bread and jam until, on the third day, walking up Empire Hill, he saw the remains of a picnic—some meat and bread, both covered with ants. He blew the insects off the food and ate it, delighted to have the gnawing pains of hunger quelled somewhat by this unappetizing fare.

About an hour later Lee met a Mr. Crowley, Superintendent of the Empire Division of the Panama Canal Construction. Bob told Crowley that he must have a job. When the superintendent asked Lee what he could do, the young man admitted that he had no particular skill or trade, but said that he had just come off a Carolina farm and knew how to do hard work—to dig ditches, to plow, to carry heavy loads, and added: "And I'm not lazy." Crowley looked the lad up and down, felt his muscles, and then gave him a job as track foreman at $83.33 per month, a room in the bachelor quarters for Government employees, and a ticket entitling him to eat at the Government Hotel.

The sun was setting in the west and the stars were just beginning to show themselves when Bob Lee found himself alone. Looking up into the sky, he thanked God "for everything, and for everybody who helped along the way," and not in the least for Superintendent Crowley who had given him this chance to work in the bottom of the Panama Canal as foreman over fifty-five men.

In Government Hotel that night there was one boarder who ate beyond the highest imagination and who, while he was still at the table, heard one of the waiters remark to another: "That new guy can eat as much as you can stack in a cupboard." Could it be that the waiter was talking about Bob Lee?

Eight and a half months were spent in the Canal Zone. The eyes and heart of the young adventurer were ever fixed upon the goal of his desire—to have money enough to begin his education. He did not mind the hard work nor the confined and unpretentious quarters, for he was used to both and had expected nothing else. He was saving his money, although he sent a portion of his earnings home regularly. And he was getting an education of another sort at the same time—a knowledge of the ways of the world and how to handle men. So that he was content.

Three letters that earnest and lonely Bob Lee sent to his mother from the Canal Zone will reveal more vividly than anything that we could say the heart and undeviating purpose of this young man.

> Empire, C. Z.
> Sunday Morning
> December 15, 1907

My dear darling Mother—

It is Sunday morning now, and though it is not like Sundays at home, I am going to have a talk with you.

This morning as I woke up, I lay in bed and thought of you for a long time. I didn't know I did love you so much, until I got so far away.

I am not going to stay here for long, mamma, just long enough to pay back what I owe and to get a little to go to school on. Then I'm coming back and for four years I'll be right at Furman, where you and papa can come often and see me, and hear my speeches on each commencement day. Then, in other years, when I get my wife, you all can come and live with us. That's a long time off—but it will surely come true, I bet.

I miss you so much, mamma, and often at night as I kneel to say my prayers, I find myself almost crying for a glimpse of your face.

I am getting along all right in my work so far. I have to work 10 hours a day, and have to walk about four miles a day going to and from my work. I have a gang of Jamaica Negroes now, and I like them better than the Spaniards, for they talk English.

I have to work hard to keep my job, for last Saturday they turned off eighteen foreman right here in Empire, and many of them more experienced men than I. If I lose my job, it won't be my fault.

I won't get any pay for the month of Dec. until Jan. 13. I meant to send you a dollar for Christmas, but I had such a time getting a job, and had so much other expense, before getting it, that I spent every cent I had.

I got a letter from Tom the other day, and as you know, I promised to send him some money when I got here, but I had to break my promise—much to my regret and sorrow.

I just haven't got it, and I fear Tom will think hard of me for it. If I had known what a time I was going to have getting started, I wouldn't have promised—I wanted so much to help him go to business school, but a fellow just *can't*, if he hasn't any money.

It costs so much to live here—you can't get board for less than $27.00 a month, if you get anything fit to eat, and a fellow can't eat just anything in a country like this.

I wish I had some of your good cooking, mamma; I just hunger for it all the time.

I am doing my own washing and cooking now, for

The Old Springs' Mansion Built c. 1904 by Slave Labor; (L. to R.) James Hampton Lee, Mrs. David A. Lee, Thomas K. Lee (Babe in Arms), Mrs. Robert B. Lee (Mother of D. A. Lee, Robert G. Lee, David Franklin Lee, Frances Lee, Miss Molly Clark (School Teacher), Benjamin Massey Lee, and David A. Lee. Picture was taken in 1893.

The Lee Boys at the Old Springs' Mansion, 1892; (L. to R.) James Hampton Lee, Benjamin Massey Lee, David Franklin Lee, Robert Greene Lee, and Thomas Kirkpatrick Lee

At Lee; Farm, Fort Mill, S. C. in 1904; (L. to R.) Samuel A. Lee, Benjamin Massey Lee, Mrs. D. A. Lee, David Franklin Lee, Fairy Lee, and Robert Greene Lee

Bob, Sam Fairy, Ben, and Tom Lee, in May, 1907

I want to pay back all the money I owe, and to save a little besides.

Mamma, I am glad Mr. Witherspoon thinks lots of me. I just love him. He was so good to me when I was going to school last year. I am going to write to him soon.

You don't know how I miss my S. S. class. I would give so much to be there on Sundays and teach them. Mamma, tell Sam to please write me. When the mail comes and there is no letter from any of you, I feel bad, sure enough.

I must close now. *Please, please, please* write me a long letter and tell me all about everything and everybody. God bless you, dear mother,—till we meet again, and through the days that pass, while we are separated, I want you to pray for me, and remember me as always true and devoted to you.

Yours in undying love and unwavering faithfulness.

Your own son,
Bob

Mamei, S. A.
May 14, 1908

My dear Mother—

Tonight before I go to bed, I must have a good-night talk with you, and whisper my same love for you. I've been thinking lately of Saturday, May 16, your birthday, and as I think of it, it seems I can see far down on the old Catawba River, in the humble home where you were born.

I wish I could go there now, and linger around that old homestead, where you played as a child, and grew to pure, sweet womanhood. But tonight I'm far away from it all, and far away from you—my precious mother—but though I am far away, remember that God is keeping your boy, and that He in His own way and time will bring him safely back to you.

Sunday I go to Gatun to work—my work there will be harder than here, for Gatun is one of the really big places on the Isthmus—but I'll be so glad when I get there, for I'll get to hear a sermon now and then, whereas here I never hear such.

I'll be home in September, and while I haven't been able to save much money, still I have no murmur to make, and am glad I came here.

I am well as usual—never felt better in my life—am never sick and weigh almost 170 lbs. When I first came here, many folks told me I'd have to drink "something hot"—a little whiskey, or coffee, or some kind of stimulant. But not for me. I haven't drunk a thing since I came here but cold water, and some of the fellows that take their daily *dram* and *toddy*, are thin as rails; some of them get sick more than I.

How are you feeling now, mamma? Be sure to take a good care of yourself, for *some day*, when I get through school, I want you to hear me—you know what.

I have a lot of work to do before Sunday, so will have to stop in a little bit. Have to make out a whole pile of service vouchers, for a whole lot of men, and it is particular and important work.

It sure rains here. Rainy season is on now. Every day it rains, and if it doesn't rain, it just simply pours.

Write me all about everything, mamma, and remember me in your prayers.

I send you a dollar. Take it and get you something for yourself—a little birthday gift to remember me by.

Yours in tenderest love,
Robert G. Lee

P. S. *Buenas noches, mi dulce madre,*
   Escribe á me muchas cartas pronto.
   Cuando usted escribe cartas á me
   Yo soy muy muy alegra siempre
      Y munca triste. Pero yo quero ver usted.
Mamma, the above is Spanish, and means this—
   Good night, my sweet mother.
   Write me many letters soon.
   When you write letters to me
   I am very very glad always
   and never sad, but I want to see you.

I can speak Spanish now. If I had time to study it or talk with anyone in Spanish, I could learn.

Dice mi hermana chiqueta escribir una carta á me.

Tell my little sister to write a letter to me.

Bas Obispo, S. A.
June 10, 1908

My dear and honored Mother:

I think you have been the best mother and the best woman in the world. I think often of all the years you have toiled so faithfully, and loved us so tenderly.

Tonight, with the sweet music of the guitars in my ears and the tender songs of this faraway land, I went out and looked at the beautiful moon and thought of you, and prayed for you.

I think of the years you have toiled in the fields; of the nights when, after the day's toil was over, you watched by the cradle of your babies, and now, we have grown big and old. Only God knows all you did for us.

We children owe you more than money, mother—more than honor and love. We owe you ourselves—our lives. Even now, mamma, I rememer how I used to say my prayers at your knee, and now since I have gone out into the world, and have learned of its awful sin, I wish sometimes that I could always be a child.

Write me soon, dear mamma, and tell me all. I haven't received a letter from you in so long. Had a letter from Tom. Glad he is getting along so well. He is a grand fellow—I knew he would win, win, win.

I'm getting along fine in my work so far and guess I'll be here at Bas Obispo for several months.

Well, I guess this is all for this time, as it is getting late. I enclose a dollar for you. Take it and get something for yourself—just something to remember me by.

Love,
Your boy,
ROBERT G. LEE

"Bachelor quarters" for canal workers proved to be an abandoned box car down at the very edge of the Chagre River. Bob's car-mate was a Norwegian named Harold Neilson, and he is remembered today by Dr. Lee as one of the "most unforgettable characters" that he ever knew. Neilson was a Christian, a Christ-like Christian, of which there are only too few. A man of prayer, a faithful reader of the Bible, Neilson was unselfish, courteous, and practised the New Testament principle of preferring others above himself. Whatever the weather—hot or cold, rainy or dry—however uninteresting the preacher might be, or however doleful the music, Lee's car-mate was faithful in attending church, and fervent in worship and in giving to the work of the Lord. He proved to be a great inspiration to the young man from Carolina, and will be remembered vividly by him until they meet again "on the shore beside the sobless sea," and evermore.

In August, 1908, Bob Lee was ready to return to the States and, after visiting his folks in Fort Mill, to enter Furman Fitting School. He had not much money, but sufficient to get started. But on the very day of his scheduled departure from Colon, he was stricken with black-water fever. He was carried to the hospital, stripped of his clothes, and put in a tub of ice. He lost consciousness after that. Black-water-fever either kills, or dies itself, within forty-eight hours, and when Bob regained consciousness he knew that the fever was dead and not he. But he also learned that once again he had missed the boat. Bitterness entered his heart briefly and he questioned God.

Why should such a thing happen to him? This delay would eat into his small nest-egg after he had sacrificed so much and worked so hard with one purpose in mind, to serve God. It was not long before he had his answer: the ship that Lee missed had encountered a severe storm, all the cargo was thrown into the sea, but worse still, several lives were lost. Lee confessed to the Lord his doubts and trustlessness, and begged His forgiveness. A week later, with a heart filled with gratitude to God and a spirit of rejoicing and hope, he bade farewell to Colon and took ship for home.

Chapter V

PREACHER-BOY ON THE WAY

COLLEGE AND COURTSHIP

It was good to Bob Lee to get back home in Fort Mill, to receive the loving embrace of "Ma" and "Pa" and other members of the family, to feel the soil of Carolina under his feet again. This was in September, 1908, just a few days before school would open. But "Pa" was heavily burdened about some debts that he owed, and Bob, in his sympathetic and ever generous way, did not hesitate a moment about what had to be done. So that his father's indebtedness might be liquidated, Bob gave him the money that he had struggled so hard to earn, and set out for Furman Fitting School, in Greenville, South Carolina, frustrated once again seemingly, but not downhearted. After paying the modest matriculation fee that the school required, young Lee had exactly thirty-six cents left to begin his educational career.

The year in preparatory school was to be companion in privation and labor with every year Lee could remember. Undaunted where others might have been discouraged or might have fallen by the wayside, Bob Lee pressed on. He had come to expect

little else than hardship and its surface handicaps,
but he accepted them cheerfully rather than re-
signedly. If work and more work were the price that
must be paid to reach his goal, the end was worth the
means. He was possessed, as his teachers would tell,
of unremitting determination. Beyond that, he had
the urgency of the Spirit of God that he was born
to be a preacher, and a preacher he would be, whatever the cost.

Various odd jobs were taken that prep-school year,
such as milking Dr. Poteat's cow, carrying students'
laundry on commission, and whatever else he could
put his hand to. But in spite of these extra tasks,
young Lee's scholastic work seems not to have suffered, as the following data from a report card in
his files indicates:

FURMAN FITTING SCHOOL
February 23,1909

	Term: January 4—February 20
Algebra	97
English	99
Geometry	97
Greek	96
Latin	95
Deportment	Excellent
General Average	97

One of the jobs he performed for two and a half
years, through his sophomore year in college—this
was as paper-delivery boy. His route, measured some
years later in an automobile, was eight miles, that
is, with the necessary crossing and re-crossing of
streets. In these nearly three years delivering papers,

Dr. Lee estimates that he covered some 6,000 miles by foot.

In the autumn of 1909, Lee entered Furman University as a freshman. He found time to participate in extracurricular activities, including athletics. In his senior year he was captain of the track team. He had run the half-mile in one minute and fifty-five seconds at the Fitting School, a time that stood as a record in the South for ten years.

An incident that occurred in junior year is worth mentioning. Bob acted as a cheer leader at the baseball games. He used to get a lot of fun "riding," in a good-natured and fun-loving way, some of the players of opposing teams. When the Presbyterian College of South Carolina played Furman College in Greenville, one of the stars of the team was Ellis Fuller. Lee was the leader of some lusty "booing" of Fuller, and it was carried on in such good spirit that the two became warm friends, a friendship that has grown immeasurably through the ensuing years.*

Between preparatory school and college, Bob Lee sold maps in the King's Mountain area. It was not easy to secure orders, but the young agent found it an even more difficult task to collect the money when he delivered the goods. Of course, he met with the usual routine of excuses and refusals. One man, taunting Lee, told him that he would buy a map and throw in a nice dinner if the map agent would plow three rows in his field. It was a strange way to

---

* Dr. Ellis A. Fuller is now President of the Southern Baptist Theological Seminary of Louisville, Ky., and in the Robert G. Lee scrapbooks are cherished letters received over a score of years from his erstwhile opponent on the ball field.

get an order, but Bob rolled up his sleeves and astonished his tormentor with the speed and skill with which he accomplished the "dare."

All in all, map-selling proved to be rather non-lucrative for the young man. He decided that he could earn more money in doing the work of a laborer. A place almost sure to offer such work would be a seaport city. Mobile, Alabama, was about the nearest such city, and so, spending some of his meagre savings, Bob went by rail to the port and hired himself out to carry bags of cement. It was a back-breaking job, but he had physical strength to spare and managed to put aside almost every cent he earned there, for his small room and board cost very little.

Several years ago Dr. Lee returned to Mobile for a series of meetings. He retraced his steps, remembering with mingled heartache and gladness the time when he was "in the cement business." Writing from Mobile to a friend, he said:

> Yesterday I went out to see the old house where I boarded, and the house next door. I cried inside with joy as I thought of the little old suit case and the room I slept in, and how little I had, and how I would not even buy a newspaper or get a shoeshine because I was trying to save money to go to school. And now, within 100 yards of the same little, old boarding house, I am staying in a lovely hotel, and my picture is in the morning paper. How good God is to me! How gracious!
>
> "Surely goodness and mercy *have followed* me all the days of my life!"
>
> How long it shall be ere I shall dwell in the house of the Lord, I do not know—I only know with such days

as last Sunday [at Bellevue Baptist Church, Memphis, Tenn.] and such days as we are having in this great church, I do not want to go to Heaven now.

While Lee was still at the Fitting School he attended the Riverside Baptist Church in Greenville one night, and there he heard a duet, "Whispering Hope." The alto part was taken by Miss Bula Gentry, and Bob told a friend with whom he sat: "I'd like to speak my hope to meet her."

The introduction was made after the service. After Bob expressed his pleasure in meeting Miss Gentry, she asked: "Are you in college?" Now Bob Lee was rather old for preparatory school. His belated educational opportunity brought him to Furman Fitting School at the time of life when other young men would be juniors or seniors in college. And so Bob, very diffident as a young man, was rather embarrassed to be obliged to admit the truth. But he did, saying: "No, I'm in the Fitting School." Her response, so graciously and seriously expressed, won "for keeps" a heart that was already beating at double time. "Well," she said, "it won't be long, will it, until you will be in college."

Lee and his companion followed Miss Gentry home, for our young friend was too bashful to think of asking whether he might accompany her. He used to say that there were three things that he could not see how anyone could do: write music, work algebra, and talk to girls. He could chew their gum back in childhood days in Fort Mill, but he never could learn, he said, to talk to them.

Because Mr. Gentry had been killed in an accident

several years earlier, Mrs. Gentry took in boarders from time to time to help meet household expenses. Thus several months later, when Frances Lee, Bob's sister, was to come to Greenville to hear her brother speak in an oratorical contest, he arranged for Frances to stay at Mrs. Gentry's. Emboldened by this further contact with Bula, Bob suggested that he might come and visit her and her mother some time, which he was urged to do. But not until the following year, when he could say that he was a "college man," did he make his first call.

The Gentry home was on Lee's newspaper route. As acquaintance with Bula grew, Bob would sometimes throw his paper against her window, and, upon occasion, would insert a personal note in it. But opportunities to preach began to come his way, and by his junior year he no longer needed to deliver papers. Fees from churches where he ministered were sufficient to enable him to rest somewhat from the hard manual and physical labors of earlier years.

It was during these college days that Lee served as student pastor in the Baptist Church in Lima, South Carolina. His salary for this, his first pastorate, was fifty dollars a year. The young preacher was very zealous in his work there, so on fire for the Lord that a little ice in the pond, where he was to baptize nine young people one Sunday, daunted him not a bit. He broke through the ice, waded out into the water waist-deep, and carried on the service. None of the newly baptized converts caught pneumonia, but there were chattering teeth in their heads for twenty-four hours at least.

Upon one occasion, the church having grown during his ministry, a movement developed in the church to give the young pastor an increase in salary, a rise to seventy-five dollars a year. To this, one of the deacons objected strenuously, expressing himself candidly: "I love this young preacher. But we can't afford to bite off more'n we c'n chew. We're payin' for as much as we're gittin' right now."

Bob Lee's courtship of Bula Gentry was out of the ordinary, to say the least. But nothing other than this would be expected of Lee, who is not an ordinary man. He had to woo his beloved in whatever free time he had, and that brought him to her home at many odd hours and under sometimes peculiar circumstances.

During the summer of 1910, Lee held nine weeks of continuous revival meetings, sleeping in a different bed every night, eating in a different home every day. This in itself is sufficient almost to kill an ordinary man. Let the skeptics try it sometime, and see. When could he call upon Bula with such a schedule? Whenever a train connection brought him to Greenville—sometimes at 5:30 a.m., and sometimes at 11:30 p.m.—Bob paid her a visit. Strangely enough, she seemed glad to see him, whatever the hour!

During the school terms, too, he was inordinately busy. One year he was president of his class; he also served as president of the Literary Society, president of the Student Y.M.C.A., was editor-in-chief of *The Furman Echo* in his senior year, and was a member of the track team, the cheering staff, the

Evangelistic Band, and so forth. No suitor who is worth his salt will allow anything to prevent him from seeing the object of his affection, and Bob Lee was indeed worth his salt.

One time, before Bob ever mentioned the subject of marriage to Bula, he took her with him to one of his country churches. He knew he was born to preach, and he wanted to see at first hand how she would fit into the generally thankless task of being a preacher's wife, and how the people would feel toward her. He confesses, however, that there was never the slightest doubt in his own mind that the people would love her. He simply wanted to show her off, and this was his excuse.

On this particular occasion, Lee rented a horse and buggy so as to take Miss Gentry to church in style. Much to his embarrassment, the horse would only "guide" to the left, and so the young man had to go far out of his way to reach his destination.

When Bob asked Bula to marry him, she hesitated, saying: "I don't know that I could be a preacher's wife. I can't speak in public."

"Who asked you to speak in public?" he replied. "I can do that. I am asking you to be my wife."

Bula consented. Bob had been quite ill in this, his junior year. He was in the hospital for a while, and Bula was very attentive to him, for she knew that she loved him. Then "Dad" Lee had to take the young man home for about six weeks. But Bob must have recuperated very well, for upon his return to college he not only passed his exams with high marks, but won a heart as well.

At long last senior year came, with its days of deep friendships, and decisions and doubts about the future, when college years would be past. Autumn, winter, and finally spring filed up to today and faded into eternity. Commencement was approaching, with its accompanying events. Except for the graduation exercises, more attention was given, perhaps, by Furman faculty and students to the senior oration, which took place on the final day before graduation, than to any other thing. Elimination contests were held early in the year, so that at the final contest, only four members of the graduating class were left to vie for the gold medal that was to be given to the winner. Bob Lee was one of the four boys.

From the time that he was selected as one of the contestants, young Lee vowed that his written copy and the oration itself would be the very best that he could do, and that he would leave no stone unturned to make it that. How he wanted to win that medal, a very high step toward his goal to become a preacher! First, he chose his subject, "Civilization's Debt to the Scientific Inventor." Then, after tremendous research, he wrote his theme. It contained 12,000 words, however, whereas the contestants were limited to 2,500. He re-wrote it, therefore, eliminating all that he thought could be spared. The second draft contained 10,000 words. With merciless pen, heart-broken because he must strike out words and phrases that he wanted to employ, he cut it once more. The result still totaled far above the maximum allowance, for it had yet 6,000 words. He re-wrote it again, and again, and again, perhaps fifteen times in all. He substituted semicolons or commas for conjunctions, and cut and cut some more, until at last he counted the words again—2,500 to the word.

Next, Bob Lee memorized his oration. To rehearse it he went out into the woods and fields, speaking his lines to stolid trees and phlegmatic cows. He not only wanted to win that contest, but he worked to win it, and he prayed to win it. For weeks upon weeks he rehearsed it. He kept a copy of it up his sleeve, and at every opportunity, literally hundreds of times, he delivered his oration. He *must* win the contest—because his old father and mother were coming to commencement to hear their preacher-boy, the boy who had dreamed so many dreams and worked so many hours to be a preacher; and because Miss Bula Gentry, whom he loved dearly, would hear him also, and had promised, should he win the orator's gold medal, to reward him with a kiss.

The day of the contest dawned at last. When evening and Lee's turn to orate came, he spoke fluently, as one born to the rostrum. Interrupted by an outburst of applause, he was not disturbed but rather stirred to greater eloquence. It was a masterly address, and when the winner's gold medal was awarded by the judges—the Hon. W. L. Daniel, ex-Gov. Martin Ansell, and Dr. George W. Quick—it was given to Robert G. Lee. The preacher-boy was on his way.

Bob came down from the platform to be congratulated by hosts of friends, to be embraced with pride by his parents, and to hear the acclaim of Miss

Bula. As he stepped toward her he waved the emblem of his double triumph above his head, and, not without blushes on both their parts, the two young people laughed joyously.

Later that night Bula Gentry rewarded Bob Lee as she had promised. We do not look beyond the veil where none ought to intrude, for this was no cheap display of affection often expressed, but the sacred experience of those who have but one love to give.

At the graduation exercises, the Furman University diploma was awarded to Robert Greene Lee, winner of numerous oratorical medals and scholastic honors, by Dr. E. M. Poteat, president of the institution, the very man who, some years earlier, had influenced an embarrassed country boy in Fort Mill to take advantage of his right to study and to learn.

Chapter VI

THE PREACHER ALMOST STUMBLES
ON A LATIN ROOT

MARRIAGE AND EARLY MINISTRY

In the autumn of 1913, Robert G. Lee, A. B., became principal of one of the grade schools in Greenville. At the same time, he was serving two country
churches as pastor, preaching on week ends, alter-
nating between the two places—occasionally going
out between Sundays to conduct funerals.

Bob Lee and Bula Gentry were engaged to be
married now. There was no formal announcement,
but there had been mutual understanding, a pledge
inviolate, between the two young people for some
time. Their friends, and certainly Mrs. Gentry, were
aware of their love and their plans, even though
Bob and Bula may have thought, as so many have
thought through so many generations, that their
engagement was a secret.

It was at about this time that Bob Lee wrote to
his mother, telling her of Bula Gentry and lamenting
the fact that he could not afford to buy his girl a
diamond ring, something he longed to do and which,
he thought, she had every right to expect. He enclosed
a gift of five dollars to his mother, for her to use in

whatever way she pleased. In response, he received this treasure from her, which he has guarded as a precious jewel for nearly forty years:

Dear Bob:

I got your letter and the $5. I don't want you to be making it hard on your getting through Furman by sending me money. I'd suffer myself much before I'd see you suffer the least bit.

It is sweet of you to say you love me. It does me good, and—some day—the knowledge that you said so will bring you joy.

Your father is not so well. A letter from you would be a tonic. He is proud of you. Wonder why. Ha! Ha!

We have a new preacher. He asked about you. Made me glad to be able to tell him you were doing fine. Some of the folks don't like the new preacher. But your pa and I always stand by the preacher the church calls. We had him out for dinner yesterday. He said I was a mighty good cook. I guess I ought to be after cooking for a big family for all these years. Your pa told him we wanted the church to be stronger for our being members of it.

I was amused seriously at what you said about your girl. You say you are sorry you can't give her a diamond. Well, having "nary" a diamond is no handicap to right living and pure love. If she doesn't love you *without* a diamond, she wouldn't love you *with* one. There are some boys worth a girl's winning without a diamond, and some boys not worth having with a pocketful of diamonds. Be careful as to the girl you choose. I'll love the girl who loves you. Live so you can offer her as much at the wedding hour as you expect of her.

We are praying for you every day. I want to live on in my preacher-boy after I am dead. So take care of your body. Study hard. Preach your best. I am counting on you. I gave you to God before I saw your face. Don't rob God of what I gave Him.

Bye-bye,
MOTHER

One will go a long way to find any sounder philosophy, better reasoning, or finer common sense than is written in the short sentences of this letter, on every subject entertained in it, from cover to cover. This was the heritage that Mother Lee left to her preacher-boy.

Never having been one to let grass grow under his feet, Lee borrowed some money from Prof. Ben E. Greer, who later was elected to the presidency of Furman University, and contracted to have a house built, giving Greer, for security, a first mortgage on house and lot. In this house on Elkins Street he planned to be married and to live after the wedding. It was a small house, built by a colored contractor, who, Lee says, was as honest as he was black. The little house held all the hopes and happiness that a castle could contain. The cost was $1,800.00.

The first that Mrs. Gentry heard about the actual wedding plans was when her future son-in-law called upon her and invited her to the wedding. To the house that Lee built with borrowed money she came gladly, of course—along with Prof. and Mrs. Ben Greer and the boys of the class which "Professor" Lee taught in the grade school. Here the young couple were married on November 26 1913, by the bride's brother-in-law, Rev. Frank G. Lavender, then a pastor in Virginia. After the ceremony, Mr. and Mrs. Robert Greene Lee went to Princeton, South Carolina, where Mr. Lee (who had been an ordained minister of the Baptist Church since 1910), united in marriage Mr. James Stone and Miss Annie Lee Arnold. Thus, five hours after her own wedding, young Mrs. Lee served as matron of honor at the wedding of another bride.

From Princeton, the Lees, happy as lovers protected from storm by one roof, departed for Atlanta for their honeymoon. They stayed at the Piedmont Hotel, in room 520. To this day, Dr. Lee, a man of deep and incurable sentiment, visits the hotel when speaking engagements take him to Atlanta, and, if room 520 is unoccupied, he looks in upon it as if it were an old friend to be grasped by the hand.

Although a newly-wed and out of college only six months, Robert Lee had begun his career as pastor and preacher four years earlier, April 3, 1910. He was ordained to the Gospel ministry, according to the procedures used by Baptist churches in the Southland—examination as to conversion and doctrinal beliefs and call to the minstry, by "prayer and the laying on of hands"—by his home church, where his mother was a charter member, where his father served as deacon, where his oldest sister's husband was Sunday school secretary for many years. Among those who had part in the "laying on of hands" were his father and one who had taught him in Sunday school as a lad.

During that sacred and solemn time, 1910—1919, that is, over a ten-year period, Lee pastored ten country churches. He was not, however, a "mover" in the sense of staying only a little while at a place; for during nine of the ten years he was the shepherd of two, and sometimes three, flocks at a time, partly while a college student and partly while a grade school teacher and principal. During this period the once-feeble ambition to be a college teacher as well as a preacher, and both in one person, became mysteriously strong. Though he seldom mentioned this plan as to his strivings to be a teacher, Lee now wanted to occupy a "chair" in some university, never forsaking preaching and the pastorate, however, which always held first place in his affection. But the teaching profession was next in importance.

The first church to call Robert Lee, even before he was set apart as a preacher by "prayer and the laying on of hands," was the *Lima Baptist Church,* situated in the North Greenville Association, and on a hill almost mountain high. Lee served this church, which has already been mentioned in connection with a baptismal service, when the brethren had to break the ice for their pastor to administer the ordinance, from 1909 to 1911. Dr. Poteat recommended Lee for this post. With faith in God and trust in Dr. Poteat's word, the church called him, never having heard or seen him. The "meeting house" as the mountain folk called it, was a one-room building. There were forty-three members. Salary to the young preacher was, at first, fifty dollars a year, even though small gifts from here and there, and never recorded on the church books, made welcome increase. It was a blessed place. Judging from the letters written others about Lima Church, to no Jew of old was Jerusalem ever dearer than was this church to the young pastor.

In going to Lima, Lee would take a little train facetiously called by many in Greenville and in little towns along the route, the "Swamp Rabbit Special."

Though not as great as was his joy in seeing lost people saved, at Lima, Lee had a "mountain-top" experience that taught him God's help in time of trouble as surely, he says, "as the disciples beheld Jesus in transfiguration glory on a high mountain apart." This is how Lee has told that experience all over the nation:

When I was in Furman University, little money came my way. What did come said "Howdy" and "Good-bye" almost in the same breath. As to my money, greeting and farewell were almost "one flesh"—never capable of separation. Once, in the "green and salad days" of my sophomore year, dollars with me were as scarce as hen's teeth and not to be found in my pockets any more than you find blonde hair on green frogs—and daily, almost hourly, I wondered how I'd get money for expenses. Blackness was added to blueness one day when, just before I went to the class room for "Latin larnin'," I received a letter from Dean Cox sympathetically assuring me that he knew what financial difficulties were mine, reluctantly announcing that I owed the University eighty-four dollars, and insistently making declaration that I should—yea, *must*—pay that amount by Monday "just ahead"—since the books must be balanced and my "carry over" was of long standing.

When, with that letter before my eyes as vividly as a zig-zag flash of lightning, I gloomily entered the class room, that eighty-four seemed to be on the spectacles of Prof. Martin, the number of every page and paragraph of the Latin grammer. Class over, I went to my room in Griffith Cottage. On my door was the figure three, but somehow, as I unlocked the door, it seemed to increase and change shape and become an eighty-four. On the mantle was my alarm clock that had aroused me at three A.M. for many nights—as I arose at that time to make ready for carrying newspapers. Vigorously pounding it was —seeming to tick out "eighty-four, eighty-four, eighty-four." After locking my door, I pulled down the shades of the windows. In the darkness, I knelt and talked to God. I talked with Him about how He had saved me when I was a boy on the farm, how He had called me to be a preacher—and that I was at Furman trying to get an education so that I could preach the Gospel. I told God I knew nobody on earth to whom I could go and ask for eighty-four dollars. I begged Him to help me out of my financial pit—and that right early.

That was Friday—blue Friday heavily fringed with black—when I prayed. The next morning I took the little train, laughed at by some as the "Swamp Rabbit Special" —and headed for the mountain station where I heard, above the voice of friends who met me, the click-clack of the metallic lips of the telegraph instrument in the wooden station house—seeming to say "eighty-four, eighty-four, eighty-four." As I got in the buggy, the pounding hoof of the horse on the dirt road seemed to pound out "eighty-four, eighty-four, eighty-four."

At the church service that Saturday afternoon there were seventeen people present. The first hymn we sang had an eighty-four in it. With heavy heart and not with as much faith as I should have had, I went through the preaching service and the monthly "bizness meetin'" that followed.

Then, "church over," I went to spend the night at the home of Mrs. Sally Goodwin whom, till this day, though she is now forever with the Lord, I call "Second Mother." A widow she was with many noble children. That night after supper, several of us sat around the old fire place, talking pleasantly and roasting chestnuts over the flames in that dear mountain home. About ten o'clock, I said: "I am tired. I want to go to bed. Let us read the Book— and have prayer." All this we did.

And when I started up the stairway to the "prophet's room," Mrs. Goodwin said: "Mister Lee, wait a minute. You know I had never thought about it until yesterday— that you are working your way through college. And

I've been thinking you might need a little money. You've been such a good pastor—and I couldn't ever pay you for all you've meant to us. But—you wait here a minute." As I stood on the lone step of the stairway of that dear mountain home, she went into a room adjoining the stairway. I heard her unlock an old trunk and let the lid fall and then lock it again. Then back she came to me—a sweet smile upon her face and above the smile, two eyes sparkling compassionately. "Shut your eyes—and hold out your hands!" she said. I did as she said. Then she dropped something into them. Then she asked me to open my eyes. I did so—and in my hands were twenty five-dollar gold pieces. Talk about your beautiful sunrises and gorgeous sunsets! The glories of both combined could not equal the beauty of that gold money in my hands. I began to laugh and cry. And it is none of your business what else I did. But, after thanks and good night were spoken, I went up the stairway to my room. And then, on the old-fashioned bed, covered with a quilt in which were many squares of cloth of various colors, I put a five-dollar gold piece on twenty of the squares and knelt down and, after viewing that golden landscape o'er, thanked God for answered prayer—and for such a friend in time of trouble as was this precious widow who did as much as for me as ever did the "widow-woman" of Zarephath for Elijah.

It was while pastor at Lima also when Lee, again without money, again pressed with expenses at Furman, rode a bicycle eighteen miles from his room to the home of Mrs. Ella Trammell—hoping and praying she would lend him some money. Large and portly woman, she was sitting in a huge rocker on the back porch when the preacher, hot and perspiring, dismounted from his "two-wheel chariot." After greetings, the young preacher made known to her his desire to borrow some money—one hundred and fifty dollars. The good woman, without any hesitancy,

went in the house and got the money. Lee, jubilant
and tearful, put the money in his left-hand trousers
pocket and made ready to ride the eighteen miles
back. Mrs. Trammell detained him until she got a
big horse-blanket pin and pinned up his pocket
"so as to hold the money in." Lee, telling of this dear
woman who made him the loan, taking no note,
asking no interest, said: "My ride back to the campus
was an eighteen-mile triumph."

The country church, *Fairview,* near Greer, South
Carolina, called Lee as pastor shortly after he began to
serve at Lima. Here he went and visited once a month
—preaching and holding a business meeting on Saturday, and preaching on Sunday morning. As in the
case of Lima, the congregation at Fairview called him
"sight unseen." Here it was upon recommendation
of Furman's dean, Prof. H. T. Cox. Before Bob's arrival, there was much excited speculation on the
part of the many members as to how the new
preacher would look and preach, some saying they
hoped he "wouldn't be fat and overly long-winded."
Lee has never laid claim to the former, but as to the
latter, well, he does not like a congregation to have
"little stomach for much meat."

There was a time, some years ago, when the great
British Bible teacher, Dr. G. Campbell Morgan, expressed himself publicly to the effect that Robert
G. Lee had "little stomach for much meat"—though
he used a different figure of speech and was unacquainted with the one of whom he spoke. The occasion was during the annual Bible conference at
the Baptist Tabernacle in Atlanta. Dr. Lee, then a

young man, had a couple of hours in Atlanta between trains, and so he went to hear the famed
British preacher. Dr. Morgan was still speaking
when Lee observed that it was time for him to leave
if he were to make his train, and so, while the sermon was still in progress, he got up and left the
service. While he was making his way to the door,
Dr. Morgan paused in his message to remark, for
all to hear: "There goes a young man with a small
cup."

Here, at Fairview, Lee presided at his first church
business conference. An argument arose between two
of the brethren over a certain delicate matter. Inside
the church, though advised hesitantly by the young
preacher, they could not settle the argument by word
of mouth; and the decision by vote of the congregation was delayed. But outside, back of the church
building, the two "at-odds" brethren "had it out" with
fists. Young Lee was not only startled, but deeply distressed. He had never seen blood spilled among the
saints before and was amazed at this un-Christian and
unscriptural behaviour, or *mis*behaviour. But his
heart was comforted when the following Sunday
morning the "at-odds" brethren voluntarily came
forward at the close of the sermon and made tearful and shamefaced confessions before the whole
congregation, asked forgiveness of God's people, and,
after embracing each other, pledged the young
preacher that "it wouldn't happen again anyhow
or any time."

At Fairview, Robert Lee conducted his first funeral service—for the little baby of Mr. and Mrs.

Lee Lanford. In his three years' ministry at Fairview (1909-12), where he went once a month and preached twice a month, on Saturday afternoon and the Lord's Day morning following, he baptized fifty-one who professed Christ as Saviour.

Near Laurens, South Carolina, somewhat off the highway and among tall pines and oaks, is Harmony Church (1909-11)—the church house being used two Sundays out of each month by the Baptists and two Sundays out of each month by the Presbyterians. The same organ, hymn books, Bible, pews, pulpit, and tables were employed by both congregations—save that the Presbyterians never used the Baptist pool for baptism! Two members of the Harmony Baptist Church had, a short while before, heard Robert Lee preach two sermons on different subjects one Sunday morning, one with only a half hour's notice, in the Beulah Baptist Church out in the country, and they believed if he could preach two sermons in one morning he could preach one acceptable to the Lord once a month. Harmony, where Lee served from 1909 to 1911, just two years, was not his first pastorate, but a number of his "firsts" occurred here. The first time in his life that he was promised an annual salary—$150.00 for once-a-month preaching—was here. The first money ever paid him for preaching was here. The amount was $18.50, paid him in February, 1910, by Mr. W. S. Powers, whom Lee calls "one of the best men who ever lived." Here the young preacher, ever ambitious to achieve, held his first "protracted meeting," when there was twice-a-day preaching for six days. Nine were won to Christ. An offering for the pastor amounted to sixteen dollars, paid to him with this comment by Brother Powers: "It's not much, I'm 'shamed to say," but to Lee sixteen dollars loomed large.

Here, for the first time, he preached one sermon without using any notes. Here he baptized for the first time. The name of the convert was Bertha Lee Helms. Here he administered the Lord's Supper for the first time. Here he had his first funeral for a grown person. Here he paid the tithe of his salary for the first time.

Harmony was a good name for this lovely church. The evidence of the Spirit's presence was felt here so frequently. The singing, too, was unusually good, reaching the hearts of the people.

Robert Lee expected something other than harmony upon the first occasion that he ever lashed out at a congregation, though it was certainly not the last time in his years of ministry. He observed evidences of a dirty habit—the stains of tobacco juice on the walls of the little church. So he rebuked the men of the church publicly with more force than tact, anticipating that there would be reverberations of intense and stormy nature. But the rebuke was accepted meekly, for they knew they were in the wrong. The following week, the women of the church washed the walls. There were no tobacco stains thereafter.

The next three pastorates were also held more or less simultaneously.

Princeton, South Carolina, 1911-13. Young Lee was pastor of this church just before he was married. He had a very fine revival meeting here when many professed the Lord Jesus Christ as their Saviour.

He was instrumental here in having a cement baptistry built out in a pasture. Rejoicing in the "visit of Heaven to earth" in the revival that swept the community, the people gave willingly of their money to build it. Here Lee baptized, along with forty others, the Britt twins, establishing in the performance of the ordinance a practice he has followed several times since—immersing twins at the same time, as at Edgefield, South Carolina, the twin sisters of J. Strom Thurmond; the Everett twins, and the Poole twins, in Memphis. The salary at Princeton was $75.00 per year, the amount being stated in the letter notifying Lee of the action of the church in extending him a call. The sister of former Governor Robert Cooper of South Carolina was once a member of this church.

Waterloo, South Carolina, 1911-16. The salary at Waterloo was $100.00 a year. With sad heart, believing he ought to live in a place of less luxury if God directed, Lee resigned his teaching position in the Grade School in Greenville, and taking his wife from the lovely little home there, moved to Waterloo. Here he stayed for one year, acting as principal of the High School in addition to his church duties. Neither he nor Mrs. Lee found any joy in Waterloo in the ancient house which he rented, which looked "almost as old inside as Noah's Ark." Lee declares that in this ancient house that he occupied, the rats were so numerous and bold, and such frequent visitors, that, in the little room he used for a study, he kept a hatchet, strong of handle and sharp

of blade, against the wall, and with this weapon
"guillotined" many a rodent, large and small, as the
invaders stuck their heads out of holes gnawed in
the baseboard. Pastor Lee led the congregation in
the construction of a new church building in Waterloo.

Waterloo is memorable above many places, however, in the hearts of Bob and Bula Lee. For it was
during their residence there that a little daughter,
Bula Gentry, was born to the young pastor and
his wife, the mother going to Greenville for the
great event, which took place on January 2nd, 1917.

Long Branch, South Carolina. Here, in this country
church, Lee served from 1912-16. The salary was $150
per year, for two sermons a month. Once, when a
hailstorm beat up the crops of the farmers quite
badly, two of the deacons asked Lee if he would take
a cut in salary. Lee answered: "If it's wise to take the
wings off Mercury's feet, cut her!" By the time he
went there again, a month later, when the crops
had somewhat recovered from the hailstorm and the
brethren had learned about the wings on Mercury's
feet, he was assured that his salary would not be cut.
During Lee's term as pastor here there were, as
the church records show, sixty-four additions to the
church, the majority by profession of faith and baptism. Two of the outstanding characteristics of the
Long Branch Church were the large congregations
that overflowed the auditorium and the unusually
fine singing. At Long Branch, Ellis Fuller helped
Lee in a revival meeting held for one week during
a hot summer.

Four other churches should be mentioned here. There was *White Oak*—located on the outskirts of Greenville. Bob Jones University is now just across the road from this little church, candy-like in architecture and ornamentation, and with its graveyard adjoining. Frequent in attendance there, as members, were Mr. and Mrs. Bates, who were very hospitable to Bob Lee, and he spent many happy hours in their home. He used to tell Bible stories to their little girl, who is now Mrs. Ellis A. Fuller. At White Oak, Lee served three years, at a salary of $300.00, and here he baptized quite a number who were saved.

At *Mountville, South Carolina,* where the salary was $300.00 per year, where Ellis Fuller's parents were members, and where Ellis himself was on the roll for a while, Lee preached for about a year, 1916-17. Some, not many, received Christ during that period. But there was joy over the few.

Only a few miles from here was *Cross Hill, South Carolina,* where the Lees lived after moving from Waterloo, and where the young preacher engaged in warning sinners and waking up sleepy saints to greater spiritual vision. Lee was becoming a high salaried preacher now, for Cross Hill paid its pastor $600.00. But his tenure of office was short in this place, 1916-17. He baptized quite a few young people, and had a part in starting a movement to build a new church building. But he left before the program was really under way.

In 1917, resigning all churches he then pastored, Lee moved to *Saluda, South Carolina,* to become pas-

tor of and to give all his time and talents to just one
church at a salary of $1,200.00 per year. He rented his
own house and provided his own car. The name of
this church was the Red Bank Baptist Church. During
his short stay in Saluda, in addition to his preaching
responsibilities and pastoral duties, Lee acted as
personal landscape gardener for the church, thus
displeasing a few by "lowering the dignity of the
ministry," and pleasing many by showing he had forgotten nothing he had learned on the farm and that,
though a preacher, he could handle mules. Feeling
that the setting of the church building needed beauti-
fying, the pastor hired a team of mules and he himself plowed up the lawn, grading and seeding it, with
rather good results.

While pastor at Saluda, Lee was asked by
the President and Board of Trustees of Furman to
take the chair of Latin at Furman University. At first
it seemed that his somewhat strange desire to be
a college professor, in addition to being a preacher,
would be realized. He was somewhat in debt, for the
Lee's baby daughter, whom they called Bula G., had
laid hold upon their one purse as well as upon
both of their hearts. The extra financial expenses in
connection with a growing family influenced him
somewhat to accept the offer. To the deep regret
of his congregation, Lee resigned his pastorate in
Saluda in the late spring of 1918.

Mr. W. L. Daniel, one of the Trustees of Furman,
was deeply grieved by Bob Lee's decision, and wrote
and told him so. It was Mr. Daniel who had awarded
Lee the gold medal for oratory in his senior year at

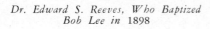

*Dr. Edward S. Reeves, Who Baptized
Bob Lee in 1898*

*First Baptist Church,
Fort Mill, S. C.,
Where Robert Lee
Made His Confes-
sion of Faith in
Christ, Was Bap-
tized, and Ordained
to the Gospel
Ministry*

Oak Grove Church, Where Bob Lee Preached His First
Sermon, "The Lord Is at Hand," at 18 Years of Age

"Pa" and Mother Lee in Fort Mill, S. C., in 1908

college, and the noble gentleman believed that Bob had been called to preach the Gospel and not to teach an ancient language.

On his way to New Orleans to do graduate work and to freshen up on Latin at Tulane University, he stopped at Mrs. Gentry's home in Greenville, where Mrs. Lee and the little daughter stayed until the Tulane days were over. The day before he took train for New Orleans, a pulpit committee from the First Baptist Church, Union, South Carolina, called on him and stated that they were ready to call him to be their pastor if he would assure them that he would accept when called. But though the offer included a salary into the thousands and a parsonage, Lee refused all overtures of the committee. The preacher-professor bee was still "buzzing in his bonnet."

Later on, Lee himself became unhappy about the situation. He was, of course, honored to have been invited to head the Latin Department at Furman University. But, after all, his life, his training, his calling, and his longing were to preach. He did not intend to cease preaching even with the new work. Yet he, in debt and worried by debts, faced the fact that one of his reasons for accepting the post at Furman was the necessity of a larger income.

With sober mind and heavy heart, having to be away from his wife and daughter for some months, Lee arrived again in New Orleans. He had not been there since he carried bananas and rolled barrels of molasses on the wharf. With expenses at Tulane ahead and unpaid debts behind, Lee was uneasy as to how he would come out. He rented a cheap room on Camp Street, matriculated at Tulane, and began the study of Latin and Spanish. The young preacher, with all monies going out and none coming in, preaching none, longing for companionship with his wife, and missing the cooing of his baby, received word that the child was seriously ill. He found the Tulane days a time of scrimping and study and unspeakable loneliness. To save money, he ate sparingly. To save carfare, he walked many times from the Tulane campus to his room near Lafayette Square, a distance of several miles. One of the hardest things to bear during these days was that he had no chance to preach.

While he was at Tulane, providentially—and we are convinced that it was God's hand and nothing less—the Trustees of Furman University passed a resolution that no faculty member could hold a pastorate and continue to remain on the faculty. But Lee did not know of this resolution until some time later, when he returned to Greenville from his studies at Tulane, in September.

Back in Greenville, and still ignorant of the new policy of the University, Lee's heart was filled to overflowing. He was united with his loved-ones once more! A larger work than he had ever anticipated was open before him—to preach, as he had always expected; and to teach Latin at Furman University! In such a spirit of joy, expectancy, and hope, young Lee went to the bank to make arrangements for a loan, so that he could build a little home. The banker, a Trustee of the University and a friend of Bob's also, knowing the purpose of the loan, felt it his duty to inform the young man of the change of policy that would prohibit his preaching if he was to teach Latin. Lee could hardly believe his ears! But further inquiry confirmed what his banker friend had told him.

The decision between teaching and preaching was now squarely up to Bob Lee. He did not hesitate an instant. Since his conversion there had been, and still was, a burning volcano within his heart to preach the Gospel. So it was that in spite of the fact that he now had no pastorate, no money, and was involved in certain debts, approximately $4,000.00, he rejected the teaching job. When he told Mrs. Lee about it, she answered with the same spiritual acumen and common sense that has characterized her understanding and encouragement throughout the many years that they have enjoyed together: "That's good! The Lord never intended that you should dig around among Latin roots. He called you to be a preacher."

Within a short time, and upon recommendation by Mr. Daniel, Lee was called to be pastor of the First Baptist Church of Edgefield, South Carolina.

Chapter VII
PLEASANT PLACES ALONG THE WAY
A Second Decade in the Ministry Begins

It was on October 12th, 1918, that Robert Lee, eager once again to be at the job of preaching and pastoring, the ministry to which God had called him early in life, arrived at Edgefield, South Carolina, to begin his pastorate at the First Baptist Church, known to its older members as "the Edgefield Village Church." Gone now was his overly ambitious and erratic desire to be a preacher and college professor at the same time; in fact, a professorship was here buried forever in the grave of Lee's memory.

Robert Lee had a happy ministry in Edgefield, a town noted for culture, its stately houses of *antebellum* design, its love of the Confederacy, its Woman's Christian Temperance activities, and the many political figures who claimed it as their home— men such as Senator Ben ("Pitchfork") Tillman, who served thirty years in the United States Senate after his two terms as Governor of South Carolina. For, in addition to Tillman, the following governors of the state came from the Edgefield District, even as the present Governor, J. Strom Thurmond, identifies himself as from Edgefield: Andrew Pickens, Jr., Pierce Mason Butler, James H. Hammond, Francis

2,1868

W. Pickens, M. L. Bonham, John C. Sheppard, John Gary Evans, and Governor Thurmond.

Edgefield, moreover, was the home of Preston Brooks who, back in the days when the North and the South were in agitation over the slave question, raised his cane against Charles Sumner, of Massachusetts, in defense of the South. Then, too, at the Edgefield Village Church, Dr. William Bullein Johnson, who was the first President of the Southern Baptist Convention, served for twenty-two years as pastor.

When Lee went to Edgefield, the church had less than four hundred members and a Sunday school that was about forty per cent of the membership. This church was larger than any he had served up to this time, and the opportunities of his ministry were broadened.

Members now living, who recall how the Lee family arrived unannounced and unexpectedly on an early train that drear October morning, tell how the preacher, his wife, and little daughter, were greeted, not by friendly people who would have been there had they been informed as to his arrival, but by the sight of twenty or more coffins, stacked up on the station platform for burial of some who had died under the influenza scourge which was sweeping the nation. The Lee family walked from the smoke-stained station to the little house that was to be their home. The address had been made known in a letter from the owner of the house, written to Lee the week before, which stated: "Your household stuff you shipped by freight arrived Monday

past. The car is on the siding awaiting your coming.
The well has been cleaned out and you will find the
key to the house next door."

It was an ancient and ugly house, with a squat
chimney, small front porch, narrow hall, three rooms,
an ell—and a leaky roof. There was no front yard. A
big oak tree, as though it were making a gesture
of pity, spread its branches over the tiny, ramshackle
building.

Going to the house next door, Lee announced to
its mistress that he was the new preacher and would
like to get the key to his house and, if she did not
mind, borrow a broom from her. Key in one hand
and broom in the other, the preacher unlocked the
door to the house, and he and his family "took up
residence." While Mrs. Lee swept, the next-door
neighbor surreptitiously spread "the alarm." Lee
found a drayman, helped him unload the furniture
from the freight car to the drayman's wagon and
from the wagon to the house, and by the time that
news of the preacher's arrival had spread, the house
had been arranged. A few members of the church
called and expressed regret that the welcoming committee had not known of the coming of the family.
Neighbors brought in some breakfast. The church
clerk came and expressed the belief and hope that
the preacher's family would be quite comfortable
here. Comfortable? Well, it was not so bad when the
sun was shining or the stars were out, but there
were many occasions, when it was raining, that the
young pastor had to hold an umbrella over the stove
while his wife cooked the meals. The Lord Jesus,

however, had not where to lay His head, so what matter a little privation to His servants? Often they thought of this, and often they clung to the words of the Apostle Paul: "I have learned, in whatsoever state I am, therewith to be content" (Phil. 4:11). But how nice it would be, thought Lee, to be obliged to learn "how to abound"!

Robert Lee had come to Edgefield owing around $3,000.00, being still indebted for his schooling, for furniture, and other things. He had to watch every penny, therefore, and make it count; at the same time, he needed to be an example in liberality to his congregation. Sometimes he wondered how he could possibly make ends meet, how he would ever pay up all that he owed, which he knew he should do as promptly as possible, so as to "owe no man anything."

One morning he came down to breakfast with a heavy heart, for he knew that he had a note due at the bank, for $100.00, that day. Before he and Bula had prayer together, Bob asked her: "How much money do you have?"

"About forty cents," was her answer.

"Did you know that I have a note due at the bank today, for $100.00?"

"Yes," she said, and continued to stir the oatmeal.

"But what am I to do?" her husband asked her. "I can't pay it."

"Then have it renewed," she replied with all seriousness.

"I have already had it renewed twice," he said. "I don't want them to think at the bank that I'm careless about my debts. They are very much on my heart."

Bula replied with calm practicality: "There is nothing else that you can do but to ask Governor Sheppard or Mr. Mims to renew the note. But first, let's pray about it." And then the two of them prayed, led this time by Mrs. Lee, telling the Lord of their need—which, of course, He already knew— and asking Him to help them.

About two hours later Lee went uptown to the bank, to speak to President Sheppard about a renewal. But before he reached the bank, in fact, just as he was crossing the street to enter the building, he was hailed by a large and stout farmer, "Bruns" Hollingsworth, a member of the church. The pastor re-crossed the street and Mr. Hollingsworth took him by the arm and led him up a stairway in the telephone building, and on a half-way landing, putting his hands on Lee's shoulders and looking him in the eye, said: "Preacher, somehow I've been thinking about you this morning. You've been a good preacher to us. You've brought joy into our home by getting hold of our wild boy, and I can't ever pay you for it. But I sold my cotton this morning, and I thought you might need some money."

Without another word, Mr. Hollingsworth put his hand down into a pocket in his huge overalls and pulled out a roll of bills that made Lee's eyes bulge. Pealing off one $100.00 bill, the farmer folded it and placed it in the preacher's hand, closing Bob's trembling fingers over it. Lee began to cry and laugh all at once.

"Don't make a fool of yourself," Mr. Hollingsworth said, not without sympathy and amusement.

"I'll be as big a fool as I want to be," was the pastor's reply, and then, turning and hastening down the steps, Bob started, "like Zacchaeus," he says, toward home.

He had not gotten far when he heard his benefactor's voice again: "Hey you, come back here!" Reluctantly Lee retraced his steps, fearful that he would be told that a mistake had been made, and that the money was too much—that the farmer meant to give him ten dollars. But Mr. Hollingsworth had no such thing in mind. Rather, he led the preacher into the meat market, bought him a quarter of a cow, wrapped it himself and put it on Bob's shoulder, saying: "Now go home and eat till you bust."

One cannot doubt that God's hand is upon him when he experiences such examples of His grace.

The terrible flu epidemic was on a rampage at this time. Visits to the village cemetery testified that there were many vacant chairs in the village households. All churches were closed. During this time of enforced absenteeism from the churches, the new preacher visited in the homes and got acquainted with all his people—and, a few months later, knew young and old by face and name.

Lee wanted to "get going," and to set the church "a-going," and chafed at the delay. The young pastor, so the people of Edgefield testify, expressed sympathy for those who wanted to go to church and were not permitted to do so, and rebuked the people who, when the churches were open, would not go.

Before many months had passed, Lee began to be troubled about the indebtedness of the church on its building. He did not say a great deal about it except to the Lord, but, through succeeding months, began to wrestle more and more earnestly with this problem. Early in February of the following year, he believed that he had the mind of the Lord as to what ought to be done. However, he still refrained from talking about it until the conviction should be so certain that he would know it was from God. Meanwhile, Mrs. Lee was his only confidante.

Finally, after wrestling one night far into the early morning in prayer, somewhat as did Jacob at Jabbok, Lee's decision was reached. He resolved to make it known to the congregation on the following Sunday morning. When he and Mrs. Lee were at the breakfast table, he said to her, "Do you know what I'm going to do next Sunday morning?"

She answered: "No telling! But what?"

"I am going to ask the people to pay off the church debt," he said. "And I am not going to tell a soul —and you must not tell a soul."

Mrs. Lee asked but one question: "Are you sure of what you are doing?"

Bob assured his young wife that he was positive that this plan was the will of God, and so she replied: "Go ahead!"

On Sunday morning, February 17th, 1919, the young pastor made the startling announcement to the quiescent congregation that he felt the indebted-

ness was not honoring to the Lord, that it was
a waste of God's money to pay eight per cent interest on the debt, and that he was looking to them
to bring sufficient money in cash on the following
Sunday morning to liquidate the debt entirely, and
he mentioned the amount—around ten thousand
dollars. His exact words were: "Next Sunday morning we will pay off our church debt. All gifts must
be dough on the barrel head. Nobody must give over
five hundred dollars; what he gives more will be
returned. But we want everybody to have a part."

Quickly, somewhat severely, yet with courtesy,
with his usual dignity somewhat thrust aside, Ex-
Governor John C. Sheppard, a faithful and attentive
member of the church, and from the very first a
warm "complimenter" of the pastor, holding hat and
gold-headed walking cane in hand, arose and asked,
in consternation and in a loud voice: "Do I hear my
ears aright?" His brother, clerk of the church, a
man of like dignity and nobility with his brother,
stood up, saying: "That's what our young preacher
says"—in such a tone of voice as to indicate that he,
at least, would fain persuade the pastor to withdraw
his quixotic proposal.

More than the usual friendly greetings and chattering among the membership followed that morning
service. Everyone was excited. Some expressed themselves as feeling that the young preacher was somewhat unbalanced, others said that they approved of
the idea, still others doubted that any such miracle
could happen. District Attorney Thurmond, a devout
worshiper with strong religious convictions, was

heard to remark: "Fine young preacher, but impractical, *very* impractical!" One thing was certain: all were amazed, all so curious as to what the outcome would be that there was little doubt that the First Baptist Church would have a packed house on the following Sunday morning.

During the ensuing week, if the pastor's announcement did nothing else, it certainly gave the populace of Edgefield a topic of conversation. Lee's name was on the lips of everyone. Wherever he went he was gazed upon with a certain awe, and frequently men and women who had been luke-warm as church members, and others who had never attended the church at all, stopped him on the street to speak with him about his courageous announcement.

In a sermon which Dr. Lee has preached all over the land, in which he relates the history of this debt-payment event, he tells of one businessman, Mr. B. B. Jones, who had been "at outs" with the church about certain policies with which he could not agree, and who had withdrawn his support of the church, both as to his presence and his purse. Seeing Lee downtown one day, he called the young pastor over to his store and asked: "You are the new preacher, I take it?"

"Yes, sir! Where have you been all this time?" the preacher asked.

"And I understand you announced, without asking anybody, that the church debt would be paid next Sunday," Mr. Jones stated.

"Yes, sir—and the fellow who has no part in it will

look like a wheelbarrow in an auto parade," Lee replied.

"Are you sure it will be done?"

"Just as sure as that I know God lives."

"And I understand you said nobody must pay
over five hundred dollars?" Jones asked.

"That's right."

"Well, you have more grit or less sense than anybody who has ever been in this town."

Without more talk or more ado, Mr. Jones asked
Lee back to his desk and wrote him out a check for
five hundred dollars, saying: "Now, if anybody asks
you if old Brag Jones is going to help pay the debt,
tell 'em what you please."

Feeling all week that all members of the church, for
their own souls' good, ought to have some share in
paying the indebtedness, Lee looked often at the
five-hundred-dollar check Mr. Jones had given him,
and, after talking much to many people about having
a part in the debt payment, looked forward to the
next Lord's Day—in hope and unwavering faith.

True to expectation, on Sunday morning there was
not a seat to be had, and people were standing. Pastor
Lee delivered a sermon of usual length, and following
this he led the congregation in prayer. Then he
announced that the offering for the debt payment
would be taken.

His instructions as to the act of payment were
that each member should stand, call his or her name,
state the amount to be given, and bring that amount
to the front, placing it on the table. Immediately, and
with eagerness, Ex-Governor Sheppard was on his

feet. He addressed the pastor: "I want to have the honor, sir, of giving the first five hundred dollars."

"Sorry, Governor Sheppard," said the young preacher, "but Mr. Brag Jones has already given me a check for five hundred dollars." Then the pastor dropped on the table the check he had carried nearly all week.

Governor Sheppard walked down and put his five-hundred-dollar check beside it. Mr. Broadwater gave the same amount. So also did "Bruns" Hollingsworth, and the E. J. Norris family. Others rose to their feet, called their names, and told how much they were going to give—some indicating three hundred dollars, some two hundred, some ten dollars, and others only one dollar; but before the service was over, there was not a single person, children included, who had not made some offering.

A committee was appointed to count the money, which was done immediately, and few, if any, left the building until the result of the tabulation was made known. The receipts for that morning service, including the gifts that had been handed to Lee during the week, amounted to slightly more than fourteen thousand dollars in cash—some four thousand more than was actually needed to pay the debt. With what joy the people heard this news! They had all had a share in the giving, and as is the case when the Lord's people contribute generously and sacrificially to His cause, the givers were the greatest blessed, their hearts being warmed and their faith strengthened.

At this same glorious hour, while some laughed,

some cried, others refrained themselves from shouting, while still others hugged each other, Mr. B. B. Jones, the same who had been displeased with the church, arose and, with tears on his cheeks, brought all to quietude by saying, in a quavering voice: "Folks, before we are dismissed, I want to say I am ashamed of us for letting our preacher live in the sort of house he is now in. I make the motion that we use all we don't need to pay the church debt as part payment, and add to it all we'll need to build a new house, and that the pastor be chairman of the committee." The motion, with many "secondings," was carried.

The church records of that notable day reveal that the pastor asked B. B. Jones, Abner Broadwater, and Bettis Cantelou to serve on the committee. A lot was bought, just across the road from the church. A beautiful ten-room house was built. And it was a great occasion when the pastor's family entered in to possess "the house the preacher built."

For the payment of the church debt, Lee had "dug deep in his jeans," and, because of trying to meet the monthly payments on his personal debts, was wanting in clothes for himself. One day Mr. Jones, who was now a warm-hearted friend of the preacher, met him on the street and, as Lee's diary reveals, said rather severely: "Say, preacher, are those the best clothes you have?"

"Yes, why?" Lee answered, somewhat abashed.

"Well," said Mr. Jones, of whom Lee had become very fond, "I want to see my preacher dressed up, 'specially on Sundays. You go down to Augusta and tell Mr. Farris, the tailor, to make you the finest

Prince Albert suit he can make and an extra pair of trousers. Then you get you some shirts, socks, collars, ties, shoes, and, if you want, a hat and gold-headed cane like Governor Sheppard's."

"Why, fellow, that'll cost you six hundred dollars," said the young preacher in surprise.

"Doesn't make any difference if it costs a thousand," Brag Jones replied. "I can't preach, but I can dress up a man who can."

"I'll be on my way in half an hour," Lee said with enthusiasm. And he was. Three weeks later, in all the glory of his new "togs and tails," the pastor appeared before the congregation. But he admitted later that he had an awful time preaching that day because he felt the folks were thinking more about his suit than his sermon.

It was at Edgefield that Robert G. Lee's ability as an organizer and promoter began to shine brightly and make itself felt. Though busy with the building of the parsonage, he gave himself in conversation as he visited and in preaching from the pulpit on Sundays to getting his people to believe in and make real the every-member principle. Against the attitude and over the protest of some who looked on any new plans as unnecessary innovations, he advocated the every-member canvass, by which each member of the church was asked to give so much per week for the financial support of the church and the causes supported by the church. He asked of the deacons if there was any objection to his making the canvass himself. There was no objection on their part to trying it out to see how it worked. Lee made the canvass, going from house to house, store to store, office to office, securing pledges for a "unified budget." He was jubilant over the results, and the church officials were exceedingly well pleased about the increase in offerings. The annual report to the Edgefield Association showed thousands of dollars' increase in the amount of money brought to the Lord's treasury. Lee, always busy day and night at doing things himself, enlisted many others who had had no part, or a little part, in the work of the church.

Although he was a very busy pastor, Bob Lee's penchant for learning was so strong that he sought some method whereby he might advance his education. He could not, in his active life, take the time to go to a university for graduate work as a resident, and yet he had the inclination to earn a Doctor of Philosophy degree. At length he heard of the Chicago Law School, where he thought he might be able to make special arrangements, and so, toward the end of 1918, he wrote a letter to the Chancellor of the School, stating that he would like to pursue his studies toward such a degree, and explaining that he was not in a position to take up residence in Chicago.

Chancellor Tobias wrote and told him that the Chicago Law School did not grant graduate degrees unless the student spent one year in residence. He did say, however, after considerable correspondence, that Lee's educational record was such that—he graduated from Furman *Magna cum Laude*—some provision might be made, and in due time this was done.

Pastor Lee worked hard on the subjects that were

assigned him, among which were Christian Ethics,
Jurisprudence, Sociology, Economics, Psychology, Philosophy, and International Law. The dean of the
school commended his work highly, complimenting
him particularly on his diagram brief on International Law. His thesis was on the subject, "Civilization's Debt to the Inventor." In June, 1919, Mr. and
Mrs. Lee went to Chicago and attended the Commencement Exercises, at which time Lee was a-
warded a Ph. D., a conferment of the Chicago Semi-
nar of Science, Collegiate Department of Midland
University. Chancellor Tobias said of Robert G. Lee:
"He classifies among the most scholarly students we
have ever had."

In many ways the church at Edgefield continued
to grow, and so did its pastor. He began to become
increasingly in demand as a speaker in other cities
and towns in South Carolina and neighboring states.
The membership enlarged and there were many
baptisms, signifying conversion on the part of those
who, having confessed faith in Christ, submitted to
this initial ordinance of a Baptist Church.

One of the members of the First Baptist Church
of Edgefield was J. Strom Thurmond, then a student
at Clemson College, the son of the District Attorney.
South Carolineans will recognize the name immediately as that of the present Governor of South Carolina, while the nation as a whole will recall that
Governor Thurmond was the Dixie-crat candidate
for President of the United States in 1948, under the
States' Rights ticket.

Pastor Lee was frequently a welcome visitor in

the stately old country home of the Thurmonds.
Upon their confession of faith in Christ, he baptized
the twin sisters of the present Governor of South
Carolina. A hard worker himself, Lee greatly admired Governor Thurmond's father and mother, who
worked hard themselves and saw to it that their
children did likewise.

On April 3rd, 1921, Pastor Lee, with heaviness of
heart because of the sorrow his going caused others,
preached his farewell sermon at the First Baptist
Church of Edgefield, having received a call which
he believed to be of the Lord, to assume the pastorate
of the First Baptist Church of Chester, South Carolina.
During his stay at Edgefield, he had seen the membership of the church increase by one hundred and
twenty-nine, seventy-nine of the new members coming
by letter, and fifty by confession of faith and baptism.
There was real spiritual blessing throughout the
years that Robert Lee served in this place, and in
addition there was the material blessing of the
church debt payment and the construction of a new
parsonage. He had the joy of seeing three of the
young men of the church begin their studies to
prepare themselves to enter the ministry, and he
himself contributing generously in a financial way to
enable these boys to get an education.

The lasting influence in Edgefield of this young
pastor cannot be described better than by quoting
from the remarks of Dr. John Wimbish, Pastor of
the Edgefield Baptist Church in 1946, when, a
quarter of a century after Robert G. Lee left the
pastorate there, he returned to Edgefield for a series

of revival meetings. Wimbish says that in Edgefield they date time by four letters: BL and AL—"Before" Lee and "After Lee."

We quote in part:

They called him "Sweetheart Lee," because said they,
"Everybody loved him." And indeed they did. For when
he delivered his final sermon as Pastor of the First Baptist
Church on Sunday, April 3, 1921, people came from miles
around to bid him adieu.

As they gathered in solemn assembly on that April
morning, all agreed that the church had never had a
pastor more generally or genuinely beloved. Many tears
were shed; many sighs were heard.

But his arrival in this unique little city was quite in-
conspicuous. Many have told me of it. Unattended and
unheralded, he and Mrs. Lee and their little twenty-one-
month-old daughter found their way to the small cottage
on Jeter Street.

He was then a tall, slender, dark-haired man, and
when he stood in the pulpit of this great old church to
deliver his first sermon as pastor, he selected for his
text, Judges 20:11: "The children of Israel went up against
the city knit together as one man."

Oh, how that sermon moved the congregation. His
magnetism was strongly felt; his rapid alliterative style
interesting, his word-pictures moving.

But before they learned that their new shepherd of
the flock was a great orator and preacher, the people discovered that his tender compassion for those in sorrow
was something akin to that of the Good Shepherd.

It was during the influenza epidemic that he arrived,
an epidemic that swept across America like a prairie fire
and left crepe hanging at many doors. Someone said to
him, "Brother Lee, everybody in Edgefield is running
from this dread disease, and you are always running right
into it."

For the pastor found his way into many homes where

the entire household was stricken by the weird malady, and sometimes took up his abode there for several days, washing dishes, preparing meals, and keeping tireless vigils through the night.

On his first Christmas in Edgefield he played Santa Claus to a family of neglected children whose father no longer cared for them. To the poor sad mother it appeared as if old Santa would not come near their little shanty that year, but the young pastor, as usual looking for someone to help and some cheer he could bring, found this mother and five little children. In his sweet, gentle manner, he talked with them and subtly learned what each child wanted Saint Nicholas to leave in his stocking. And so, Santa Claus did visit that home on Christmas Eve night, and the next morning there was much rejoicing as each child found the desire of his heart in his stocking—all because the young preacher cared.

People began thronging the church to sit at the feet of this man as he held forth the Word of God. To listen to one of his sermons was like "setting sail with Drake or Hawkins in search of new worlds and golden spoil."

Every message proved to be an intellectual treat as well as a spiritual feast. These South Carolineans of old Edgefield were quite accustomed to speech-making, for they had heard the best of the silver-tongued orators of the South expostulating their theories of government and their theological convictions. But here was a man whose eloquence excelled them all. There was something fresh about him, something that had the tang of a June morning and the glory of an autumn sunset—something genuine and positive and irresistible.

Indeed a "Son of Thunder" he was. For though he could be as gentle as a lamb, in the next instant he could exhibit the fury of a lion. And every real pastor knows the importance of that religious fury at times.

A short while after being installed as leader of this church, he realized that much improvement could be made on the Board of Deacons . . .

Here it might be well to enlarge
cident. Young Lee was more intereste
ress of the church than in the feelin
He often said that the feelings of n
be given priority over the welfare o
matters, spiritual and financial. He de
all the good men who were deacons i
noble men who had loved and served,
before their young pastor was born
Lee got the conviction that some splen
were of "deacon timber" were not l
in the work there, not given the opport
which they really deserved to have
that other worthy men should be
recognition and made to feel responsi
welfare of the local church.

Without asking anyone's advice, L
deacons together and, after prayer and
that he was going to ask the unusual
quested them to resign and to help sel
good men who were worthy to take

With a few mild protests on the
silence on the part of one, and with
fidence in their pastor's leadership, they
their resignations were presented the n
the church "called into business ses
were selected by the church, and the
cons, for the sake of the ongoing churc
per at the pastor's home for the incomi
was a good thing for the deacons wh
so long to learn that, in honor pref
they did not have to be deacons to s

the stately old country home of the Thurmonds. Upon their confession of faith in Christ, he baptized the twin sisters of the present Governor of South Carolina. A hard worker himself, Lee greatly admired Governor Thurmond's father and mother, who worked hard themselves and saw to it that their children did likewise.

On April 3rd, 1921, Pastor Lee, with heaviness of heart because of the sorrow his going caused others, preached his farewell sermon at the First Baptist Church of Edgefield, having received a call which he believed to be of the Lord, to assume the pastorate of the First Baptist Church of Chester, South Carolina. During his stay at Edgefield, he had seen the membership of the church increase by one hundred and twenty-nine, seventy-nine of the new members coming by letter, and fifty by confession of faith and baptism. There was real spiritual blessing throughout the years that Robert Lee served in this place, and in addition there was the material blessing of the church debt payment and the construction of a new parsonage. He had the joy of seeing three of the young men of the church begin their studies to prepare themselves to enter the ministry, and he himself contributing generously in a financial way to enable these boys to get an education.

The lasting influence in Edgefield of this young pastor cannot be described better than by quoting from the remarks of Dr. John Wimbish, Pastor of the Edgefield Baptist Church in 1946, when, a quarter of a century after Robert G. Lee left the pastorate there, he returned to Edgefield for a series

of revival meetings. Wimbish says that in Edgefield they date time by four letters: BL and AL—"Before" Lee and "After Lee."

We quote in part:

> They called him "Sweetheart Lee," because said they,
> "Everybody loved him." And indeed they did. For when
> he delivered his final sermon as Pastor of the First Baptist
> Church on Sunday, April 3, 1921, people came from miles
> around to bid him adieu.
>
> As they gathered in solemn assembly on that April
> morning, all agreed that the church had never had a
> pastor more generally or genuinely beloved. Many tears
> were shed; many sighs were heard.
>
> But his arrival in this unique little city was quite in-
> conspicuous. Many have told me of it. Unattended and
> unheralded, he and Mrs. Lee and their little twenty-one-
> month-old daughter found their way to the small cottage
> on Jeter Street.
>
> He was then a tall, slender, dark-haired man, and
> when he stood in the pulpit of this great old church to
> deliver his first sermon as pastor, he selected for his
> text, Judges 20:11: "The children of Israel went up against
> the city knit together as one man."
>
> Oh, how that sermon moved the congregation. His
> magnetism was strongly felt; his rapid alliterative style
> interesting, his word-pictures moving.
>
> But before they learned that their new shepherd of
> the flock was a great orator and preacher, the people dis-
> covered that his tender compassion for those in sorrow
> was something akin to that of the Good Shepherd.
>
> It was during the influenza epidemic that he arrived,
> an epidemic that swept across America like a prairie fire
> and left crepe hanging at many doors. Someone said to
> him, "Brother Lee, everybody in Edgefield is running
> from this dread disease, and you are always running right
> into it."
>
> For the pastor found his way into many homes where

the entire household was stricken by the weird malady, and sometimes took up his abode there for several days, washing dishes, preparing meals, and keeping tireless vigils through the night.

On his first Christmas in Edgefield he played Santa Claus to a family of neglected children whose father no longer cared for them. To the poor sad mother it appeared as if old Santa would not come near their little shanty that year, but the young pastor, as usual looking for someone to help and some cheer he could bring, found this mother and five little children. In his sweet, gentle manner, he talked with them and subtly learned what each child wanted Saint Nicholas to leave in his stocking. And so, Santa Claus did visit that home on Christmas Eve night, and the next morning there was much rejoicing as each child found the desire of his heart in his stocking—all because the young preacher cared.

People began thronging the church to sit at the feet of this man as he held forth the Word of God. To listen to one of his sermons was like "setting sail with Drake or Hawkins in search of new worlds and golden spoil."

Every message proved to be an intellectual treat as well as a spiritual feast. These South Carolineans of old Edgefield were quite accustomed to speech-making, for they had heard the best of the silver-tongued orators of the South expostulating their theories of government and their theological convictions. But here was a man whose eloquence excelled them all. There was something fresh about him, something that had the tang of a June morning and the glory of an autumn sunset—something genuine and positive and irresistible.

Indeed a "Son of Thunder" he was. For though he could be as gentle as a lamb, in the next instant he could exhibit the fury of a lion. And every real pastor knows the importance of that religious fury at times.

A short while after being installed as leader of this church, he realized that much improvement could be made on the Board of Deacons . . .

Here it might be well to enlarge upon this incident. Young Lee was more interested in the progress of the church than in the feelings of anyone. He often said that the feelings of nobody should be given priority over the welfare of the church matters, spiritual and financial. He devotedly loved all the good men who were deacons in the church, noble men who had loved and served, some of them before their young pastor was born. But Robert Lee got the conviction that some splendid men who were of "deacon timber" were not being utilized in the work there, not given the opportunity to serve which they really deserved to have. He believed that other worthy men should be given official recognition and made to feel responsibility for the welfare of the local church.

Without asking anyone's advice, Lee called the deacons together and, after prayer and the statement that he was going to ask the unusual of them, requested them to resign and to help select some other good men who were worthy to take their places.

With a few mild protests on the part of some, silence on the part of one, and with expressed confidence in their pastor's leadership, they resigned and their resignations were presented the next Sunday to the church "called into business session." Others were selected by the church, and the outgoing deacons, for the sake of the ongoing church, gave a supper at the pastor's home for the incoming deacons. It was a good thing for the deacons who had served so long to learn that, in honor preferring others, they did not have to be deacons to serve Christ; it

was good for the church to utilize men otherwise
unused: and it was good for the selected men to
assume greater responsibility and to make wider
use of their talents.

It is not often that a pastor asks a Board of
Deacons to resign and finds them doing it in a
Christ-like way, with no diminution of their love
and loyalty to the church. As someone said at the
time: "The pastor asked the fellows, and they did
it without bellows."

But now back to Dr. Wimbish's comments:

> Yes, Lee was a great leader, this brilliant young preacher
> from old Fort Mill, South Carolina. And he was a great
> pastor, spending hours every day in personal visitation
> among the people of the city. They tell me he could be
> seen walking at various times of the day and night, enter-
> ing homes throughout the county, ministering with the
> Word and with his gracious love and humility, so like the
> Master's . . .
>
> Though he served the Edgefield church only two and
> one-half years, Dr. Lee had a full ministry . . . It was
> while in this pastorate that he prepared and delivered for
> the first time his famous sermon, "Pay Day—Some Day."
> Since its first delivery at a Wednesday-night prayer
> meeting service in Edgefield, multitudes have been
> brought to Christ as he has preached this remarkable
> message all over America.
>
> Many there are who remember the day when he an-
> nounced from the pulpit that the church debt would be
> paid the following Sunday and the sensation that was
> created among the membership . . .
>
> I quote once again from the local paper regarding the
> eventful Sunday:
>
> "A great day. *He* was there. Day previous dark and
> gloomy. Sunday morning all shadows had fled. And all
> the people came to hear the preacher present the cause of

the church indebtedness and to do their part. And if any
came to scoff, this time they remained to pray."

Yes, God said "Amen" to the faith of the young pastor
by performing a miracle that Sunday and the church debt
was entirely liquidated. Dr. Lee still points back to that
experience as the greatest miracle of his ministry . . .

But the time came when Robert G. Lee felt God was
leading him into another part of the battle-line. The
First Baptist Church of Chester, South Carolina, extended
him a call. A spokesman of the Edgefield Church said in a
letter to one of the leading newspapers of the State:

"If Chester should be so fortunate as to secure him,
they would indeed be blessed. Edgefield as a community
and the First Baptist Church and the country desire greatly
and unanimously that he remain with us. He has been
great in his undertakings, and eminently successful in their
accomplishment, great in his influence and in his preaching,
and we would not be willing to part with him."

But he felt God was leading him, and on February
20, 1921, he penned his resignation. I give you herewith
excerpts from that writing:

"With courage to do the right as God gives me to see
the right, I hereby offer my resignation as pastor of the
church, the same to take effect the first Sunday in April,
that Sunday included . . . Moreover . . . I beg . . . that
you bid me Godspeed as I gird on my armour to fight His
battles in another section of His far-flung battle line."

And so, on April 3, 1921, he preached his last sermon
as Pastor of the First Baptist Church of Edgefield, using
this combination of verses as a basis of his parting message: Philippians 1:3: "I thank my God upon every remembrance of you": Exodus 14:14: "And the Lord
said unto Moses, Wherefore criest thou unto Me? Speak
unto the children of Israel that they go forward"; I Corinthians 2:9: "But as it is written, Eye hath not seen, nor
ear heard, neither have entered into the heart of man, the
things which God hath prepared for them that love Him."

To the people a shadow seemed to be across the sun
that April morning. The orioles flashed through the

groves of hickory unnoticed and the thrushes that perched amidst the branches of the oaks in the old church yard had a rather plaintive note in their melody and the wind that sighed across the meadow was in a minor tune.

Yes, Robert Greene Lee came and left a trail of glory across Edgefield County.

In September of 1946 we had the great preacher back to conduct a revival meeting in his old church, so dear to his heart. When he arrived in the city and entered the living room of the home which he himself had built, tears filled his eyes. Emotions welled up within his breast, for on wings of memory, he went back a quarter of a century to the days when he and his devoted wife and little girl, Bula G., had resided there.

"This house does something to me," he said. "It was in that back room that the doctor stood at the bedside of our little girl and said, 'Preacher, she will not live to see the light of another day.'

"And it was right in this breakfast room here that another doctor said, 'Brother Lee, the physician's diagnosis is not always correct.'

"And the doctor was wrong, for the Great Physician took the case in hand, and my little girl recovered."

The people came to hear him preach [for this revival series in 1946], young people, old people, those who remembered him "in the dear dead days beyond recall," and those who had known his name as a household word since infancy. Yes, they came to hear him preach and were moved to tears and to action by every sermon. Many were gloriously saved, among them two Catholic young people, whose mother and grandmother had recited to them over and over again the stories of this consecrated servant of the Master and his days in Edgefield.

While with us he spoke to the combined student body of the Edgefield schools, and on that morning while sitting on the platform, gazing into the faces of the little children of grammar school age on the front rows and the young people of high school age farther back in the auditorium, I witnessed an unforgettable scene. Under the masterful ability of the preacher-orator, I saw those young people of such diversified talents and ages weep, and laugh, and shout, and cry. It was indeed a unique occasion. I have never experienced another scene like it; I doubt if I ever shall again.

People from hundreds of miles around came to hear him preach. Indeed caravans of automobiles came from distant cities. People sat in the windows of our church, the aisles of our church, stood in the doorways and out in the yard. We even had people seated in the baptistry and along the edge of the platform, all with breathless expectation. They listened as he preached the unsearchable riches of Christ Jesus, and on the night designated for him to preach "Pay Day—Some Day," even though it had rained steadily all day and the rain continued to fall in torrents, the people came by the hundreds, indeed by the thousands.

The Chief of Police in our city brought all of his men into service to take care of traffic, and on this night he estimated that 2,500 people sought to hear this unusual man preach his famous sermon, one of the most poignant, heart-searching messages ever preached by any man in any age.

The Honorable J. Strom Thurman, Governor of the State of South Carolina, who is a member of our church, was greatly stirred by his messages and said, "I want to have my picture taken with the greatest preacher living today."

I am happy to call him my friend. And as I peruse his magnificent record as a servant of the Master, I thank God for the day when he spurned the professorship at Furman University, saying "Gentlemen, I would not give up preaching for the Presidency of the United States."

If ever a man could rightfully sing the old Negro spiritual, "I know 'de Lawd has laid His hand on me," I feel Robert Greene Lee is that man.

Dr. Lee, going to Chester, South Carolina, on April 10, 1921, served as pastor of the First Baptist Church for a period of about sixteen months. Although this

was a brief stay, notable things occurred in relation
to the ministry and growth of the church, and other
interesting incidents took place in the life of this
zealous and ambitious preacher-boy.

At Chester, only thirty miles from Lee's log-cabin
birthplace, the work began with zeal on the pastor's
part and with enthusiasm in the hearts of the people.
Soon crowds overflowed the church building. Refusing to unite with other denominations for a Sunday night union service because he did not believe
such a course could be sufficiently evangelistic to win
the lost, and under severe criticism for this "refusal
to be brotherly," as some critics expressed it, Lee
stuck to his preaching-last and, as church records
and scrapbook clippings reveal, baptized converts
nearly every Sunday night.

During the first summer in Chester, Robert Lee,
finding the church auditorium too small to hold the
crowds, began to hold church services on the lawn.
On one occasion the pastor invited the town band to
play at a lawn service. It was to be more than a musical entertainment, for the program was to include
a Gospel message at the conclusion. Tremendous
criticism fell upon Lee's shoulders which were,
however, broad enough to bear it. There may have
been some justification for the suggestions made
that the pastor was indulging in sensationalism, but
he felt that whatever accusations there might be,
his purpose—to attract unsaved men and women to
the service—fully warranted the means of bringing
it to pass. And it turned out that Lee was himself
justified; for a great crowd gathered for the service,

and when the invitation was given to receive Christ as Saviour, seventeen people stepped forward to confess His Name before men.

Later, he rented, for fifty dollars per week, a huge tent that Gypsy Smith, the evangelist, had used, and began holding a series of evangelistic meetings in it. Frank McCravy led in choir work. A great wind storm came up and blew the tent down, but, not wanting to close the meeting, which Lee was convinced was of the Lord, he had the tent erected again. No sooner was it put up and the final ropes tied, than it blew down the second time. Again, after about fifty good women sewed up rents in the tent with huge needles and thread, it was erected, and again it blew down. But undaunted, Lee called the women to assist once more, had the tent put up again, and carried on with his meetings night after night.

This was the greatest "protracted meetin'" that Bob Lee had held to this time. There were about one hundred and fifty professions of faith in Christ, and in addition, scores re-dedicated their lives to the Lord or pledged themselves to enter His service. As a result of these meetings, so many requested baptism that Lee felt that it could not be handled properly in the baptistry of the church. Consequently, he decided to immerse these people in the Sandy River that flowed along the edge of the city of Chester. As often with his decisions, he asked nobody's counsel. Some of the deacons of the church objected to the baptism being administered in the river, suggesting that this open-air baptismal

service would be undignified and might even cause
some to be taken by a carnival spirit.

Quite a group of these men, noble men all, called
on their pastor at the parsonage and begged insistently that he should not have the baptismal service in the river. Lee asked them to trust him, and
in due course they acquiesced. About one hundred
and twenty men and women, boys and girls, presented themselves at the river for baptism on Sunday
afternoon, and twenty-two others, timorous perhaps,
or concerned lest there be undue levity at a service
of this kind, preferred to wait until the evening to
be baptized in the church.

It was reported by the newspaper, *The Chester
Reporter*, that between three and five thousand
people gathered along the banks of the Sandy
River as spectators that Sunday afternoon. They
heard Lee give a brief talk on the symbolism of
the baptismal ordinance, followed by a request for
reverence and the spirit of worship, and by prayer.
Then, for one hour and a half Pastor Lee baptized, a-
mid profound silence throughout the assembled throng.
Deacon J. T. Perkins remarked, after the service
was over: "Pastor, I have heard more laughter and
seen more misbehaviour at funerals than I observed at the baptism today. It was a sight that I
shall carry with me to Heaven."

During the tent meetings that were mentioned
earlier, a young man who was on a South Carolina
chain gang, hearing of the meeting, asked the guard if
he might attend a service. Strangely enough the
guard consented, requiring a pledge from the young

prisoner to be back at the jail at 10:30 p. m. This chap, dressed in prison garb, walked the eight miles to the tent and was converted during the service that evening. But the meeting was not over until 9:30, and he saw that he would not be able to get back to his quarters by the appointed hour. He told Pastor Lee of his difficulty, and the preacher took the prisoner back in his car, getting him there on time. Lee watched the guard put the chain back on the young man's ankles. The prisoner said to the preacher: "Isn't the sky pretty? Certainly prettier then when I came into the prison."

This boy was made a "trusty" after this. Later, he felt called of God to preach the Gospel and had made arrangements, with the preacher's assurance that he would help him get through school, to finish high school and enter college. But after a few months, the young man was smitten with tuberculosis and was sent to the hospital in Oteen, North Carolina, where, a year or so later, he died—rejoicing until the end in his salvation, and dreaming until the end of being a preacher.

Under Lee's ministry at Chester, the enrollment of the Sunday school soon doubled, and after a few weeks the men's Bible class which, upon Lee's arrival, had no members, boasted a membership of more than one hundred. The pastor, deterred not by the objections and dire prognostications of some, launched a vigorous and successful campaign for the building of a new Sunday-school building, which still stands as a beautiful and useful monument to the faith and zeal of this man of God, and to the willingness of the people to follow a man who believed and dared.

Bob Lee has always carried a bent for writing. At Chester he competed in a short-story contest put forth by *The State,* a newspaper published at Columbia, South Carolina. He won second place and a prize of one hundred dollars in the contest in which over four hundred writers competed, the title of his story being, "Flames and Cinders." Lee would enjoy doing more of this kind of writing, but he has no time for it.

But, in connection with this short-story business, he himself tells another. After he won the hundred dollars in *The State* contest, he noticed another announcement of prizes for short stories. Lee sent one in entitled, "Mills of Grief." Some weeks after he submitted this story, the fiery preacher cut loose in his pulpit one Sunday with all the words of rebuke he could summon and denounced trashy and tainted literature, telling his congregation that nobody had a right to sell such trash and no one, unless he wanted "to swim through fifty feet of sewerage to get a teaspoonful of truth," should read them. After the service, one of the members of the church, a keen lawyer, came to the pastor and said: "Brother Lee, I want to see you tomorrow and show you something." They agreed to meet in the lawyer's office next morning. The lawyer, with a few words, handed him a magazine called *The Wampus Cat,* hardly to be classed with highly reputable periodicals, in which was the announcement in bold and glaring type that Robert G. Lee was the winner of the first prize in the short-story contest and that a check would be sent the winner at an early date. Lee had not seen the magazine and knew nothing of having been placed first among the contestants. The chagrined preacher wrote a letter to the editor of the publication telling him not to print his story because he would not consent to having it published in a magazine of such sordid nature. The editor protested strongly. Against the editor's protest, the preacher was adamant. The editor did not print the story.

But this was not Lee's only embarrassing experience at Chester. A distant relative by marriage, the sister of Mrs. Lee's brother's wife, died in a neighboring town. The family requested that Bob come over to conduct the service. At first he did not feel he ought to go, but they persisted in their request, and so at last he consented, and he and Mrs. Lee drove some distance, through quite a storm. Upon their arrival, to Lee's astonishment, the pastor of the local church, at which the deceased had held membership, was present and was prepared to conduct the service, for no understanding had been come to about a special request. Lee was quite embarrassed and did not know just what to do, but upon the gracious insistence of the local pastor, performed the service. The pastor's kindliness, however, did not lessen the young preacher's painful embarrassment. He learned a great lesson that day, namely: never go back to marry or go back to bury members of other pastors' churches.

At Chester another matter was brought about which might have involved the preacher in greater embarrassment than both of the incidents related

Bob Lee (in Dark Shirt and Suspenders) Working on the Panama Canal in 1909

At Furman Fitting School, 1909 (Lee, second row, second from right)

Bob Lee as Freshman at Furman University, Aged 23

above. A young lady of unquestioned consecration, who loved the Lord greatly and who sang in the choir, had a voice that was raspy and sometimes unpleasingly loud. One day, the preacher went to the choir director and said: "Do you know what's wrong with the choir?"

"Yes," the men answered, "everybody knows the one who makes what's wrong!"

"Why not ask the lady out?" suggested the preacher.

"Ask her out?" the director almost shouted, "I'm not that big a fool!"

The preacher went to the Sunday-school superintendent and a similar conversation took place, the superintendent saying: "I'd have all her kinfolks on my neck."

Lee then went to the chairman of the deacons and discussed the situation in the choir, with the chairman frankly admitting that he did not have spunk enough to ask the faithful choir member to leave the choir.

What, then, could be done? The preacher decided to ask the young lady to withdraw from the choir. For this purpose he went to the uptown department store where she worked. When he walked up to the counter where the young lady was serving, she greeted him with profuse words of gladness, and then asked: "What can I do for you, preacher?"

"Do you really want to know?" he asked, calling this young lady by name.

"Of course," she replied.

"I want to ask you to get out of the choir," the preacher said with tender bluntness.

With confusion and a slight flush of face, the young woman asked him, "Why?"

"Because you can't sing any better than I," the preacher said, "and it would help the choir for you to get out."

There was a long pause. Lee wondered if she was going to be angry. But she was lovely. "All right, preacher, I'll get out," she said, "but I want you to understand one thing: I am going to sing all I want out in the congregation."

Dr. Lee assured her that would be perfectly all right. That night the young lady was absent from choir practice for the first time in many months. And the next Sunday, she was not singing in the choir, but in the congregation. Thoughtful Christians may learn some real lessons from this episode, among them that it pays to be forthright in Christian service, if the frankness can be expressed in love and a kindly way; and that it is pleasing to the Lord not to have hurt feelings which, after all, are evidence of the activity of the flesh.

Amid all the joyous life which was the preacher's in Chester, the first stirrings about receiving and accepting a call to New Orleans are found in Dr. Lee's scrapbook, where there is a copy of a letter that he wrote to his friend, Ellis A. Fuller:

Chester, S. C.
June 9, 1922
My dear Pal:
I received your church calendar this morning while on a short stopover in Chester, during an interlude in my

meeting at my old home church, where I was baptized and ordained—and where my father and mother are now members.

Your few scribblings on your calendar burned themselves into my heart, like letters of fire—when I think that you have had forty-two additions in so short a time and that you baptized seventeen last Sunday—"Thank the Lord"—and may He give you mighty power.

My love, my prayers, my friendship, my all, are ever with you, and for you—never forget that He who fights *for* God, never fights *without* God.

You ask what the First Church [of New Orleans] said in asking about me. I prefer to remain silent on that question just now, but will quote word for word from a telegram I received from New Orleans the other day.

> Rev. Robert G. Lee
> Chester, South Carolina
> New Orlean's largest city South. Second port United States. We want First Baptist Church to become the first church in all the land. To that end, at regular service Sunday night, a call was extended to you to lead in this work and the vote was unanimous.
> CICERO A. RAMSEY

In reply, I sent the following telegram:

> I recognize the honor bestowed, opportunity afforded, responsibility imposed, and the ordeal of decision thrust upon me by the call extended me by First Baptist Church, New Orleans. The call will be seriously and prayerfully considered. Cannot render either an affirmative or negative answer until after consultation with you, third Sunday June.

So, you see, from this, that I may not be in South Carolina much longer. I am not sure, and will not be sure until after my visit to New Orleans. Please keep this matter *sub rosa*. From what I have been told, the opportunity is wonderful beyond words to express. Pray for me

that I do just God's will for His kingdom, laying aside
all personal aspects of this.

Love,
Bob

In due course Robert G. Lee accepted the call to
New Orleans as being of God, and left Chester in the
very early autumn of 1922. During his pastorate at
the First Baptist Church in Chester, there were
415 additions to the church, 300 of these being by
confession of faith and baptism.

Chapter VIII
FRIEND OF SINNERS; JOY TO THE BRETHREN
A Baptist in a Roman Catholic City

Insofar as Dr. Lee was aware or was able to determine later, no member of the First Baptist Church of New Orleans had ever heard him preach when he received the call to become its pastor. The Chairman of the Pulpit Committee was Mr. Cicero A. Ramsey, the Superintendent of the Sunday school. Reference to Mr. Ramsey's telegram has already been made. Other communications from this gentleman are to be seen in Dr. Lee's scrapbooks, and with them are communications from Dr. B. H. DeMent, President of the Baptist Bible Institute,* who was occasionally supplying the pulpit of the First Baptist Church at that time. Dr. DeMent's warm-hearted letters, urging Dr. Lee to consider deeply and prayerfully the call of the church, marked the beginning of an affectionate and abiding friendship between the two men of God, each one the equal of the other in capacity to love sincerely and whole-heartedly.

It was after he received the official call to the church that Dr. Lee first preached there, on the third Sunday of June, 1922. On July 5, Mr. Ramsey sent Lee a telegram, stating:

---

* Now the New Orleans Baptist Theological Seminary.

133

CHURCH MEMBERSHIP GETTING RESTLESS. PLEASE WIRE
YOUR DECISION.

Dr. Lee responded as follows:

MY SISTER** DIED THREE HOURS BEFORE I COULD REACH
HOME FROM NEW ORLEANS. CONSEQUENTLY UNTIL RECENT
DAYS COULD NOT FULLY WEIGH MATTERS AND PRAY OVER
THEM. LIKE GIDEON I MUST BE SURE OF GOD'S WILL.
WILL WIRE MY DECISION SATURDAY. KINDEST REGARDS
TO WHOLE CHURCH MEMBERSHIP.

On Saturday Dr. Lee telegraphed his acceptance.
This is the telegram he sent:

FOR MY DECISION READ CONSECUTIVELY FIRST THESSA-
LONIANS THIRD CHAPTER ELEVENTH VERSE. SECOND EPISTLE
JOHN TWELFTH VERSE. ROMANS FIFTEENTH CHAPTER
TWENTY-NINTH VERSE. SECOND THESSALONIANS THIRD
CHAPTER FOURTH VERSE. PHILIPPIANS FIRST CHAPTER
TWENTY-FIFTH AND TWENTY-SIXTH VERSES. ROMANS FIF-
TEENTH CHAPTER THIRTEENTH VERSE. READ THESE VERSES
TO CHURCH ASSEMBLED. GOD BLESS ALL.

Dr. Lee's unique message, translated into the
Scriptures themselves, was read in the church on the
following day:

Now God Himself and our Father, and our Lord Jesus
Christ, direct our way unto you. Having many things
to write unto you, I would not write with paper and ink:
but I trust to come unto you, and speak face to face, that
our joy may be full. And I am sure that, when I come
unto you, I shall come in the fullness of the blessing
of the Gospel of Christ. And we have confidence in the
Lord touching you, that ye both do and will do the things
which we command you. And having this confidence,
I know that I shall abide and continue with you all for
your furtherance and joy of faith; that your rejoicing may

**Frances L. (Mrs. James T.) Young.

be more abundant in Jesus Christ for me by my coming to you again. Now the God of hope fill you with all joy and peace in believing, that ye may abound in hope, through the power of the Holy Ghost.

Of course there was great rejoicing among the membership of the New Orleans church, and Mr. Ramsey wrote acknowledging the acceptance of the call as follows:

July 18,1922

Dear Brother Lee:

I received your telegram in due time, but made no announcement to anyone except Dr. and Mrs. Caine, before the close of the Sunday-school hour on Sunday morning; at which time I advised the church and Sunday school assembly that I was in receipt of a code message on the previous day, and not having at my office a code book, I was not in a position to interpret same; but felt that the church members assembled could assist, and to that end would ask that they open their Bibles and read the code ciphers as given in this telegram. It was a very happy ending in which the organ and choir and congregation joined in rendering "Praise God from Whom All Blessings Flow."

CICERO A. RAMSEY

Dr. DeMent sent this letter almost immediately:

My dear Brother and Pastor:

Here is my heart and hand and purse and life in glad co-operation at the old First Church, N. O.

I have read your acceptance as it appeared in the *Times Picayune*. It was unique and impressive.

I believe the Lord is going to use you in a large and permanent way to meet the wonderful opportunities at the First Church and in the Metropolis of the South.

Cordially yours in Him,
B. H. DeMent

And when Dr. DeMent was called Home some years later, Dr. Lee said of him: "He certainly kept every promise made in the letter."

It was on Saturday, September 16, 1922, that Dr. and Mrs. Lee, with Bula G., arrived in New Orleans. They were met at the station by a committee from the church and driven to the pastor's home on Peniston Street. What memories flooded the heart of the new preacher! Vividly he recalled his first experiences in that city, when he was Panama-bound as a young man. The lonely, forlorn farmer-boy was a far cry from the now up-and-coming Baptist preacher. Once he had longed for a single word from a friendly passer-by. Now he and his wife and child were greeted by a committee of warm-hearted Christians. "As if the new pastor were worthy of any such fuss made over him!" he thought.

Dr. Lee preached his first messages as pastor on the following day, September 17, and on Tuesday night of the next week a reception was given to the Lees so that all might get acquainted with the preacher and his family, and that they might come to know the members of the church. Immediately they seemed to have fallen in love with each other, and equally promptly the sheep of the flock learned that their new shepherd was not only a beloved brother, but that he was also a faithful minister—and that he was there for business. His whole mien indicated this.

Lee began to visit the people in the succeeding week, and within three months he had called upon every living member of the church. The membership, numbering 758 people on the roll, was less than Lee had anticipated, for some had been dead as

long as three years without notice having been made
of the fact. New goals were set for Sunday school
attendance. Announcements were sent out that the
pastor wanted to see at least 500 people in the Sunday
school, a far larger number than had ever attended,
and the response was enthusiastic. On the first
Sunday 299 had been present, plus a child one of
the teachers brought in from the street to make an
even 300. The following Sunday 545 came for the
Sunday school services.

The preaching services were well attended also,
and one of the joys of the pastor's heart was the
church choir and the splendid mixed quartette under
the most able leadership of Paul Jacobs, a Jewish
Christian whom, Dr. Lee says, was the most understanding and co-operative choir director he has ever
worked with.

Some few months later, at the suggestion of Mr.
Jacobs, the pastor agreed to give the Sunday evening
service over entirely to music. That afternoon he
went visiting, giving no thought to a sermon for
the night service. But Jacobs and he did not reckon
upon the faith and perseverance of Mr. James H.
Tharp, one of the deacons, who was not informed of
the plan to have "a musical service only." Nor did
they reckon upon the interruption and work of the
Holy Spirit in the service that night. After the
musical program had taken up over half an hour,
the pastor called on Mr. Tharp to pray. This good
brother arose and prayed earnestly that Dr. Lee
would preach with power such as he had never
had before, and that souls would be saved that
night. Lee, right in the midst of the prayer, went to

Jacobs and whispered that he must leave out an anthem or so, because the hand of God was upon him for a sermon. The pastor, coerced and guided by the Holy Spirit, delivered a sermon *ex tempore* to the conversion of eight people and the blessing of many.

Because of the very strenuous program that Dr. Lee undertook in New Orleans, following a similar energetic ministry in Chester, his health broke down after only a few months. He was obliged to go away for a complete rest, but he had already endeared himself to the hearts of the people, and their love, as well as their prayers, followed him.

Dr. C. B. McFerrin, editor of a health magazine and head of a health clinic in a distant city, was visiting in New Orleans. He was an enthusiastic friend of Lee's and regular in his attendance at the First Baptist Church services, although he was not a member of the church. Without request from anybody, he helped in a generous way to defray the ailing preacher's hospitalization. No doubt he will share in the rewards of the New Orleans ministry when the Lord's people stand before the judgment seat of Christ.

When Bob Lee returned to the pulpit after about ten weeks' absence, thirty pounds heavier, not only was his health restored but he seemd to be able to attack the tasks, wrestle with the problems, and fulfil the ministry with even more vigor than had been his earlier.

The First Baptist Church of New Orleans certainly had a dynamic leader in its pastor. Innovations of one kind and another were used, in addition to the tremendous Gospel preaching that went out from the pulpit week after week, to lure visitors and unsaved people into the church. The advertising that appeared in the Saturday papers was not sensational, but it was directed to catch the attention of visitors from other cities and states, and to draw into the services New Orleans citizens also, that is, those who were unattached as far as church affiliation was concerned. But the pastor did not stop with newspaper advertising. He rang doorbells, visited hospitals, jails, hotels, and wherever else he could get a lead to attract others to the church. His salary was now $4,000 a year, but the way he helped in the education of boys and girls who needed assistance, and the way he came to the aid of some "smooth talkers," one might have believed that he was receiving many times that amount. Lee could never forget his own boyhood and the lack that he had experienced in respect to material things and educational opportunity. Any young person who showed the slightest inclination to increase his scholastic training found a ready listener in Dr. Lee, and an outstretched hand to help along the way.

One of the methods that the pastor used to increase the usefulness of his ministry was that of appointing a committee of laymen in his church to hand out cards to visitors to the services, thus obtaining their names and addresses. Two friends of the author, Mahon and Lucille Crawford, signed such a card one Sunday morning in September, 1924. A bride and groom who had only resided in the city for one week, accustomed to the friendliness of Memphis, their home city, and the many acquaintances there, the Crawfords were feeling their first pangs of homesickness in New Orleans. The day following their visit to First Baptist Church, the energetic pastor was calling upon them in their boarding house. The happiness that his visit and his subsequent sweet friendship introduced into their lives will never be forgotten. First of all, Dr. Lee determined what the Crawfords' relationship to Christ was, whether they had received Him as their Saviour. Mr. Crawford, who had been baptized as an infant in the Methodist Church, had never made a public profession of Christ, but was won to the Lord by Dr. Lee, who baptized him. Mrs. Crawford, a Baptist for years, had been, to this time, merely a professing Christian. Lee encouraged them both to "line up for Christ" in the city of New Orleans. The Crawfords are now active and influential members in the Bellevue Baptist Church of Memphis, Tennessee, where Dr. Lee is presently the pastor.

It is not possible, in cold type, to portray the earnestness and holy zeal with which Lee prosecuted his commission. Men sometimes lose sight of the fact, in the fulfilment of many duties, even though those tasks may be carried out with enthusiasm, that theirs is a God-given service. Lee did not succumb to this fault, but bore in mind daily that he was a vessel of God who was supposed to be filled with the Spirit. Notations upon sheets of paper found in his files indicate that during these days in New Orleans he was taking constant stock of himself. Among these papers we find sets of resolutions that he made concerning himself, of which these are a few: to watch his thoughts, to be absolutely honest, to take care of his body, to improve his mind, to conserve his enthusiasm, not to give way to bitterness, to read the Bible systematically and thoroughly, and to give the Lord Jesus much thought in the round of daily ministry.

During the year 1924 there was considerable correspondence between the Pulpit Committee of the Grove Avenue Baptist Church, Richmond, Virginia and Robert Lee concerning the possibility of Lee's becoming the successor of Dr. Len G. Broughton as the pastor of that church. In due course, on September 7, 1924, a telegram, signed by H. R. Pollard, Jr., was sent to Dr. Lee containing the following message:

LARGE COMMITTEE UNANIMOUSLY ENDORSED YOU TODAY. LETTER FOLLOWS.

The letter that came within a few days declared that a committee of fifty had unanimously agreed to recommend to the Grove Avenue Baptist Church that a call be extended to Robert G. Lee. But the New Orleans pastor replied by telegram:

AFTER MOST SERIOUS THOUGHT AND EARNEST CONSIDERATION MUST DISAPPOINT YOU AND YOUR SPLENDID PEOPLE BY NOT ACCEPTING YOUR INVITATION TO BECOME YOUR PASTOR. PLEASE EXPRESS MY ABIDING GRATITUDE AND APPRECIATION TO THE COMMITTEE FOR SUCH REAL CONSIDERATION AND COURTESY. GOD'S BLESSING AND ALL MY PRAYER.

Correspondence is also found during the year 1924 as to Dr. Lee's helping a young man go through Furman University. Another item in one of the scrapbooks shows a pledge made out to Furman University for $125.00, signed by Robert G. Lee, and paid.

Every man engaged in public ministry for the Lord receives certain gracious and complimentary letters which are accepted with deep thanksgiving. But among Dr. Lee's papers are to be found not dozens or hundreds of such letters, but literally thousands of them. The first one that we have run across is from Horace M. Wolfe, dated June 29, 1924, and sent from the Baptist Bible Institute of New Orleans. Writes Mr. Wolfe:

My dear Brother Lee:

As I was thinking of how Christ came and gave His life and gave up Heaven for a period to redeem fallen man and got none or little appreciation for His work while on earth, I am writing you to tell you, while you are still living, that I have read after Spurgeon, Truett and other great preachers, but I have never heard or read after a man who I believe to be the preacher that you are.

I want to put flowers on your living life and not on the grave, and that is why I'm telling you this, for I fully believe what I have said, and God forbid that I should say it for flattery. I say it with the sincerity of my thought and soul.

My greatest regret when I go out of the city to preach on Sunday is that I cannot hear you preach, but I claim your earnest prayers as I endeavor to preach the Gospel of Christ in my feeble way, and thank God that it is not I that I preach, but Christ our Lord.

Among the many loyal and faithful members of the First Baptist Church of New Orleans was a consecrated woman, whose husband was a Jew, an unbeliever. This woman attended the church regularly, and occasionally her husband accompanied her. Lee was the only man whom he would consent to hear preach. Whenever this couple came into the church, the wife would offer a prayer silently, calling to God's mind His promises, and remembering the Word of God: "Faith cometh by hearing."

Several years later, after Dr. Lee had taken up the pastorate in Memphis, he returned to New Orleans to deliver the Convention Sermon of the Southern Baptist Convention. The lady of whom we have been speaking came to the meeting and told Dr. Lee that her husband had been ill for some time and could not get out to the service. She asked Lee if he would drive out to see her husband, which the preacher did. The two men were left alone in the room. After some minutes, the wife of this Jewish man was about to enter the room where her husband and Dr. Lee were. At the portal of the door she heard Dr. Lee's voice in prayer, so she waited. She observed the preacher sitting there with his back to the door, and he was holding the thin, white hand of her husband between his two hands. She thought that perhaps a decision had been made for Christ. At the close of the brief prayer Dr. Lee leaned over and kissed the hand of the dying man. After the preacher departed, the only comment that the old Jewish man made was: "I believe in Dr. Lee and everything he said. That was a beautiful prayer he prayed." He died shortly thereafter without ever making a confession of Jesus as Messiah and Saviour, but his wife had the assurance that Dr. Lee had been used to win her husband that day by the bedside.

As 1924 turned into 1925, Bob Lee was busier than ever before, for his outside ministry had enlarged to such an extent that he could hardly keep up with the schedule. Early in the year he conducted a series of meetings in the First Baptist Church of Shreveport, Louisiana. Shortly after the campaign ended in Shreveport, Dr. Lee received a letter from Dr. Dodd as follows:

> My dear Dr. Lee:
>
> Our final count indicates 179 additions during our meeting, and one joined Wednesday night at prayer meeting. 101 of these were for baptism. Our hearts are still singing. It would have done you good to hear the testimonies last night at prayer meeting.
>
> I shall always be grateful for the privilege of this intimate association with you. May every blessing attend your way to life's last flickering light.
>
> Sincerely and fraternally,
M. E. Dodd

At about this time Dr. Lee, who had been serving as Director of the Baptist Bible Institute, was elected to be a Trustee on a new Board that was formed. Dr. DeMent wrote him, saying:

> My beloved Pastor:
>
> Just a word to say thank you for your faithful service as Director of the Baptist Bible Institute in the days not long passed and to welcome you to all the duties and joys of a Trustee on the new Board. What a joy you are to the President of the School! I thank God at every remembrance of thee, my Brother. Just this word of appreciation. God bless you.
>
> Most cordially yours,
B. H. DeMent

In May of 1925, a very sad event occurred. On May 4, Bob received a telegram from his brother Ben, reading as follows:

> WE LOST OUR MOTHER AT FOUR THIRTY-FIVE THIS MORNING. ANSWER.

This telegram arrived on Sunday morning. Dr. Lee said nothing about it to people in the church, but taught his women's class in the Sunday school and preached a sermon in the morning hour of worship. At the close of the service, he made the announcement of his mother's "Home-Call," and then he hurried to catch a train to take him home. With the Spirit's help and in the strength that the Lord gave him, he assisted in the funeral. Prior to Dr. Lee's having left the service on May 4, however, many came forward to unite with the church by letter or by profession of faith. There can be little doubt that Bob Lee, the preacher-boy, was remembering something that his mother had said to him in a letter received some few years before: "I want to live on in you, long after I am gone."

The expressions of sympathy and love that Dr. Lee received at this time were many indeed. We cannot begin to mention them. But in one of the scrapbooks, pasted alongside of the notice of Mrs. Lee's death and these telegrams pyramided one on top of another, are two letters of another kind—letters that Bob Lee had written to his mother toward the end of her life. One of these is dated June 4, 1924, approximately one year before Mother Lee passed away. It was addressed to Dad and Mother and says:

> I was so glad to get the letter telling me that Mother was able to walk around the house again. It makes us all so happy. That is nothing short of a miracle of the Lord's mercy and favor toward us, and a mighty testimony to the truth that the Lord answers prayer.
>
> Mother, if you feel like it and can, I wish you would write me just two or three lines. I have not seen a word of your handwriting since last August. It would do me

so much good to see just one more letter in your writing,
provided it does not weary you or hurt you to write.
With the love of my heart,

Your preacher-boy,
Bob

The other one was written somewhat earlier. We
quote without further comment:

Dear Mother:
I go way back in memory today to the little house
where I was born. I wish so often I could see you and
be with you some, but it seems to me I am so far away
and my work makes such demands on me that I cannot
get off but seldom to see you. But I love you, love you
ever.

Your boy,
Robert G. Lee

Once again calls began to come from other
churches. In early October a telegram was received
from Mr. Charles O. Cook, Chairman of the Pulpit
Committee of the Columbus Street Baptist Church
of Waco, Texas, asking Dr. Lee if he would be interested in accepting a call to be pastor of that
church. The negotiations never went far enough to
have an official call issued, however. Another inquiry was received from Beaumont, Texas. At about
the same time, Mr. John P. Thomas, Chairman of the
Pulpit Committee of the Citadel Square Baptist
Church of Charleston, South Carolina, wrote to
Dr. Lee urging him to accept a call to that church.
We shall have more to say about this later.

In September of 1925 the Great Commoner, William
Jennings Bryan, went to be with his Lord. A me-
morial service was held at the Jerusalem Temple in
New Orleans on October 4, and Dr. Lee gave the ad-

dress. It is reproduced below, taken from notes in Dr. Lee's possession.

William Jennings Bryan—The Man

In this brief twenty-minute period, the limits of which I shall not violate, adequately and fully to speak of Bryan the Man is as impossible of achievement as putting the Amazon River in a teacup, as confining the lightnings of Sinai in a barn lantern, as putting all the flowers from a vast plain in one vase, as impossible as shooting all the arrows from the full quiver of half a century from one bow string in the fraction of an hour.

But unnumbered are the hosts today who say of Bryan what Anthony said of Brutus on the blood-soaked plains of Philippi centuries ago:

> His life was gentle, and the elements
> So mixed in him that Nature might stand up
> And say to all the world, "This was a Man!"

A man he, sixteen ounces to the pound! A man he, thirty-six inches to the yard! A man he, twenty-four hours to the day! A man he, to the last step of his eventful life journey! A mighty man of valor, to the last hour of his luminous day!

About him, as about all great men, is an element of mystery. Great men, like fertilizing fountains that flow down from the hills of divinity, are as streams of water in a dry place. They empty into the broad river of history, which does not flow unvexed into the Eternal Sea, and the current of their influence winds on forever. However we may differ as to the attained or unattained objectives of his life, we agree that his career as a man is without historic parallel in our nation. However much our words are in disagreement in speaking of his career and his ideals and policies, we all know that his career as a man is as strange as legend, as beautiful as romance, as real as sunlight, lightly touched, here and there, with tragic pathos. However our appraisals vary, all men, friends and foes alike, in one mighty chorus of confirmation, agree that he was a seer who saw clearly and afar, a hero who dared valiantly, a great heart who felt deeply, a trumpet voice who spoke mightily, a lion-hearted fighter who never sulked, a mighty statesman eagle, quarreled at but not hindered in his lofty flight, by the noisy human sparrows of his day who envied but could not attain unto his eminence.

A sad day it was for our land, and for the world, when the eyes which had flashed fires of indignation against the wrong in one thousand battles and had radiated gentleness and light and good humor through all his long eventful career were closed! But William Jennings Bryan forever stands before the world as one of the tall sons of the morning. His spotless character, his imperious will, his impassioned eloquence, his magnificent and practically faultless physique, his commanding personality, his unbesmirched statesmanship made him one of the most arresting figures of any century. Multitudes did he baffle with his bigness! Multitudes did he enchant with his goodness! Multitudes did he master with his magnetism! Multitudes, who disagreed with him and who stood out against some of his policies, did he win to enthusiastic personal admiration. The death of no President called forth such volumes of newspaper matter. The picture of no departed President has been so widely published. The death of no national figure has been more widely mourned. Teaching us what? Teaching us that a thousand deaths cannot lay him in the grave. No disease from within and no danger from without can destroy him. He bears upon his face the stamp of the immortal. Conspicuously does he stand out among the deathless men of all ages!

I—Consider His MANY-SIDED and MARVELOUS PERSONALITY.

A man of most universal genius! The cartoonists who caricatured him and some of his policies; his political enemies who fought and feared him; his friends who cherished for him a worshipful affection; the skeptics, the infidels, the agnostics, the atheists, the materialists, the evolutionists (and not one in a million of all of them would refuse to swap deathbeds with him)—these, all these, along with the cohorts of the whiskey traffic who laughed at his scrupulous temperance ideals and feared his power when unleashed against them—all, and many others from other walks of life, acknowledge his many-sided and marvelous personality.

He was an ORATOR—and the fires of his eloquence will forever remain unsmothered in the speeches he has left us! He was a WRITER—and keen logic, transcendent truths, refreshing messages, great plans both political and humanitarian, fell from his pen like golden pollen from stems of shaken lilies. He was a REFORMER—and descended upon the civic unrighteousness, the political corruption, the subtle schemings of demagoguery as a flame of fire. He was a PROPHET—and dreamed dreams of a more righteous America and a more righteous world and of a golden age of morals. He challenged and warned against the iniquities in our land which were as the iniquities which made old Rome a branchless tree, dishonorably barren, which made old Greece a crumb in history's rubbish heap, which made old Babylon a dirty doormat for irreverent feet, which made old Egypt a shabby sexton of splendid tombs, which made old Spain a drowsy beggar watching a broken clock. He declared in no uncertain tones that the grinning skeletons of Nineveh and Tyre declared that "the wages of sin is death"—for a nation as well as for an individual. He was a STATESMAN—ever uninfluenced by any flattery, ever unmoved by any threat, ever unafraid of any Macbeth of villainy, ever untainted by any Midas of avarice, ever unbesmirched by any Ananias of falsehood, ever untrapped by any Ahab or Jezebel of corruption and hatred. He was a LAYMAN-PREACHER—who, in public life and private life, showed no religious relax, who was not ashamed to talk to the boy in the elevator about Christianity, who hated the smiling ease with which old faiths are chucklingly thrown off and new ones grinningly taken on. He was a FARMER—and he loved the open furrows, the smell of the good brown earth, the color of the faithful old hills, the fertile patience of the unexhausted

prairies, the majesty of immeasurable stars, the homeliness
of wayside weeds, the variety of seasons with their punctual
return, and the lure of the Western skies where he
seemed to catch "the glory of God's robe where the last
fires of sunset flamed." He was a BUSINESSMAN—to whom
honor was more precious than rubies and a good name
"rather to be chosen than great riches." He was a
SOLDIER—whose hands were unstained by plunder. He was
a SCHOLAR—possessing no superficial mental illumination
that lacked the urge of sacrificial passion, possessing no
haughty conceit that looks with contempt on the least
of God's creatures. He was a THINKER—unhampered by
petty antipathies and petty dabblings—a man with eras
in his brain. He was a LEADER—unspoiled by the admiration of the world and the adulations of his friends; never
haughty in victory; never supercilious in an hour of
triumph; forever devoid of all rancor and malice in defeat;
never embittered; never surrendering to the enemies of
human freedom. Three times, in 1896, in 1900, in 1908,
he was candidate for the presidency of the United States.
Three times was he defeated. But never was he embittered.
He loved to tell upon himself what an old Negro
woman in Mississippi said on one occasion. The white
people were talking of Mr. Woodrow Wilson's running
for the presidency. She said: "Who dat runnin' fer de
presidency?" When told that it was Mr. Wilson she said:
"How come dat? I thought Mr. Bryan mos' ginnally
always run!" He was a WORKER—and he could toil
terribly. In him there was no desire to seek ease through
tasks that did not tax his strength. In him there was no
passive acquiescence in small attainments. In him there was
no slothful timidity in attempting great things! In him there
was no fainting in the burden and heat of the day; in
him no stopping for excessive rest when problems and
burdens rested on him with the weight of a hundred
worlds.

He was an official in the United States Government.
And in all the positions of trust in which he was placed
and with which he was honored by vote or by appoint-

ment, he ever preferred the duty he owed to God to any danger or criticism that was apt to come from men. Faithful was he, never changing possible ideals for working compromises, never changing righteous principles for loose expediences, never diluting the stringency of his convictions, never changing serene wisdom for sharp subtlety, never substituting the oil of flattery for the unvarnished truth, never making life a scheme, an artifice, and less of an exalted crusade, ever irresistibly indignant in the presence of fraud or injustice. His orbit was certainly his own, and the track of his wheels can never be confounded with that of any rival. Some names there are whose light shines brightly for a brief time, after the manner of falling stars, but Bryan's emblem is the sun, whose going forth is unto the ends of the earth and whose shining brings universal service.

II—Consider HIS ABILITY AS AN ORATOR.

As an orator he fulfilled the dreams of the divine Orpheus, who drew multitudes to him by the eloquence and magic of his speech. In his speaking he was august in his simplicity, majestic in his humility, compelling in his self-assertion. Along with Demosthenes, Pitt, Oliver Cromwell, Gladstone, Spurgeon, Webster, Calhoun, Lincoln and Wilson, he will have his shining place in the centuries because in all his speeches he championed righteousness and challenged iniquity. The political Pilates, the industrial Herods, the journalistic Jezebels, the financial Ahabs who uttered themselves against him will be remembered only in dooms of infamy and woes of shame, while Bryan's name will stand forever unstained and unclouded.

As an orator he was at times a lamp glowing softly; at times a furnace burning fiercely; at times a zephyr whispering softly; at times as lightning flaring furiously; at times a river flowing smoothly; at times a cataract thundering mightily; at times a fountain gushing forth refreshing waters abundantly; at times a red-hot Vesuvius pouring forth lava; at times a gentle mouth filled with real consolations; at times a mouth in which was a two-edged sword. As an orator he came forth exultantly from the tabernacle of Democracy set high in the heavens of the nations of men, rejoicing as a strong man to run a race.

In political fight his words leaped forth as sparks fly from the hammer falling on an anvil. His eloquence often swept the audience into a frenzy of applause, as a forest fire, driven by a great wind, sweeps through a forest. Often in political fight, when he spoke, every word was a thunderbolt, every sentence a flare of lightning, every paragraph an earthquake. His fame as an orator spread abroad, and few auditoriums were large enough to contain the crowds which flocked eagerly to hear him.

In the Democratic National Convention, which met in Chicago in 1896, in a building which seated fifteen thousand, it was an occasion of intense excitement, for the silver question had brought on a class and sectional struggle in which the gold faction charged repudiation, while the supporters of free silver accused their opponents of greed and conspiracy. Many gold delegates were unseated. President Cleveland's policies were condemned. A commendatory resolution offered by a minority was hooted down with catcalls and insulting cries and shrill hisses. During the heated debate many well-known public men set forth their arguments and invectives—among them Ben Tillman, "pitchfork" senator from South Carolina, Hill of New York, Russell of Massachusetts, and others. Then Mr. Bryan appeared before that excited crowd and spoke, ending with the impassioned declaration: "You shall not press down upon the brow of labor this crown of thorns; you shall not crucify mankind upon a cross of gold!"

In this speech he was "an animated aurora with all the variations of luminous sunset." His power over that audience made one to think of the Man of Nazareth, who stilled the storm on Galilee with the words "Peace, be still!" That speech raised him from the divided leadership of a faction to the unchallenged mastery of a powerful political party. In the Baltimore convention, he was the most commanding figure, and turned the tide from Champ Clark to Woodrow Wilson—and his support of Mr. Wilson during the ensuing campaign assisted in his election. Without effort he possessed a kingly authority. He carried everywhere and all the time the atmosphere of gentle supremacy.

A question was asked centuries ago. This the question: "How did you know that Theseus was a god?" The answer: "I recognized Apollo by his speech; Mars by his thunder-bolts; Minerva by her wisdom, but I know that Theseus was a god, because whatsoever he did, whether he sat, or whether he walked or whether he spoke—whatsoever he did—he had supremacy over men!" So it was with Bryan.

As an orator his lips and tongue, as someone has so aptly said, were the physical instruments of the most musical and commanding voice of this age, and which spoke to more people, many times over, than the lips and tongue of any other man who ever lived in the world. As an orator he had nerves of silk and sinews of steel. People listened to him like children frightened at the roar of a storm, or like slaves to the reading of an emancipation proclamation, or like a lover to the sweet and passionate whisperings of a lover. As an orator he often gathered and gleaned from the Bible—the Bible which was to him the friend of his fireside, the comrade of his solitude, the comrade of his travels and the light of his darkness!

III—Consider Him As a Mighty Advocate of Peace.

Born just before that awful struggle between the States—when a million people marched North and more than a million marched South and died when brothers' fingers clutched at brothers' throats—there seemed to be in him some of the recoil against war that women feel when their dead are before them. A babe he was, during one war; a colonel he was, during the Spanish-American war; Secretary of State he was, during part of the World

War—and he hated war. Not that he was afraid to fight. Not that he was afraid to draw his sword. Not that he fainted at the smell of gun powder or trembled when bullets whined and cannon boomed! Not that he wanted peace at any price. But the fact remains that he hated war—and was a strong advocate and worker in the cause of universal peace. Yes!

Yes, he hated war. And the reasons Dan Poling gives for hating it were summarized in Bryan's life: he hated war, for he knew its folly, and had seen it waste the substance of the world in riotous carnage. He hated it with terror—the terror of one who has seen its frenzied butchery. He hated it with passion—the passion of one who has held his dying against his breast. He hated it with disillusionment—the disillusionment of one who has gathered up its bloody fragments. He hated it with agony—the agony of one who has sons to be numbered and daughters to be offered should its guns grow hungry again. He hated it because of the young men it spits upon bayonets and like offal across continents sown to passion and watered with blood.

I am speaking the words that Poling uttered when I say he hated war because of the child it orphans and the bride it widows; because of the betrothed it leaves unmated, the father it leaves sonless, the mother it robs of the fruit of the womb; because of the evil passions it unleashes to feed upon the innocent. He hated it because of the virgins it casts to the lions of lust; because of the good will it destroys, the truth it perverts, the murder it decorates, the brotherhood it rapes, the black damp of suspicion it hangs over the councils of men. He hated war for the crimson blood-bubbles it blows over all the seas and for the poisoned breath it gives the wings of the wind. He hated it for the men it maims, for its ruined cities, for its polluted rivers, for its desecrated altars, for its fences of skulls and bones that girdle the globe. He hated it for the hearts it breaks, for the minds it crazes, for the souls it damns.

But to continue in the words of Poling, he believed.

And because he believed—believed that the song of the angels over Bethlehem is a prophecy; believed in the ultimate might of right; because he believed in God and had cast the anchor of his faith behind Jesus Christ, Prince of Peace—he seemed to see the dawning of the day when nations shall beat their swords into plough-shares, their spears into pruning hooks, and when men shall learn war no more forever!

And because of this, he was a soldier in every good cause, in every intellectual, moral, spiritual, and humanitarian battle for the right. He, never stooping to any low word or low deed to carry through any plan, truly "endured hardness as a good soldier of Jesus Christ."

As has been said of others we can say in larger measure of him: he was a man in whom the noble grandeur of our mountains towered; a man in whom the quiet beauty of our plains nestled; a man in whom the patience of God's stars shone; a man in whom the noble rage of our seas sobbed; a man in whom the modesty of God's violets bloomed; a man in whom the determination of God Almighty burned—our statesman sun by day and our warrior moon by night in every good cause. Not one flower will ever wither in his wreath of glory. Not one gem will ever tarnish in his crown.

"Blow, blow, ye golden trumpets, over the immortal dead. Play, play, ye unseen harps, over the undying dead! Shout, shout, ye angels of joy, over the deathless dead! Sing, sing, ye minstrels of glory, over the living dead!" Following in his footsteps, our feet are shod with celestial lightnings, for in Christ his impetuous temper found utterance and mighty expression against wrong; in Christ his mighty intellect found anchorage; in Christ his versatile personality found fulfilment.

"And when he fell in whirlwind, after a stormy conflict with the foes of the Bible, he went down as when a kingly cedar green with boughs goes down with a great shout upon the hills, and leaves a lonesome place against the sky!"

On one occasion, while in New Orleans, Dr. Lee had a "brush with the law." A young woman, named Nellie Wright, was on trial for her life because of a certain crime. Dr. Lee visited this young woman in the jail and came to the conclusion that she was innocent. He made such a statement from the pulpit, and Judge Marr came out with an accusation to the effect that Dr. Lee was preaching "anarchy and revolution."

On the following Sunday Dr. Lee read, in his pulpit, the accusation that appeared in the newspaper, *The Item,* and then gave a five-minute reply to Judge Marr, quoting verbatim eight statements which he had made in his sermon, namely:

Statement 1: "Something has happened which has made hundreds of hearts beat in horror and sorrow—something which has made the Law active that justice might be satisfied."

Statement 2: "Surely tonight, calmly and solemnly, we can ponder this awful tragedy to our profit, to the good of others, and to the warning of many."

Statement 3: "Real editors lift discussion out of the partisan muck up to the prophetic mountains. They are an antidote to rabid nationalism; they are an offset to violent partisanship."

Statement 4: "Statesmen who pass iniquitous laws live in those laws, cursing successive generations; authors of base books survive in those books like a chronic pestilence."

Statement 5: "Ninety percent of the children brought to one court said they had never attended Sunday school. One New York judge declared his experience on the bench taught him that our boys can be saved only by the essentials of Christianity."

Statement 6: "We need more fences of precaution at the top, then we will have less need of hospitals at the bottom. More prevention at the top will give us less tragedy at the bottom. We need to build moral fences, spiritual fences, cultural fences, fences of truth and righteousness—to see to it that the wine glass and the gaming table and the dance hall and improper amusements do not break these fences away."

Statement 7: "Can we dwell on the avenue and think nothing of the slums? Smallpox says 'No,' typhoid fever says 'No,' war says 'No,' crime says, 'No.'

Statement 8: "Were I juryman to vote or were I judge to sentence, I would give the limit to bootleggers who defy the Eighteenth Amendment, to all whiskey buyers and sellers who know that every drop they drink comes to them tainted with some man's perjury of his marriage vows."

"These mere statements quoted verbatim from my sermon manuscript," said Dr. Lee, "are but drops from the 'anarchy and revolution and disregard for law' which I preach. And that is my last word to Judge Marr on this matter."

New Orleans is a Roman Catholic City. Under the powerful Gospel preaching of the pastor of the First Baptist Church, an astounding number of Roman Catholics (one hundred and thirty-five, according to the records) came to know the grace of God in Christ, and that the salvation which they professed was not and could not be through works of any kind, but entirely by faith in the completed and complete work of the love of God on Calvary's Cross. Perhaps no Protestant minister ever to hold a pastorate in this colorful city has been used to win more Roman Catholics to the Saviour; certainly none loved their souls more than did Robert G. Lee, nor tried harder to lead them to Christ.

It was not unusual for Dr. Lee to receive letters such as this one, selected from his files:

Dear Rev. Lee:

This is a great religious city, lots of beautiful faith and lovely people. I went to my church [Catholic] Sunday at 7 a. m. and then to the Baptist Sunday school and services, with one of the ladies in the office. I enjoyed it thoroughly and suppose I will go again.

What do you think? One morning last week I woke up at 3:30 and who do you think I was thinking of? Rev. Lee was on my mind and the words he used in his sermon, "I am willing to spend and be spent, even though you love me less," which I know, are the words of St. Paul.

I thought this was a strange thing, and would like for him to know how these words, as given by him, impressed me.

This girl was later led to Christ, but one of the most lovely trophies from Roman Catholicism was a Mrs. Smith, who was thoroughly converted the first time she heard Dr. Lee preach. Such a radiant Christian she was, her heart filled to overflowing with the joy of her salvation in Christ, that she came to be known by everyone in the First Baptist Church, where she was very active, as "Mrs. 'Happy' Smith."

Sickness came upon her, and she sent word to Dr. Lee one Sunday, asking two things: that the congregation should sing her favorite hymn for her, *Standing on the Promises,* for that was her testimony now; then, that the pastor come to see her when the service was over, for she knew she was going to die, and she wanted to see him once more before she should depart to be with Christ. It goes without saying that her requests were happily complied with.

There had come to New Orleans, following World War I, two Roman Catholic young men—one having served in the French navy, and the other with the German fleet. Both of these lads found the First Baptist Church at about the same time, and both were converted through the Gospel, under Dr. Lee's ministry. Now brethren in Christ, these former enemies of both God and each other were led into the waters of baptism on the same evening.

A rather unusual experience, with a Roman Catholic girl, came to Dr. Lee one Monday morning. Let him tell the story as he has given it in churches or at Bible conferences throughout America. Lee calls the story "The Surrendered Desert," having preached on that subject on the Sunday night that he first saw the girl.

Though I had spoken four times, and though I had given forty minutes to a wedding and had administered the ordinance of baptism Sunday night, I felt that I must be at my office early. I asked Mrs. Watson, my secretary, to meet me there at 7:30. She did, being there before I arrived. When I went into my office, she came in and said: "A young lady has been waiting to see you."

"Who is she?" I asked.

"I do not know. She did not tell me her name; and I felt I should not ask her. But she was waiting here when I came."

I said: "Send her in."

In a moment there walked into my office a young woman who was making an effort to be calm, efforts perceptible at once. I arose to greet her, and asked her to be seated. She was, I judged, about eighteen years of age. Extravagantly dressed she was, with a huge white fur neckpiece around her neck and shoulders. A frilly little hat perched perilously on the side of her head. One hand,

her left, was gloved, and she held a right glove in her
left hand. There was a haunting look about her eyes and
a slight frown on her brow; and she looked as though
smiles had been strangers to her face for a long time. And
when she spoke, it seemed that laughter had been an
alien matter to her mouth.

"Last night I heard you preach, but I was not in
the auditorium." She appeared to be somewhat old beneath her mask of rouge, her youth tainted with vicious-
ness.

"I am sure you were not," I said lightly, "for had you
been here wearing that I would have seen you."

I smiled. She grew a bit more serious.

"But I stood on the corner of Delachaise, just outside, and heard you preach. I hated you and all you said
until you said that God accepts a surrendered desert. And
I knew then I must see you. I have no father or mother;
no brothers, no sisters that I know of. Would you let me
talk to you as though you were my father and loved me—
my mother and understood me? I am a human desert."

"Yes," I said, "all you tell me shall be kept as a sacred
secret."

Then she talked with me—at first in a subdued voice I
could hardly hear, as though she were afraid others would
hear her. Sympathetically and intently did I listen as she,
with a hesitancy that bordered, at first, on distrust,
verbally turned the dirty pages of a life of sordid shame
and sin. It was like watching one empty out a garbage
can on the parlor floor. It was like standing near a
smoking fire and getting smoke, that hurt, in one's eyes.

After she had finished the sordid recital, she looked
at me as one crying for help and yet as one who would
be defiant should I not help; as one in despair calling and
getting no answer from hope; as one struggling in a
muddy sewerage river grasping for the last plank that
drifted slowly by. Her words had shocked me. My heart
was in my throat. She looked at me with eyes that burned
strangely, as one tired of sin, tired of life, tired and
distrustful of everybody.

Robert G. Lee, A.B.,   as a Graduate of Furman University, 1913

*Lee's First Pastorate, Lima Baptist Church,
Lima, S. C.*

*Baptismal House and Pool at Harmony
Baptist Church, Near Laurens, S. C., Where
Lee First Performed the Baptismal Ordinance*

*Vessels Used for
the Lord's Supper
at Harmony Baptist
Church*

"Do you think there is any chance for a girl like me to get back, to get out of the ditch and on the road again? Will God—*will* God—accept my surrendered desert and make it blossom? You said He would. Is it so?" Her words were ominous with distrust and fear—and penitence. My lips seemed to freeze to my teeth.

The recital of things she had done seemed to daze me into speechlessness. I did not, *could* not, speak at first. She took my silence for reluctance and cried out, almost shrieked out, as though she wanted all the world to know: "If you don't think so, if what you said last night is a lie, then you'll read of 'em fishing my body out of the river tomorrow—if they can find it!" Her voice had in it the wail that bordered on a snarl. She had stood to her feet and was gripping the corner of my desk with trembling fingers. Her whole body was aquiver.

Then I spoke. I told her that all I said the night before was so—that Christ would be far more than words could tell to all who with repentance toward God and faith in Christ surrendered to Him. I told her that Christ would accept her surrendered desert, and restore the years the locusts had eaten—and make her, though smutty from contact with the devil's pots, to be as "a dove covered with silver, and her feathers with yellow gold" (Ps. 68:13).

To come quickly to the end of a darkened road, I will simply say that she accepted Christ, knelt in prayer, and promised to "see me again." As she went out the back door from my office, she took off the costly white fur neckpiece and dropped it in the rubbish can just outside the door.

Later, I baptized her—nobody, not even my secretary, knowing ought of her terrible sin, knowing anything of her having been the dirty toy of dirtier men for three years.

These unworthy hands of mine baptized her. These eyes saw her smile as I put her face slowly under the water. Next day she 'phoned me that she was "leaving town," to start anew.

Five years later—in another city—she came to my house
with a young man. She stood before me at the marriage
hour in our home, a fine young man beside her, a young
man whose life, while in his teens, was one of awful sin.
He, too, had been redeemed. Both of them told me they
were getting married "without any secrets," that they had
opened all the pages of both books when they talked of
marriage and became engaged, that they had forgiven what
needed to be forgiven in each other and that they were
forgetting the past, starting over in beginning life together.

I saw them as they left our little home. They stopped
on the edge of the sidewalk and looked up at the stars,
as though they were praying to God; and then they kissed,
and went away arm in arm, heart to heart, hand in hand,
soul to soul.

I know where they live now.

Their surrendered deserts have become gardens of the
Lord.

And their little children are beautiful flowers in the
garden.

To that time, Robert G. Lee was never happier in
his life than he was in New Orleans. He felt that
his ministry was making a genuine impact upon the
old city that he loved so dearly; his influence in the
church and the affection that he held for his
people, and they for him, were deeply gratifying;
outside opportunities were constantly arising, and he
was free to accept them; and he and his family
were well. He had led the church in the erection of
an educational building, situated behind the church,
at a cost of about $100,000 and things were prospering
in every way following his three years in this
Roman Catholic city. Lee felt that his valley was
green indeed. He was as nearly satisfied with the
way things were going as a man of his energy and

abounding zeal could possibly be. Consequently, the initial call, and several that followed with persistence, to the Charleston church were answered in the negative. On the last occasion that word came from Charleston, it was by long-distance telephone. It was Wednesday evening, and Dr. Lee was teaching the teachers of the Sunday school at a regular weekly meeting. One who was there has remarked: "I shall never forget the look that came on his face. He had suffered in agonizing prayer to know what God wanted him to do in this matter, and here they were calling him again." Dr. Lee informed Mr. Thomas that he would let him know within a few days. Then he put out the fleece.

No one who has never sought the mind of the Lord in a matter of this kind can possibly understand what it means when a definite "fleece" is put out, whereby some seemingly unusual thing is asked of God in order that He may demonstrate His will to a troubled and groping child of His. As Dr. Lee weighed the situation, he continued to feel that he could be used widely in his present pastorate. Yet he realized that Charleston, an old city which does not welcome new methods, was a great opportunity for an evangelistic ministry, something to which it had never, to that time, responded. George Truett, A. C. Dixon, D. L. Moody, and others had preached their hearts out in Charleston, South Carolina, without finding nearly the response that they longed for or felt the right to expect. In fact, Lee himself was later informed by certain members of the Charleston church that if he tried to hold a "revival meeting," he himself would have his heart broken. If he should go to Charleston, then, there would be great opportunity to give impetus to evangelism in that needy city. He knew also that the Citadel Square Baptist Church had a large indebtedness, and he felt that they needed a leader who would drive himself and stir the congregation to liquidate this debt or to refinance it, at least. These and other things weighed upon him. Some accused him of wanting to go to Charleston because the church was the largest Baptist church in the state. He affirms that this is not so and did not influence him in any way. He did not want to go to Charleston, but whenever he said "No" to the calls that came he had no peace of mind.

At the time that the last call came, it had been raining for days and nights as it sometimes does in semi-tropical climates. Dr. Lee's "fleece" was that if God wanted him to go to Charleston, He would stop the rain and that, on the following morning, when he, Bob Lee, awakened, the sun would be shining. Having committed the matter to the Lord, Lee went to bed and slept like an untroubled child. When he awoke the next morning, the sun was shining brightly through his window. With all his great sincerity Dr. Lee believes implicitly that this was in answer to his prayer, and the Lord gave him complete peace as to his decision as soon as it was made. He sent a telegram of acceptance to the Pulpit Committee in Charleston somewhat similar to that which had been sent when he first went to New Orleans to the First Baptist Church there.

The membership of the First Baptist Church in New Orleans was stunned by Dr. Lee's decision. The final and official call came on November 5,

1925, in a telegram from Mr. T. S. Wilbur, Chairman of the Board of Directors:

> CHURCH'S CALL IS UNANIMOUS. EVERYBODY IS DELIGHTED. WE AWAIT YOUR COMING WITH GREAT CONFIDENCE. YOU CAN COUNT ON OUR HEARTY AND LOYAL CO-OPERATION.

A few days later Dr. Lee was in Atlanta for meetings, and there he received a wire from Mrs. Lee as follows:

> FOLKS MUCH SURPRISED AND GRIEVED AT STRONG POSSIBILITY OF YOUR GOING TO CHARLESTON. THEY HARDLY KNOW WHAT ACTION TO TAKE BUT FEEL AND HOPE THAT YOU CAN REMAIN HERE FOR YEARS. MONDAY NIGHT MEETING MAY BE INTERESTING. HAVE HAD TIME THIS WEEK. ALL WELL. LOVE.

But the decision had been reached, and Dr. Lee made his plans to leave and to begin the ministry in Charleston. During his term of service in New Orleans 1,016 members were recived into the First Baptist Church, more than 300 by baptism. The prayer meetings averaged over 200 in attendance for a period of three years, and contributions totaled more than $100,000.

It would be difficult to express the great grief that was felt, not only among the members of the First Baptist Church, but in the city and in the state as well, at Dr. Lee's leaving. The congregation simply could not understand their pastor's departure. How *could* he go, whom they loved so deeply and who reciprocated that affection with every beat of his great heart? It was as if a lover, having wooed and won his beloved, turned to leave her forever at the moment that he had won her hand. On the day when Bob Lee preached his farewell sermon, there were no dry eyes, no effort to wipe away the tears that flowed so freely from deeply grieved men and women. "Dr. Lee just can't leave us now!" was the thought and wish of the whole membership. But the servant's hand had been put to the plow, and he could not turn back.

Three items in the Lee scrapbooks tell of the effect his departure had within the community and throughout the state.

The first is an old clipping from a New Orleans newspaper. Neither the name of the paper nor the date of its issue is to be seen; but this is what it says:

> Dr. Lee has been an earnest worker during the more than three years of his pastorate in New Orleans. He is a man of high ideals, a great leader, and has endeared himself to those who know him, both members of the Baptist faith and others. He has always borne a reputation of living the life that he preached, and his leaving has cast a gloom over the entire membership.

Under date of November 9, 1925, Dr. Edward D. Solomon,* Corresponding Secretary of the Louisiana Baptist State Convention, wrote:

> My dear Lee:
> It would take a great many more words than you use for me to express to you my deep regret that you are leaving Louisiana. You have been a tower of strength, a preacher of eloquence, a man of God, a friend of sinners, and a joy of your brethren. Your words, your life and your work have put us on a high plane in this state. We moan your going away, but we are grateful and thankful for your three years' stay in our state.
> I am trying to find myself so as to rejoice that we

---

*It was Dr. Solomon who nominated Robert G. Lee for President of the Southern Baptist Convention, when Dr. Lee was elected to that high office in May, 1948, for his first term.

have had three years of your life, labors, and love. I am saying to my Master that He must give me more grace, more strength now since you are going away. My love and that of my family will follow you to your new field of labor.

The Psalmist says that "even in laughter there is sorrow in the heart." I laugh when I think of the good that you have done, but down underneath I have a deep sorrow because of your leaving us. God's blessings upon you.

Yours in Christ Jesus,
E. D. SOLOMON

Finally, an editorial, "Follow Me," appeared in *The States*, a newspaper of New Orleans, which we reproduce in full below:

"FOLLOW ME"

The last recorded words of Jesus Christ are these, which He spake to His eleven disciples when they held their closing appointment with Him in the mountain in Galilee: "All power is given unto me in heaven and in earth. Go ye therefore, and teach [that is, make disciples or Christians of] all nations, baptizing them in the name of the Father, and of the Son, and of the Holy Ghost: *teaching them to observe all things whatsoever I have commanded you*: and, lo, I am with you alway, even unto the end of the world."

This is St. Matthew's version of it. St. Mark tells us that "they went forth, and preached everywhere, *the Lord working with them*, and confirming the word with signs following."

St. Luke informs us that the Saviour commanded His disciples "that *repentance and remission of sins should be preached in his name* among all the nations, beginning at Jerusalem."

The eternal and everlasting command of Jesus was spoken to St. Peter: "Follow me."

In the quotations which we have just set out from the Bible we think will be found all that there is to a preacher's chart. He has no other guide for the message he is called to deliver to a sin-cursed world. His business is the most important in the world. And the most important thing in the world is the salvation of a human soul. If he does not bend all his energies to this task of saving souls, his ministry is as profitless as was that of the unprofitable servant who hid his one talent in the ground.

No man who has reached middle life and has kept in close touch with the affairs of the Church, no man who is acquainted with the history of the great religious movements that have shocked and stirred this old world from center to circumference, but knows that the men who have led these movements, the men who have built great churches, the men whose ministry has been most fruitful, have been the preachers who have had a passion for saving souls. Luther and his great opponents, Loyola and Xavier, had this passion. John Knox had it, so did John Wesley and his great co-laborers. Bishop Butler had it, and so did that famous Brighton preacher, F. W. Robertson. Moody had it, and so did Charles H. Spurgeon. Bishop Galloway of Mississippi had it, and so did Bishop Phillips Brooks of Massachusetts. Bishop Chandler of Georgia has it, and so has Dr. Robert G. Lee, pastor of the First Baptist Church of New Orleans. Dr. Palmer had it, and so has the provincial of the Jesuits, Rev. E. Cummings, S. J.

We might string the list out to great length. Every name we have given is that of a man who has walked, as did Enoch of old, with God, and whose labors God has blessed mightily. They caught the Master's spirit, they were enthused with His final command, they took up the blood-stained Cross of Calvary and carried it exultantly before a shouting multitude, ever preaching "Jesus Christ and him crucified."

With these mighty examples before him is it not strange to find a Southern Methodist bishop, Dr. John M. Moore, exhorting the preachers of the Texas conference that they "could not avoid preaching evolution in the pulpit"?

A simple question might be put to the Modernist bishop: "Why couldn't the preachers avoid doing this?"

"Evolution," said Bishop Moore, "was progress, and fundamentalism was fixity."

That is what Celsus, the first agnostic, said of Christianity seventeen centuries before Bishop Moore was born. But the bishop belongs to the boasted modern mind which, with a slight wave of the hand, flips aside the whole past and brings it up to date.

Bishop Moore was educated in the rationalist universities of Germany, and has long been one of the leading Modernists in the Southern Methodist Church. Lately he has become bolder in expressing his faith in evolution and in deriding fundamentalism, which is but another name for the Christianity that Christ taught and which is to be found in His God-breathed Bible.

Is evolution progressive? Not so that anyone can notice it. What progress has it made? The very men who are bothering their puny finite minds with this unsubstantiated guess are now fighting among themselves over it, and one of the greatest of the clan of evolution scientists, Prof. W. E. Ritter, of the University of California, recently said this:

> If one scans a bit thoughtfully the landscape of human life for the last few decades, he can hardly fail to see signs that the whole battleground of evolution will have to be fought over again; this time not so much between scientists and theologians as among scientists themselves.

It is a common complaint among the evolution preachers like Bishop Moore that those who oppose the theory, like the great scholar and theologian, the senior bishop of the Methodist Church in the South, Dr. Warren A. Candler, never read any late books on this and other subjects. This writer not long ago heard Bishop Candler say that he had spent a large sum of money buying books on evolution and Modernism, and after reading all of them found that he had been buncoed. The books were mostly trash, said Bishop Candler. And he spoke the truth.

Virchow, whose name belongs by the side of Newton's and Pasteur's and the four or five other titans of the realm of science, said that evolution is "all nonsense." This dictum is agreed to by such modern scientists as Prof. George Barry O'Toole, Prof. Louis Trenchard More, Prof. Calvin S. Page and Prof. Oswald Spengler, names that command the respect of scientists the world over. We wonder if Bishop Moore has read their books!

J. P. Lotsy, the famous Dutch scientist, in his treatise *Evolution by Means of Hybridization*, says: "Phylogeny, i. e., reconstruction of what has happened in the past, is no science, but a product of fantastic speculation."

Bishop Moore would have his preachers preach this "fantastic speculation" rather than "the unsearchable riches of the Gospel of Jesus Christ."

The surest way to kill the Christ-spirit in a preacher or in any other religious man is to raise a doubt in his mind as to God, as to God's Bible, and as to the immortality of his own soul. This, in brief, is what evolution does. It denies God's creative power, it denies the inerrancy of the Bible, and it denies the immortality of the soul.

When something like 75 per cent of the teachers of science in this country do not believe in a personal God but do believe in evolution, when every agnostic and every infidel and every skeptic in the world denies God but affirms the "truths" of evolution, when Darwin confesses that his acceptance of the theory of evolution forced God out of his consciousness and Bishop Brown follows him with the same acclaimer, is it not a horrible thing for a bishop to tell his preachers to preach this accursed thing?

Preachers wonder why they preach to empty benches. No doubt many preachers in New Orleans have asked themselves that question. Dr. Palmer never did. He always had a packed house. Father de la Moriniere never did. Dr. Lee, the Baptist preacher with a simple Gospel message, based strictly upon the teachings of Jesus Christ, following that final command which we have quoted, has had packed houses to hear him even at night and throughout the hot summer months, when other churches were closed or empty. The reason is not hard to find. These men preached the Truth to their people. That is what Bishop Moore should have instructed his preachers to do.

The pulpit is no place for scientific theories or for any other theories. "Follow me!" is the call!

Chapter IX

INTERLUDE IN CHARLESTON

Bob Lee Goes Back to South Carolina

Although there was a sense of inconsolable loss in New Orleans over Dr. Lee's departure from that city, and regret generally throughout the state of Louisiana among those who knew of the work of the rising young preacher, there was gladness in South Carolina at the thought of his return to his native state. Numerous letters are in Lee's files expressing both sentiments. It is not easy to select out of communications from noble men the letters that will best suggest the affection in which Bob Lee was held by his brethren. We have, however, chosen two. The first is from David A. Lee, Bob's father. It will be remembered that "Dad" Lee was not enthusiastic when Bob, as a lad, expressed his burning purpose to obtain an education so that he might be a preacher. But the father was, in the course of time, convinced that his boy was on fire for God and resolute in his determination. So it was that "Dad" Lee said to him: "I'd like for you to be a preacher, provided you will be a good one; but I don't want you to be a 'one horse' preacher. We have too many square pegs in round holes already. If you can be a 'sure nuff' good preacher, I'll lie down on my back like a fellow listening to his

172

hounds run a fox, and I'll give a whoopee yell: 'Go to it, Bob! Go to it, son!' "

Here, under date of November 11, 1925, from Fort Mill, South Carolina, is "Dad" Lee's "whoopee yell":

Dear Robert and All—

Your letter to hand. So glad to hear that you aire coming back to your old state of South Carolina.

The people of S. C. needs good preaching as much as any place. You will have the biggest place in the state.

This is your birthday. God bless you today . . .

You have made my heart glad so many times in these twenty years—for the honor you have brought to me. Wish I could see you today—and kiss you. So glad to hear that little Bula is getting on so well, and that big Bula is well.

We aire all well. Love to all.

D. A. LEE

The second letter is from Bob's friend, Ellis A. Fuller, at that time head of the Department of Evangelism for the Home Mission Board of the Southern Baptist Convention. It is dated November 16, 1925, at Atlanta, Georgia:

Dear Lee:

I have been wanting to write you since I saw the announcement of your decision to go to Citadel Square. I know your work there will be wonderful. I am *for you,* night and day, in my prayers. I am grateful that my confidence in you is such that I have no fear that any of the compliments that are being paid you will affect your humility one iota. God is signally honoring you and using you. . .

Do not fail to pray for me as I attempt to lead this work. Suffice it to say that the job is big, and the man is little.

Affectionately yours,
ELLIS FULLER

The newspaper of the old home town, Fort Mill, also expressed its pride in its native son. Under date of December 10, 1925, the *Fort Mill Times* printed this article:

> From a boy of 21 struggling for an education to pastor of the largest church in the South Carolina Baptist Convention at 39 is the story of the rise of Rev. Robert G. Lee, formerly of Fort Mill, who will occupy Sunday, for the first time, the pulpit of the Citadel Square Baptist Church of Charleston.
>
> The minister's father, D. A. Lee, 70, is one of the oldest residents of Fort Mill at the present.
>
> The boy of eighteen years ago left Fort Mill with no money, but with a strong conviction and a determination to win his way through college and the seminary.
>
> In the Panama Canal Zone he earned enough to enable him to return and make his way through Furman Fitting School. Entering Furman [University], he served as pastor of several churches which in turn assisted him in his fight for an education. During his entire career he never called upon his father for financial aid.
>
> Dr. Lee recently completed his fourth year as pastor of a large New Orleans (La.) church. Before that time he held pastorates at Chester and Edgefield.
>
> It is needless to say that among the proudest and happiest citizens of Fort Mill is the aged father of the pastor.

When the Lees arrived in Charleston, the officers and members of the church gave a very lovely reception for them. They invited the ministers of the city, the civic leaders, and others who might be interested, as well as all the members of the church who cared to come. David Lee and Sam, Bob's father and brother respectively, were there, and Dr. Lee introduced them to the assemblage. Acknowledging the introduction, Bob's father said: "Since he was a boy, Bob has always said he was going to be a preacher. Nothing could stop him. I'm proud he's back in South Carolina."

Robert Lee began his ministry in Charleston, South Carolina, on the second Sunday of December, 1925.

Here in this new charge, Bob Lee made new resolves for himself and his ministry, as he had done before: he determined not to be satisfied with accomplishments to date but to go on *for* and *with* God; to improve his mind and his body; to be wholly honest and sincere; and to be unaffected by whatever portions of praise might come his way. And pasted at his desk he had a poem by Edgar A. Guest:

> To live as gently as I can;
> To be, no matter where, a man;
> To take what comes of good or ill
> And cling to faith and honor still;
> To do my best and let that stand,
> The record of my brain and hand.
> And then, should failure come to me,
> Still work and hope for victory.
>
> To have no secret place wherein
> I stoop unseen to shame and sin;
> To be the same when I'm alone,
> As when my every deed is known;
> To live undaunted, unafraid
> Of any step that I have made;
> To be without pretense or sham—
> Exactly what men think I am.

Lee was fully aware that these lines lack one thing: God is left out of the picture. But he could put God into it, and rest in the Lord and the power

of His might. This he sought to do with undeviating
determination day and night.

Pastor Lee was to need to cling to such sentiments as the poet expressed, and to hold hard upon
Christ in the days to come. He had, as has already
been indicated, perfect peace about his decision to
leave New Orleans for the work in Charleston, but
he could not help feeling deep grief about forsaking
the city where he had been so signally used of the
Lord and where there were so many people whom
he loved very dearly. And while there is no record
of the fact, neither has Dr. Lee said a word about it
to the author, reading between the lines of the
history of the time we surmise that there were
moments when he wondered whether his transfer
to the Citadel Square Baptist Church was as a
result of his own decision or God's voice speaking to
him. For things did not go as easily and co-opera-
tively as they had in New Orleans. This did not dis-
courage him overmuch, for he was accustomed to
difficult ways, so that it only challenged him the
more. But some of the things, minor matters perhaps,
which he wanted to see done, such as changing the
location of the baptismal pool, or the hour of morning
worship, or re-carpeting the aisles of the church, or
changing the time of the monthly observance of the
Lord's Supper—matters mentioned to the brethren
before he moved to Charleston—were never realized.
Some of the brethren, and the pastor never doubted
their well-meaning motives, did not see eye to eye
with Lee regarding these things which the pastor
thought would add much to the efficiency of the
church activities and the blessing of the ministry.

The Rev. and Mrs. Robert G. Lee in Edgefield, S. C., 1918

Where the Lees First Lived in Edgefield, S. C.

*The House that Robert G. Lee Built in
Edgefield*

Edgefield Baptist Church

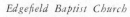

He thought them slow of heart to believe in "the serving of tables." There were certain requisites for the Citadel Square Baptist Church that he felt were his particular job—divinely appointed for R. G. Lee and no one else. It is true, he was to be the pastor in Charleston for only two years, but he had no way of knowing that in the beginning.

A few days after Dr. Lee preached his initial sermon as pastor of the Citadel Square Baptist Church, the first official meeting of deacons was held. From the minutes of the meeting, which convened on December 15, 1925, we glean that the newly-called shepherd had no intention that the sheep should lie down in one spot to eat grass. In addition to the authorization for employment of a pastor's secretary, Mr. John P. Thomas, one of the deacons, was instructed to look into the possibility of refunding the large church debt, approximating $175,000, at as early a date as possible. A budget was established for the year 1926, the highest in the church's history—$45,000. This was to be applied as follows: one third for missions, one third for church expenses, and one third for interest on and retirement of the indebtedness of the church. It was determined, also, that Citadel Square should issue a church bulletin every Sunday, an innovation.

Two letters pasted in one of the scrapbooks of this period are worthy of special note, since they indicate once again the great love that this apostle of love inspired in others. One is from Dr. DeMent, addressed not to Dr. Lee but to Dr. A. E. Hutto, Jackson, Alabama, where Lee was holding a meeting of several days' duration:

My dear Brother Hutto:

How well do I remember you in the olden days. You have my ex-pastor but not ex-friend with you for a few days. Treat him right, as no finer man or more brilliant thinker or more effective orator is in our Baptist pulpit today than Robert G. Lee. You might tell him this if you are not afraid it will make him mad! He is the salt of the earth and the light of the world. He will do to tie to now and evermore. Would that we had more like him. Give him my love.

> Hurriedly but cordially,
> B. H. DeMent

Dr. Hutto gave this letter to Dr. Lee.

Near the end of December, Sam Lee and his family visited the Lees in Charleston. Upon returning home to Fort Mill, Sam Lee wrote to his brother Bob:

Dearest Bob:

Thank you for your letter. You didn't enjoy our being with you any more than we ourselves did. . .

Bob, I want to ask a favor of you, if not too much trouble to you. Please mail me one of your church calendars every week, as I want them for a special purpose, to help me in some of my work, as lots of times I can get things from them that I cannot get elsewhere. So if you don't mind, and I know you don't, I'd appreciate it. We had a fine day at our little church yesterday. Had 189 in Sunday school, and they all promised me that they would help me push the buggy along in 1926.* I feel that I need some pushing, as I have pulled till I'm nearly done. . .

Do you know, I was right homesick for you yesterday, I don't know why, as my family were all home together, and somehow I just thought and thought about you, and how much I love you and Bula and Bula G., and how much you all love me, and how I enjoyed hearing your dear sweet voice in the church, and, oh, I don't

---

* Samuel E. Lee, vice-president of the Harris Department Store, was Sunday-school superintendent in the Fort Mill Church.

know, just seemed like I wanted to be near you for a little while.

I was sitting there in your church the night I was there, and just sat and looked at you, and thought how in the years not so very far past you worked and worked and worked on the farm until you were so tired, and it looked to me as if you were still tired, but through it all there appeared something that cancelled every tired feeling you might have. And I just thought what a job upon a poor weak human being, to be at the head of so many folks, to lead them and guide them aright. I just want you to know that my heart goes out to you in your work, and I always ask God to help you and keep you with us a long time. Somehow I don't want you to go first, but I want to go, and I want you to say a few words at my funeral,** as it's almost like poor old Mrs. Feltz said here—that she wouldn't mind dying if you could preach her funeral.

Excuse all this, but I just had to tell you. God bless you all three always, and remember, we love you— Write me when you can. Come as soon as you can.

Love to each of you,
SAM

Some personal affronts, though perhaps not intended to be such, wounded Dr. Lee deeply, and the pastor spent many hours praying that thoughtless criticisms in the church family would not cause bitterness to abide in his own heart or in the hearts of any of the members, nor cause coldness of heart toward the Lord, or the church. A soul less sensitive than he might readily have been unaffected by continued opposition in certain matters and insistence upon proceeding always according to custom. But Lee had always worked so hard himself, had always tried

---

** Samuel Lee died in 1939, and Dr. Lee did "say a few words" at his funeral.

so hard, and had so much zeal for the Lord that he was painfully perplexed by certain criticisms of his motives on the part of some who were themselves perplexed, no doubt, by the pastor's ways of doing things.

Let it not be thought, however, that the preacher's disappointment and discouragements were generally known. He kept his feelings to himself, and so did the few who disagreed with him. Prayer, time, courtesy, and hard work soon overcame any disagreement as to the misunderstandings between the pastor and some of the brethren. In a few months after Lee went to Charleston, a spiritually salutary and happy condition existed between pastor and people. By the time Lee left Charleston at the end of two years, the church membership was willing for the two years to lengthen into many. And but for the will of God, such might have been the case. Certainly in Charleston every experience, even the failure of the bank in which he lost all the money he had on deposit, were allowed of God, no doubt, for the growth of this servant of His who was to assume in days to come greater and greater responsibilities. "Tribulation worketh patience; and patience, experience; and experience, hope: and hope maketh not ashamed" (Rom. 5:3-5).

Cherished above every other experience in Charleston is the memory of the conversion and baptism of her who has been so precious to her father's heart from the day of her birth—Bula G. A dear little girl who virtually grew up in the church, she has never disappointed her "daddy" in any way. With deep sentiment Dr. Lee recalls every loving embrace she offered him, and also amusing little incidents, such as the occasion when, following the Sunday-morning service in the church, Bula G., still a little girl, took her turn in shaking the hand of Pastor Lee, saying: "I enjoyed your sermon, Dr. Lee. I was asleep." Or again, he looks back with deepest joy to a later occasion when Bula G., in sweet co-operation with her preacher father, refused to go to a dance with these words: "I never intend deliberately to do anything to displease my daddy—or God."

Richest recollection, however, is April 10, 1926, the sixteenth anniversary of Dr. Lee's ordination to the ministry. Some weeks prior to this, Mrs. Lee had talked with Bula G. regarding her need for forgiveness for her sins, and the salvation of her soul. Bula G. was nine years of age, but she was already a good reader, and shortly after this Dr. Lee found her one day, weeping as she read her Bible. The passage, in one of the Gospels, pertained to the crucifixion of our Lord. Bula G.'s daddy spoke with her, as her mother had, about Jesus' death for sin, for Bula G.'s sins, and told her that He died for her, on account of her very own sins. He explained how she might be forgiven, how she might be saved and go to Heaven—not through baptism, not through joining the church, but by trusting in Jesus Christ as her Substitute, her Saviour.

After reading Bible verses such as John 1:12; 3:18, 36; and portions of Romans 10; to which Dr. Lee guided her, the little girl said: "Well, I believe, and I love Jesus, and I want to do what He wants me to do."

The following Sunday morning—Dr. Lee did not

recall its connection with his ordination until later—
when Lee gave the invitation, he hoped devoutly that
Bula G. would come forward to profess Christ. But
she did not. The Lees prayed about it during the
day, and that night, when the choir had sung some
of the old Gospel songs and while the invitation to
come forward was still open, the nine-year-old girl
walked down the aisle with mingled timidity and
determination, and made known her trust in the
Saviour. The invitation hymn that was sung by choir
and congregation that night, not by design but
"coincidence," was the very one that was used in the
village church in Fort Mill when Bob Lee, as a lad,
made profession as to his faith in Christ as his
Saviour:

> Out of my bondage, sorrow, and night,
>   Jesus, I come, Jesus, I come;
> Into Thy freedom, gladness, and light,
>   Jesus, I come to Thee.
> Out of my sickness into Thy health,
> Out of my want and into Thy wealth,
> Out of my sin and into Thyself,
>   Jesus, I come to Thee.

On the succeeding Sunday, Dr. Lee announced to
the church congregation that he was going to baptize
his daughter that afternoon in the lake in the park.
As had been the experience at Chester, there were
many protestations about the open-air baptismal service. Some of the dearest Christian friends in Charleston expressed distress and told the pastor that, on
account of strollers in the park, some of whom would
view the baptism only as curiosity seekers, there
would certainly be levity and irreverence.

But Dr. Lee went ahead with his plan. About 1,500 people gathered on the banks of the lake. The choir sang. The pastor read from the Scriptures and explained clearly the meaning of Christian baptism. He asked for reverence and a spirit of worship, and baptized Bula G. amid such quiet that not even a whisper was heard. Tears were in many eyes; they were in Robert Lee's eyes, too, and those of his dear wife. For this was one of the high points of their Christian lives, never to be forgotten.

Among Dr. Lee's correspondents in these Charleston days are to be found the names of some who were already in prominent positions in the Southern Baptist Convention, and others who were growing in stature along with the Charleston pastor. Much of our information regarding the progress and growth of Lee is to be had from his correspondence.

Here is a letter from Chester, South Carolina, from Bob's brother, Frank:

> August 20, 1926
> Chester, South Carolina
>
> My dear old Bob:
>
> Appreciate your letter so much today. It does me so much good to have a brother who can preach like you. Am so proud of you and so happy every time you are with me. Everyone here says they wish they had you back here. Some of them are going to Charleston to hear you and I hope to get down there, too, real soon. Hope Bula and Bula G. are O. K. So lonesome since you left. God bless you.
>
> Love always,
> FRANK
>
> P. S. These Chester folks sure loved you. They are always asking about you.

Another letter, undated, comes from Dr. A. M. Vollmer, Educational Director of the Walnut Street Baptist Church in Louisville, Kentucky:

Dear Dr. Lee:

In my homiletics class at the seminary we were asked to write a brief paper, the title of which was to be "The Best Sermon I Ever Heard." I am enclosing a copy of that paper as I thought you might be interested in it. . .

Most cordially,
A. M. VOLLMER

A copy of Dr. Vollmer's paper was enclosed, in which he spoke of having heard Dr. Robert G. Lee during the Southern Baptist Convention in Memphis in 1925. "I was so stirred," says this man, "by the message, that I resolved to have him at the Walnut Street Baptist Church in Louisville. The subject of the sermon was 'What Jesus Became.' "

Then there is another letter from Bob's brother, Sam, from Fort Mill, South Carolina, dated 1927:

Dearest Bob:

Thank you for your letter. Yes, I think I can see how busy you are, or anyone who is in the work you are and have it at heart. There are thousands of things to do, if we would attempt even a part of what ought to be done, and I hope and pray that your strength will be with you for a long time, so that you may carry on. I am proud of you, because you love me, and then, too, because you are such a fine capable brother, whom everybody loves who knows you. I was right amused at Greenville. Sometimes I would be meeting different folks, some from Charleston, and many others from other parts of the state, and when they are told my name is Lee, the next thing they ask is if I'm a brother to the *preacher*. I tell them immediately "Yes"; then that makes them all the more happier to know me. I made Bula laugh there. I told her that until folks found out I was your brother they didn't pay any attention to me, as I looked so insignificant and common, I guess, as I wasn't hardly noticed until I was known as Dr. Lee's brother. Then they made out like they were just crazy about me. That's all right; I am proud of it anyway, and if I *have* to ride on your coat tail, I can sure swing on, and glad of the chance . . .

I met several people who used to be in your congregation at Long Creek, etc. All spoke highly of you, and I just looked around there and imagined I could see you on some rainy morning, out with your papers, and I just thought how marvelous, against some who had their pathway strewn with roses, so to speak, and have not made good. God surely has been good to you, and me, too although we have had some real ups and downs, and still have them . . .

The rest of that letter has been torn off.

In March of 1927 Dr. Lee was scheduled to speak in Florida, and so he invited Dr. Edward S. Reeves, the man who baptized him, to take the pulpit of the Citadel Square Baptist Church in Charleston. In the bulletin of the church for March 13, 1927, Dr. Lee introduced the speaker to the congregation in these words:

I introduce to you today the man who baptized me. Well do I remember his Christly teaching, his fine example, his encouraging words, his inspiring encouragement when I was just a boy. Well do I remember that first Sunday night in August, 1898, when his hands buried me in baptism. I commend him to you as a faithful servant of the Most High God, as a preacher who loves the Lord, as one who has served Him faithfully, as a minister who rightly divides the Word of Truth, a workman who needeth not to be ashamed.

My heart's love to all today.

Pray for us in the meeting in Florida. Will see you next Sunday. Your Pastor,
ROBERT G. LEE

Dr. Lee's great friend, Dr. DeMent, President of the Baptist Bible Institute of New Orleans, was in Ridgecrest, North Carolina, and sent a letter to his friend as follows:

Dear Royal Grand Eloquent Lee:

My dearly beloved, oh, noble and generous you are! That check is fine, bless your heart—more than I had any right or mind to expect. Rest assured it will fit in well.

I rejoice that you had such a fine meeting in Augusta and big crowd last Sunday night.

As I said, I had a great time on the 22nd. So you are off to Shreveport and Baton Rouge and may the Lord bless you. I am not trying to manage the Lord but I do wish He would send you to the First Church of Shreveport. I am praying for it constantly and as earnestly as I know how. You would fit there and I'd almost have a fit if the Lord would send you to that great church. We shall see. We must be patient and grow strong. Give our love to the Lee family. We are to drive over to Greenville tomorrow for David. Blessings on you. "*Little* (big) *man,*" excuse haste and pen—no secretary now.

Affectionately yours evermore,
Byron Hoover DeMent, Lee's Pal

During Lee's pastorate in Charleston, he held two two weeks' revival campaigns in the church. There was hesitancy on the part of some, who expressed the opinion that the pastor's heart would be broken, saying: "Charleston is not an evangelistic city. Response to invitations to receive Christ is not what it is in places that are not so staid and set in their ways as Charleston." Mel Trotter, one of America's greatest evangelists of the twentieth century, had attempted an evangelistic campaign in Charleston. During the period that Mel was preaching, in a tent just across the street from the

Citadel Square Baptist Church, he found the going
rather hard, and, where he hoped he might see
great evangelistic conflagrations, saw only feeble
candles glowing. Much distressed, almost in despair,
he visited Dr. Lee and discussed the situation with
him. Mr. Trotter told Lee that he knew how the
disciples felt who fished all night and caught nothing.
Dr. Lee was not in the city for the full series of
Trotter's meetings, but he did attend some of the
services and asked his church to support the work
by attendance and gifts.

It was because of Mel Trotter's experience, and
that of others before him, that not a few thought
Lee was making a mistake in holding a "protracted
meeting." But the pastor was insistent, and so the
church agreed to pray and work. Lee secured W. A.
Huey, then choir director of the First Baptist Church,
Richmond, Virginia, to lead the singing and to do
Christian visitation.

During the two weeks of Lee's campaign there
were 156 public professions of faith. The closing
address was the occasion for Lee's message "Pay
Day—Some Day." Twenty-eight people came forward
when the invitation to receive Christ was given, and
89 converts were baptized that Sunday night. Some
of the citizens of Charleston, who had been spiritually
sleepy until that time, began to open their eyes
and rub them a little bit.

In the spring of 1927 open intimations were received from the First Baptist Church of Shreveport, Louisiana, that they were interested in Robert
G. Lee as potential pastor of the church, though no
official call had been issued. Lee was invited to speak

in Shreveport early in June. At about the same time the first suggestion of a call to Memphis, Tennessee, came by way of an interview which Mr. J. E. Dilworth, Chairman of the Pulpit Committee of the Bellevue Baptist Church, Memphis, had with Dr. Lee in Charleston. Dilworth stated his business, and Dr. Lee replied that he could not consider going to Memphis. But Dilworth had heard that Lee was to preach in Shreveport, and so invited him to stop over in Memphis to see the Bellevue Baptist Church, which the Charleston pastor agreed to do.

True to his promise, Lee did pass through Memphis and visited the Bellevue Church. Later on, the Committee reported that all that Lee did was to thump on several pianos and remark that they were badly out of tune!

The First Baptist Church of Shreveport had had, as its previous pastor, Dr. M. E. Dodd, who was now minister of another Baptist church in California. But on the way to Shreveport, Dr. Lee was told that there was a possibility that Dr. Dodd might return. He had had a very wonderful ministry there over a period of years, and the membership and officers were deeply attached to him. Lee arrived in Shreveport, was courteously entertained and listened to, and then, when he had bid good-bye to the deacons there, they were very gracious in commending his messages. But nothing was said about any call, nor did it ever come, at which Lee was not greatly astonished, in view of the news which had been given to him. Under date of June 21, Lee received a letter from Mr. T. H. Thurmond, of Shreveport, saying that he had notified the Pulpit Committee that "if they had not recalled Dr. Dodd, or selected him for presentation to the church for final action, Dr. Robert G. Lee should be the pastor of the First Baptist Church." It was evident to Lee then that the rumor which he heard was true, which indeed turned out to be so.

There are two more letters that ought to be noted at this time. The first is on the letterhead of Louisiana State University, and is dated June 26, 1927. It is signed by Jimmie Davis, who, twenty years later, was elected Governor of the State of Louisiana:

> Dear Dr. Lee:
> I was a member of the graduating class of Louisiana College in 1924 when you delivered the commencement address—the most eloquent and the greatest speech I ever heard. Am also a member of the graduating class at Louisiana State University this year and you may know that we are glad you are coming.
> Your friend,
> JIMMIE DAVIS

Following Dr. Lee's address at Louisiana State University, Davis wrote to him again to tell him that he heard one of the teachers of the university, a man who had no interest in religion whatever, say that the message almost converted him, admitting that it had at least given him a different vision from what he previously had.

The other letter is from New York City, dated August 18, 1927, on the letterhead of the American Association for the Advancement of Atheism, Inc., and is addressed to the editor of *The Baptist Messenger*. It is in reference to an article of Dr. Lee's that had appeared in the *Messenger*. The letter states:

Gentlemen:

The scholarly article by Rev. Robert G. Lee in your issue of August 11 has completely squelched me. So much so, in fact, that I am tempted to make a proposition.

I challenge the Rev. Lee or anyone else your paper may select to debate with me: "Is There a God?" My language would be such that your paper would not hesitate for a moment to print it. Here is an opportunity to show up the leader of American Atheism as an ignoramous. Let me hear from you.

Cordially,
FREEMAN HOPWOOD

Dr. Lee did not accept the challenge, for no sensible man would enter into such a dispute. There is no basis for debate when one man is an unbeliever and rejects the Bible and the other party believes the Bible to be the inerrant Word of God. It is to be remembered that "the natural man receiveth not the things of the Spirit of God: for they are foolishness unto him: neither can he know them, because they are spiritually discerned" (I Cor. 2:14).

As to Dr. Lee's conviction about the Bible, he has expressed himself innumerable times, both from the pulpit and in print. Here is an article about God's Word that Lee wrote in Charleston:

THE BIBLE IS THE BOOK OF BOOKS

The Bible, possessing the wonder of self-authentication, is validated and confirmed by the Spirit of the living God with a divine certainty that is "incommunicable by reason and impervious to the assaults of doubt."

In the Bible, as I believe, God revealed His will and truth unto men through men—controlling the speakers and writers He selected, breathing His Spirit into them, subordinating them to His pleasure and wisdom, directing their minds and hearts and hands in such a manner

that they infallibly expressed just what He wished to say—
so that if they wrote history, He preserved them from
making the slightest error—so that if they predicted future
events, He told them clearly and distinctly what would
occur—so that if they announced doctrinal truth, it was
strictly according to His breathing in every particular.

The Bible, settled in its source (Ps. 119:89), is a
Book above and beyond all books as a river is beyond a
rill in reach. The Bible, so sure in its promises (Jer. 1:12),
is above and beyond all books as the sun is beyond a
tallow dip in brightness. The Bible, so satisfying in its
contents (Jer. 15:16), is above and beyond all books
as the wings of an eagle are beyond the wings of a
sparrow in strength. The Bible, so secure in its guidance
(Ps.119:105), is above and beyond all books as an orchard
is beyond a roadside weed in fruit bearing. The Bible,
supreme in God's estimation (Ps. 138:2), is above and beyond all books as Niagara is beyond a mud puddle in glory.

The Bible, coming to us drenched in the tears of multi-
tudinous contritions, is the Book our fathers touched with
reverent hands. The Bible, coming to us worn with the
fingers of agony and death, is the Book our mothers stained
with grateful tears. The Bible, coming to us steeped in the
prayers of myriads of saints, is the Book against which
tyranny has issued its edicts, against which infidelity
has loosed its blasphemous tongue, against which agnos-
ticism has hurled its anathemas—the Book which many
enemies, ancient and modern, have tried to exterminate—
the Book which the dissecting knives of some scientific
anatomists whack at—the Book against which some pulpits
and some college snipes aim their ill-grounded propositions
and summon to appear at the bar of human reason.

But this marvelous Book is still "the Word of God"
that "liveth and abideth for ever." And all its enemies
of yesteryears and nowadays have not extinguished one
spark of its holy fire, nor diluted one drop of its honey,
nor torn one hole in its beautiful vesture, nor broken
one string on its thousand-string harp, nor weakened its
vitality by one pulse beat, nor shortened its march of

triumph by one step. Today this Bible walks more bypaths and travels more highways and knocks at more doors and speaks to more people in their mother tongue than any book this world has ever known, or ever will know.

Consider the wonders of the Bible. It is wonderful in its inspiration, in its translation, in its preservation, in its unification, in its salvation, in its sanctification, in its consummation. Addressing itself to the universal conscience as no other book does, it creates lives and alters destinies. Speaking with binding claims, it inaugurates world-wide movements and gives birth to immortal works. Commanding the obedience of mankind, it comes into communities of unrighteousness as the leaven of regenerative force. The plot of heaven-blessed and vitalized soil out of which has blossomed our every social and national blessing, it causes philanthropic and redemptive enterprises together with educational and therapeutic institutions to arise and stand as a tribute to its vitalizing power.

And the best we can say, with tongue or pen, is but man's mean paint on God's fair lilies, but man's paste jewels in God's casket of pure gems. Our best efforts to praise it are but disfigurements. For it is the living Word of a living God—the Book supernatural in origin, eternal in duration, inexpressible in value, immeasurable in influence, infinite in scope, divine in authorship, human in penmanship, regenerative in power, infallible in authority, universal in interest, personal in application, inspired in totality. And today, wherever it is read and treasured, it breaks the fetters of the slave, takes the heat out of life's fierce fevers, robs death of its sting, and parting of its pain. Even as in the centuries gone forever into the tomb of time, it unbars to the hastening soul the gates of everlasting delight beyond the grave. Still, as in ages agone, dying martyrs cool their hot faces in its fountains. And multitudes, as saints in other years have done, pillow their heads upon the one Book which is the softest pillow a dying head can press. The Bible is forever the miracle Book of diversity and unity—always harmonious in finite complexity.

And beware lest we forget that the Old Testament and

Bula Gentry Lee and Bula G. (at two and a half years)

Robert Lee Baptizing Bula G. in Park Lake in Charleston, S. C.

A Small Portion of the Several Thousand Who Witnessed the 120 Baptisms in the River at Chester, S.C.

the New Testament alike tell of Jesus. Of the Bible truly it can be said that Christ, the Glory of God, doth "lighten it, and the Lamb is the light thereof." The name of Jesus, the Supreme Personality, the center of a world's desire, is on every page—in expression, or symbol, or prophecy, or psalm, or proverb. Through the Bible the name of Jesus runs like a line of glimmering light. The thought of Jesus, literature's loftiest ideal and philosophy's highest personality and criticism's supremest problem and theology's fundamental doctrine and spirituality's cardinal necessity, threads the great Book like a crystal river winds its way through a continent. Yes, this living Word of our living God stars Jesus.

Take Jesus out of the Bible and it would be like taking calcium out of lime, carbon out of diamonds, truth out of history, invention out of fiction, matter out of physics, mind out of metaphysics, numbers out of mathematics. For Jesus alone is the secret of its unity, its strength, its beauty. This is what Jesus meant when He said: "Search the Scriptures; for in them ye think ye have eternal life: and they are they which testify of Me" (John 5:39).

One morning, about a week after Dr. Lee returned from Shreveport, he said to his secretary quite suddenly: "I've made a mistake."

"What is it?" she asked him, thinking he had reference to something that he had said in a letter that he was dictating to her.

"I made a mistake about Bellevue. I ought to have gone there."

Dr. Lee's secretary replied, "Why don't you let them know? But perhaps they have already called someone else!"

"Oh, no!" replied the pastor, "no one could have the feelings I have if the church had a pastor."

So he sent a telegram to Mr. Dilworth. Forty minutes later a reply came from Memphis. An appointment was made for Mr. Dilworth and Mr. G. I. Fraser to meet with Dr. Lee, in Atlanta, to discuss the proposition.

When the three men came together in Atlanta, they looked over a map of Memphis which Mr. Dilworth had brought. The two deacons pointed out what other churches there were in the city and showed Lee the need of a really great Baptist church where Bellevue was then located. At the close of the interview Dr. Lee told the two members of the Committee that he would accept a call, but that they should not announce it until after a revival campaign that he was about to hold in Charleston should be completed.

As soon as the revival meetings were concluded, Dr. Lee wrote a letter of resignation to the Citadel Square Baptist Church, a copy of which was sent to every deacon. And to each deacon he wrote a personal letter expressing appreciation for favors and kindnesses shown him and for their ministry with him in conducting the work of the church.

Dr. Lee's letter of resignation to the church was as follows:

The Citadel Square Baptist Church,
Charleston, South Carolina
My dear Brethren and Sisters:
    Only a strong sense of duty and a conviction that I am doing the right thing—the thing that is best for the church now and eventually—urges me to take the painful step which I am now taking. Under the belief that the maximum achievement of any man's life is to do the will of God I take this solemn step—not impulsively, but after earnest, heart-searching deliberation and prayer. And I hope this step will cause no undue hurt to any heart and no grief to the church and no hindrance to the kingdom interests and no regret.

I believe that a pastor owes it to the world and to God and to himself to fill the place where he can do the greatest good, and reach the most people, that he may extend his usefulness. And I have always believed that a preacher, any preacher, if he is true to his calling, is a soldier of the Cross of Christ and, therefore, under orders from the great Captain of his salvation—somewhat in the same manner that a soldier in the army of his country is under orders from, and should be obedient to, the commands of his superior officer.

I know that life is short—very short. And I have always believed that a preacher should be where and go where his life, his one brief life, according to the leading of the Lord and according to his own convictions in such solemn and responsible matters will count for most in the kingdom of God.

Accordingly, I hereby offer my resignation as the pastor of the Citadel Square Baptist Church, the same to be effective at as early a date as sensibly possible and at a time mutually agreeable to both pastor and people.

I offer this resignation with genuine love to all—with a love that will not end with the severance of my pastoral relation with the membership. Wherever I go and wherever I am, in future years, my heart's garden will bloom with the unfading and fragrant flowers of kind and loving remembrance.

Moreover, I wish now, once and for all, to express my heartfelt appreciation to the membership for their many, many kindnesses and expressions of love to me and to my family. We shall ever treasure these.

With gratitude to God for His blessings upon the work these two years in which it has been my privilege and honor to try to serve as your pastor, and with prayer that the Lord will guide you in the selection of another pastor, and with confidence that you will carry on the work nobly in the future, and with unspeakable love.

Gratefully, appreciatively, prayerfully,

ROBERT G. LEE

Accepting Dr. Lee's resignation, the following resolution was adopted and placed in the records of the
Citadel Square Baptist Church;

> It shall ever be a valued part of our history that Dr.
> Robert G. Lee served us as pastor, and although separated,
> we shall be together in heart and purpose in the service
> of the Lord.

To the Charleston newspapers Dr. Lee gave his
reason for accepting the Memphis call:

> My decision to leave Charleston was prompted strictly
> by the belief that I have greater possibilities in my new
> field.
> I have been more than pleased with my charge here.
> I feel that our church has advanced. It is a grand old
> church. It is my belief, however, that it should be the
> ambition of every man to perform God's will, and I
> think it is His will that I should go to Memphis, which
> is one of the South's greatest fields. The Bellevue
> Baptist Church is not as large as Citadel Square, but it
> has great possibilities for expansion.

During the almost exactly two years that Dr. Lee
served at Citadel Square, the affairs of the church
progressed. The Sunday school reached a membership
of 1,800, with an average attendance of 1,027. This
was much larger than the Sunday school upon his
arrival. Gifts to missions and benevolences were increased. The membership of the church, which was
1,200 when Lee went to Charleston, increased to
1,690 persons during his term of office.

One hundred Sundays after he preached his initial
sermon at the Citadel Square Baptist Church, Dr.
Lee left Charleston and many friends dear to his
heart, to begin his ministry at the Bellevue Baptist
Church, Memphis, Tennessee.

Part II

A VESSEL UNTO HONOR

Preamble

—2—

PREACHER-BOY FINDS HIS HOME

It was on December 11, 1927 that Robert Greene Lee preached his first sermon at the Bellevue Baptist Church in Memphis, Tennessee. From the very moment that he mounted the pulpit for his initial address as pastor, Lee began to feel more at home there than in any other public place in all the world, an emotion that has only intensified with the passing of the years. His warm heart went out to the sheep in that pasture in a fuller way, perhaps, than ever before, and the membership at Bellevue responded in like fashion. The people immediately were so drawn to their new pastor that on April 1, 1928 a little more than three months after Lee's assumption of the pastorate, the Board of Deacons was assembled by Chairman G. I. Fraser on a special call, and the following resolution was adopted:

The Committee previously appointed offered the following resolutions concerning our Pastor, Dr. Robert G. Lee, as recommendation to the Church for its adoption; copies to be sent to Dr. Lee and *The Baptist and Reflector*, and same to be spread on the minutes of the Board of Deacons and of the church, if approved:

WHEREAS God in His infinite wisdom has shown special favor to our church in sending us Dr. Robert G. Lee for our Pastor, and

199

WHEREAS, after only three short months since his coming, we stand aghast and astounded as we review with awed silence what hath been wrought in our midst, and

WHEREAS none of us, not even the most optimistic, or the most hopeful, or even the most prayerful had a vision such as is now a reality, and

WHEREAS, as we try to think of all his accomplishments, achievements, results, already in hand, we can only marvel, not having realized before the possibilities of one so thoroughly competent, capable, consecrated a man of God as exemplified in our dear Pastor, and

WHEREAS, as the crowning achievement of his ministry here, we are permitted the high privilege of seeing each Sunday night men, women, and children in great numbers buried with our Lord in baptism, and

WHEREAS, with all these things in mind, and our hearts filled with gratitude to God, we cannot remain silent, but must give expression out of the fulness of our hearts:

THEREFORE, do we take this opportunity to express in this feeble way our great appreciation to Dr. Lee for his untiring efforts, for his great ability, for his wonderful power with God and man, and for his love for us. We thank God again for his coming. We also want him to know that, imperfect as we are, we do appreciate and love him, and hope and trust that each one of us will be what he wants us to be and do what he wants us to do.

COMMITTEE: L. C. WEINER, CHAIRMAN
J. L. West
L. L. Baker

The hand of God was upon Robert G. Lee. The Lord honored His hard-working, tireless, and loving servant who was ministering to Him and to His flock with all his might, upheld by the might of the Lord. As pastor, preacher, and friend Dr. Lee fulfilled faithfully that portion of Scripture which he had chosen, early in life, as his life-verse: "I will very gladly spend and be spent for you" (II Cor.

12:15). Paul had to confess to the Corinthian Christians, however, that the more abundantly he loved them, the less he was loved by them. But this was not true of Robert Lee in his relationship with the Memphis Christians, for he cannot but say, if he would speak the truth: "Though the more abundantly I love you, the *more* I be loved."

Lee has now been at Bellevue for nearly twenty-two years as we write, and there will be ample opportunity to consider what God has accomplished through him, as we proceed. It is time now that we should learn more of the man himself, both in private and public life, as preacher, pastor, and personality. It will increase our comprehension of the favor that God has bestowed upon him. For there are many facets in this jewel of preachers which, if it be turned with understanding and appreciation, will reflect "the light of the knowledge of the glory of God in the face of Jesus Christ."

Chapter X
LOVER OF HOME
Husband and Father

Over the mantel in the living room of the Lees' modest and comfortable home at 1668 Peach Street, Memphis, hangs an oil painting, the gift of Dr. Lee to Mrs. Lee on their twenty-fifth wedding anniversary, of the house that Dr. Lee built for his bride in Greenville, South Carolina, the house in which the young couple were married, and which was home during the early years of their lives together. The painting's presence there is symbolic of the happiness that the Lees have enjoyed and the high place that their first home, in the richest significance of the word, has in their hearts.

Throughout the years of their married lives Dr. and Mrs. Lee have spent much less time together in their home, in whatever city they may have lived, than their natural instincts and desires have dictated. But heavy duties and a full schedule of exacting engagements have kept Dr. Lee so busy that his hours in the home, except at mealtime, late evenings, and for slumber, are few and far between. Mrs. Lee, although she has been a "preacher's widow" for more than thirty-five years, has never complained. She says that she knows that the ministry is her husband's first love, and that she and the family are willing to take second place to the Lord, always.

It will be recalled that when Bob Lee and Bula Gentry were married in 1913, Lee was pastoring four churches in and about Greenville. The combined salaries of all four charges were insufficient to keep the young couple and to care for the mortgage that was being carried on their lovely little home. Consequently, Bula Lee retained the position that she held before marriage, as secretary to the president of a large cotton mill in the city. Her earnings were greater than the total of the meagre emoluments that the young preacher received from all of his churches, and financial matters were certainly less of a problem on account of her working. Bob Lee chafed a bit at the thought of his wife's continuing to work in an office, but his discomfort was a great deal less than it would have been had they not been able to use her salary to help, in these early days, with household expenses and with interest payments due on the mortgage on the house.

The Lees would be the first to claim that their married life has not been without its human imperfections, but it has been completely happy. After the early adjustments that were necessary between the husband, intense and very quick to act, and the wife, deliberate and relaxed, after a period of learning that patience needs to be exercised on the part of both parties to a marriage contract, life has been serene indeed for these two devoted servants of God.

Bula Lee has been a source of tremendous strength to her ambitious husband who, in early days, was

sometimes on the border of despair. She has tried
to advise and comfort without nagging, and she has
always refrained from making suggestions or giving
advice about his preaching, believing that her husband "gets his orders from God." Perhaps there has
been one exception to this rule, in that she has intimated to him, from time to time, that he may be
a little bit too fearless in his denunciation of evil. She
reasons that many of those who hear Dr. Lee cannot
possibly understand the love behind his rebukes,
and that it might be better, therefore, for him to tone
down what may appear, to those who do not know
him well, to be caustic speech.

One of the most wretched and comfortless experiences in all their years together fell upon them
when Robert Lee accepted the call to the church in
Waterloo and was obliged to move from the home,
built with so much romantic love and with such
high hopes, in Greenville. Their last night in that
little house was sleepless and filled with many tears.
In the morning, both of them suffering genuine agony
of soul, they left this place so precious to them, each
pretending to the other that it was perfectly all
right and that even better days were ahead. The first
baby was on the way, and it was Bob Lee's great
desire that the little child might be born in the
house at Greenville. Instead, she first saw the light
of day in a hospital in Greenville, on January 2,
1917—the baby daughter Bula Gentry Lee, mentioned
earlier in this chronicle.

No baby was ever welcomed with more joy or
loved with more unrepressed devotion than the little
child that this godly couple had prayed for. The

father had always hoped that their baby would be a girl, and the mother, expressing impartiality as to its sex, longed for a child to have its father's mind, a child that would be physically well and strong. From the beginning, the little girl was called Bula G., but there were, of course, affectionate nicknames for the little lady such as every young father and mother use for their tiny offspring—"Bitsy Gal," "Daughter Delightful," and other terms of endearment. Like other parents, every event and adventure in their baby's life was a matter of supreme importance to them. Bula G.'s first toddling steps in the aisle of the church, her first tooth, her first word, were all momentous events. When the first tooth appeared, Mrs. Lee, who was tending Bula G. in the home, ran over to the church where the father was, to tell him of it: "The baby has a tooth," she cried excitedly.

"Well, that's fine," responded the father; and then, pretending to be jealous, he added: "But I have thirty, and you have never said a thing about them."

How great was the agony of this young couple when Bula G. lay ill and at the borderline between life and death during the Edgefield days! What joy and pride they experienced as she became popular among her playmates and did well in grammar-school days, conducting herself in a fashion that was deeply gratifying to the parents. Again, in Memphis, when she was sixteen years of age, Bula G. became desperately ill and again God heard the prayers of His devoted children and restored their beloved to them. High-school days, too, brought gladness and satisfaction to Dr. and Mrs. Lee, as when their daughter made her decision as to nonparticipation in certain worldly entertainments.

Devotion of father to daughter and daughter to father—and this in no way suggests any less devotion between Mrs. Lee and her daughter on both sides— has been extremely warm and strong at all times. Once, when Bula G. was in her early teens, she and her father were sitting before a winter fire, having sacred conversation. Coming into the room, Mrs. Lee asked them: "What are you two lovebirds doing?"

"Nothing," they replied simultaneously.

"Well, what are you thinking about?" she then asked.

"I was just thinking," Dr. Lee replied, "that if I could find the father and mother of the boy who will some day be the husband of our little girl, I would crawl on my hands and knees, on glass if necessary, and ask them to rear that boy so that he will be a Christian boy, and come to the marriage altar with as much to give our little daughter as she has to offer him."

But in later years, when Bula G. began to have engagements with many boys, Dr. Lee was always courteous to her "dates." He resolved that he would never attempt to influence her as to the choice of a husband, adding, however, that he certainly did not want to be the father-in-law of a boy who was not a Christian, or who was a drinker. It was a happy day for both of the Lees, as well as for Bula G., that, when she did come to the marriage altar, it was to be united with a splendid Christian, a Navy man, Ensign Edward R. King, an Annapolis graduate who, with his parents, was a member of the Bellevue Baptist Church in Memphis. Commander King, as he now is, lives with his wife and their three little chilelen in Norfolk, Virginia. The gayest and most contented days on Peach Street are when the beloved Bula G. returns, with her little children, to visit her doting parents.

For the past few years now, Dr. and Mrs. Lee have gone back to where they started from, since Roy Lee* has also established his own home. What fun used to be had in the household when the family was together! For all of them are possessed of a sense of humor, and all are very quick of wit, and so the table and living-room conversations were scintillating, to say the least.

One day, Bula G. was reproved at the table by her father for lack of good manners while eating. Then Dr. Lee added: "If I had done that, I suspect my father would have switched me."

"Yes, sir," replied his eight-year-old daughter, with a twinkle in her eye, "but I want you to make more out of me than your father made out of you."

And on another occasion, Roy was talking incessantly about a new monkey that he had seen at the zoo that afternoon. When Dr. Lee had an opportunity, he interrupted the boy, asking him: "Did he recognize you, son?"

As quick as a flash, but very solemnly, Roy

---

*Roy DeMent Lee was taken into the Lee home in Chraleston when he was but a small child, being legally adopted after a short time. He was named, in part, for Dr. Lee's very dear friend, Dr. DeMent of New Orleans. Roy had his schooling in Memphis and entered the army during World War II, and was awarded the Medal of Honor for meritorious service. Roy, at the time of writing, holds a position in Florida, where he makes his home.

Dr. Robert G. Lee, Pastor of the First Baptist Church,
New Orleans., La. 1922 - 1926

Dr. and Mrs. Lee with Bula G. in New Orleans in 1923. In the Background Is Dr. John T. Christian, Noted Baptist Historian and Author

First Baptist Church and Educational Building, New Orleans, c. 1926

replied: "Yes, sir! He said: 'How's our paw?'"

Bula G. Attended Blue Mountain College, Blue Mountain, Mississippi, where she earned her A.B. degree and made a remarkably fine record. In his files, Dr. Lee has a statement from Dr. Lawrence T. Lowrey, President of Blue Mountain College, in respect to Bula G.'s accomplishments. Let Dr. Lowrey speak:

Miss Bula G. Lee, of Memphis, Tennessee, registered as a freshman in Blue Mountain College in September, 1934, and in 1938 she received her Degree of Bachelor of Arts and at the same time a Diploma in Speech Arts.

Throughout her college career she was one of the most outstanding students in the college, and although the graduating class of 1938 was perhaps the most able group ever to receive degrees in a given year, Miss Lee was certainly one of the most capable of the class.

Her versatility and her accomplishments were quite unusual.

Even from her freshman year she was chosen for various honors which commonly went to more advanced students. It is a remarkable fact that for four consecutive years she was a member of the Baptist Student Union Council, a member of the opera troupe, a featured participant of the exercises in the May Festival, a member of the Music Club, and a member of the Scribblers' Club. She held numerous offices in these important organizations.

She was also chosen for numerous honors. She was chief editor of *The Mountain Breeze*, our student literary journal; a featured player in the annual outstanding production of the college dramatic club; a member of the college orchestra; and successful in several fields of athletic sports, including volley ball and golf. In her junior year she was selected as the most charming girl in the college, and despite her innumberable extra-curricular activities she earned a place on the college honor roll and was a reader in the department of history.

Perhaps the inevitable consequence of all this was her

election in her senior year to a place in the great inter-
collegiate publication, *Who's Who Among Students in
American Universities and Colleges.*

Lawrence T. Lowrey

To doubt that such a commendation brought joy
to the hearts of Bula G.'s parents is to know nothing
of parenthood.

Once, while Bula G. was away at college, she
needed some money for certain expenses there,
and wrote to her father for $186.00, using, in her
letter, the well-worn expression that this was a
"C.O.D.," that is, "Call on Dad." Dr. Lee responded
quickly to her request for funds, as he has always
done, and then remarked, at the conclusion of his
letter, that he wanted to suggest a toast that she
might propose for her father, namely: "The *Kin* You
Love to Touch."

Due to Bob Lee's early life, its privation, and the
fact that he had to make his own way from boyhood,
he is of rather an independent nature, and his wife
is therefore denied serving him in some of the little
ways in which a woman longs to help her husband.
For example, he never permits her to assist him in the
packing of his bags when he is obliged to travel,
for, he says, he wants to know where to find things
when he unpacks, and to have no one but himself
to blame if anything has been left out or has been
damaged through faulty packing. In so many other
ways, however, Mrs. Lee is able to be a genuine help-
meet to her husband. She always dresses the house
up and makes it look attractive for weddings that
are held in the home. She is active in the church
without attempting to be bossy. She is a shield on

the telephone and in the home when Dr. Lee is
studying or resting, and ought not to be disturbed.
She takes a deep interest in the Sunday school, being
Superintendent of the Primary Department, upon
which she spends much time, and money, and effort,
and prayer. Although Dr. Lee is himself a man
with deep faith in the value of prayer, it is almost
always Mrs. Lee, in the home, who suggests, when a
problem arises: "Let's pray about it." Loyal to her
husband at all times, Mrs. Lee makes a charming
minister's wife, of whom he is justly proud, and
a staunch defender of her husband whenever she
hears any criticism expressed pertaining to him, or
his decisions, or his activities.

It goes without saying that Dr. Lee, the sentimentalist who visits the honeymoon hotel whenever he
is in Atlanta, who always drives by the little house
at 104 Elkins Street whenever he is Greenville, who
has among his keepsakes the ribbon that he gave
to Bula Gentry on the night that he won the oratorical contest, a paper drinking cup that was used on
the train during their wedding trip, the first letter
Bula G. ever wrote to him, and innumerable other
things that are to him of untold value—it is under-
standable that such a man, who is known for his
thoughtfulness and kindliness, would be an attentive
husband in the matter of all the little things that
are so pleasing to the normal woman's heart. His life
of uninterrupted activity deprives him of devoting
to his family the time that he would like to spend
with them, but he compensates, by the quantity
and quality of his gifts and attentions, for whatever dearth of companionship there may be. He is

extremely scrupulous to arrange his schedule so as to be able to celebrate birthdays, anniversaries, and holidays with Mrs. Lee, as he did also in respect to the children when they were at home; and this, not because he feels he ought to, but because he wants to. For the women-folk he does not forget, on special occasions, to bring gifts, or to send corsages. And now that Bula G. has her own home she receives telephone calls from "Daddy," or, if the celebration is on behalf of one of Mrs. King's little ones, from "Granddaddy."

The home on Peach Street is entirely lacking in ostentation, for both in its surroundings and within the house simplicity is the key word. It is indeed a home—a comfortable, quiet, and restful home. The large living room and spacious dining room are carpeted from wall to wall with a soft carpet of blue, the same hue that is in the carpets of the Bellevue Baptist Church. The papering on the wall, the draperies, and the furnishings have been chosen in excellent taste. There is nothing flashy, but all is in modest beauty, blue, Dr. Lee's favorite color, being the predominant tone throughout the house. Although the Lees have sometimes discussed moving to a larger residence in a newer, and perhaps cooler, neighborhood, the sentimental attachment and memories that linger about 1668 Peach Street have influenced them to come to the conclusion, again and again, that this house will always be their home. For it is theirs, the arrangement having been made with Dr. Lee, when he first took the pastorate of the Bellevue Baptist Church, that he was to supply his own living place out of his salary.

In the rear end of the home is Dr. Lee's library. The walls are lined around the room with books, and there are two extensions of shelves jutting into the room. In one corner there is a comfortable couch, and here Dr. Lee does a good deal of his studying and all of his serious reading. In common with the library of any busy man, this room, while kept clean at all times, is left undisturbed as far as papers and books, sometimes lying open where they have been laid by their owner, are concerned.

Together this happy couple serve the Lord whom they love so well. They share a joint bank account, and Mrs. Lee is free to draw funds from it at any time that she desires. Dr. Lee is very generous and sacrificial in giving his money, not only to the Bellevue Baptist Church, but to help young men and women obtain education, and in other ways. Far from complaining about this, Mrs. Lee is in complete agreement with her husband, having learned from experience what it means to give tithes and offerings unto the Lord. When Bula Gentry accepted Bob Lee's proposal of marriage and promised her hand with her heart, she pledged to God, to Bob Lee, and to herself that she would go with Bob Lee wherever he would go, would live in any sort of home necessary, would suffer sweetly whatever hardships might come their way, and she has faithfully abided by her promise.

The highlight of every week in the Lee home, when Dr. Lee is not out of the city for extended meetings, is on Sunday night, after the evening service and the baptisms, when Dr. and Mrs. Lee are almost sure to be home together, and undisturbed. There, in their little breakfast nook, they sit together, eating onion sandwiches and drinking buttermilk, and talk over at length the blessings of the day and the goodness of God, and discuss some of the problems that enter into their lives, as they come to every one of us.

Dr. Lee is, at heart, a "homebody," no different in this respect from hosts of other men who serve God and love their wives and children. Stored away in the attic, and in bureaus and desks, are all the love letters that these two have written to each other through the years, and still stored in their hearts is that first love that burned so brightly in earlier days and that does not fade but glows bright and warm in the breasts of Dr. and Mrs. Robert G. Lee to this day.

Chapter XI

LOVER OF FUN

"ALL WORK AND NO PLAY. . . "

Although every busy man knows that he ought
to take time for relaxation and rest, it is not always
as easy to arrange such a thing as to talk about it.
This is particularly true when one is engaged in the
service of the Lord, for the demands come at all
times of day and night, seven days a week, year
in and year out. Consequently, Dr. Lee does not
have much time to play, to rest his weary nerves
and body so that he may be refreshed to carry on
in the labors to which he has been called. From time
to time he may get in a game of golf or see a ball
game, but there are intervals of from one to four
years sometimes, between one round of golf and
another. He could count on the fingers of his two
hands the number of ball games he has seen in the
last few years. However, having been athletic himself
and having a wide interest, he keeps in touch with
sports as well as with a varied catalog of other things
through his reading of the newspapers and in conversation with other men.

Dr. Lee is not an expert golfer, but he could be
had he the time to devote to this game, a conclusion
that the author reached after playing with him one
day at Skytop, in the mountains of Pennsylvania. Lee
is naturally athletic, very strong, and has determina-

215

tion and the ability of concentration which enable him to do well anything that he can practice. It will be recalled that, in school days, he was quite a runner. He also coached the football team at the grade school where he taught, played baseball on the town team, though he admits that he was never very outstanding, and has entered into other sports as well. When you hear him talk about baseball, for example, you will think that you are talking with a regular fan. He has seen all the greats of a generation ago, as Ty Cobb, Tris Speaker, Joe Jackson, and other luminaries of the diamond. He will argue, at the drop of a hat, to prove that "Shoeless" Joe Jackson was the greatest natural hitter that ever played ball. Dr. Lee loves to tell the story about Jackson, who received his nickname "Shoeless" because he played baseball barefooted or with only socks on his feet in his early years, being a rather illiterate boy of the mill-village section of Greenville, who, it is said, came running one day in from right field and said to the manager of the team: "There's glass out there in right field."

The manager asked him: "Is it cutting your feet, Joe?"

"No," said Jackson, "but it's roughing up the ball something terrible."

But Lee's first love in sports, as it is with many men of his age, is golf, although he enjoys hunting and fishing very much also. At the slightest opportunity—whether he has his own clubs with him or not, whether he has golf shoes or not, it makes no difference—he will play. Since he has never had lessons, his stance would not be acceptable to most professionals, but he hits a long, straight ball, rather high. He is one of those golfers whose companions will tell him that he must "live right," for he rarely gets into trouble, and usually, in the minimum number of strokes, is on the green. Were he a good putter he would turn in some remarkable scores; but putting takes practice, and for this he has no opportunity.

Dr. Lee likes to tell the story of the time that he played golf with the famed Bobby Jones of Atlanta, perhaps the most consistent amateur who ever entered tournament golf, who held the American open and amateur championships on a number of occasions, and, during his last year of tournament golf, made what is known as the "grand slam" of golf, winning, in one year, the open and amateur championships of both the United States and Great Britain.

Dr. Lee and Mr. Jones were standing at the first tee at the club in New Orleans, and each one's partner was late. They spoke to each other, and Jones, who had never seen Lee before, suggested that, while they were waiting for their partners, they might as well play two nearby par-three holes. Dr. Lee was delighted, of course. Jones told him to drive off first, so Lee took his driving iron and sent the ball to the edge of the green, about 165 yards distant. Jones then addressed his ball and sliced a little bit, the ball coming down near a tree and kicking back into the rough. It took Jones another shot to get on the green, and two putts, while Dr. Lee put his ball in the hole with two putts.

When Jones suggested that they play the next hole,

Dr. Lee refused to do so, saying: "I want to have it to say, as long as I live, that the only time I ever played golf with Bobby Jones, I beat him."

About two years ago, Dr. Lee was visiting his son-in-law and daughter in Dahlgren, Virginia, where he played golf for the first time in about four years. In the first nine holes he managed to collect four pars, and he overheard the Admiral, who was playing with his son-in-law and himself, ask Ed King: "Did you tell me your father-in-law is a preacher?"

"Yes," King admitted.

"Reckon he is telling the truth about not playing golf in four years?"

Lee's great sense of humor, which comes to his aid many times in the pulpit when he wants to lighten up the message somewhat, is evident in all social gatherings. He has a repertoire of jokes that he likes to tell that would go on ad infinitum, if there were time for him to tell them all. But he has the gift of telling his jokes only when they fit the occasion, and thus the humor is not lost through inappropriate stories.

This is not a joke book, but the life-story of a man of God. Yet, if we would understand the man wholly, it will not be amiss for us to print a few of Dr. Lee's favorite stories in order that his sense of humor may be appreciated and understood. Bear in mind, if you will, that these little anecdotes lose something of their humor when they are put on paper. They are far better when told by one who is an excellent story-teller, which Dr. Lee is.

Perhaps the favorite of all Dr. Lee's stories, one he has told for over thirty years from one side of the country to the other, is the one about a home in the deep South where the colored maid, hearing the phone ring, went and picked up the receiver to answer it. Her mistress, Mrs. John Jones, sat in the living room and overheard the following conversation:

"H'lo." "Yas'm." "Yas'm." "Sho' is." Then the maid hung up the receiver, and went about her work in the house.

The phone rang again. Again the maid answered. And Mrs. Jones heard the same words:

"H'lo." "Yas'm." "Yas'm." "Sho' is."

Mrs. Jones called to her and said: "Mandy, that's the funniest conversation I ever heard! What were you talking about?"

"Well, ma'am," said Mandy, "Ah jus' picked up de phone and said: 'H'lo,' and some white lady on de phone said, 'Is dis Miz Jones' residence?' I said, 'Yas'm,' and den she ast, 'Is Miz Jones dere?' I said, 'Yas'm,' and she answered me, 'Long distance from Washington.' I said 'Sho' is,' and hung up de phone."

One of Dr. Lee's pet stanzas is about the bachelor girl, Miss Nancy Jones, inelegantly called an "old maid" by some in her home town in Alabama. This lady who had wrought much good in the town, died. Some people were anxious to have an epitaph written and published in the little weekly town paper. They interviewed the editor and made request of him that he write an epitaph for Miss Nancy Jones. He said: "I can't do it. I can write about a bull fight or a baseball game, but I can't write an epitaph for an old maid."

But the group was insistent and threatened him with refusal to subscribe to the paper or to advertise in it. Under this coercion which implied financial loss, he promised to write an epitaph. The following week, this appeared:

Epitaph
. Here lie the bones
Of Nancy Jones;
For her, death had no terror!
She lived an old maid,
She died an old maid,
No hits, no runs, no error.

A story told by Josh Billings, one that Abraham Lincoln was fond of, Dr. Lee likes much, as published by Frederick Shannon in his book *The Universe Within*:

A certain man, invited to an important social function, was perturbed because he lacked the conventional dress. Concluding, however, that he could ill afford to miss such a rare opportunity to get into high society, he decided to brazen his way through the ordeal. Crossing the threshold of the drawing room, he espied a line of handsomely gowned women, and, walking straight up to the nearest, said, "You are a handsome woman."

Unused to such familiarity, especially from strangers, she poured her vials of verbal wrath upon the ill-mannered stranger by saying, "I wish I could say as much for you."

Whereupon the man responded, "Well, if you were as big a liar as I am, you could."

Here is another of his favorites:

The papa hog grew so tired of the pen that he wandered down to the village brewery, where he found a big puddle of some beer which had been poured out. He guzzled up so much of the stuff that when he went home, he was staggering badly, squealing wildly, and grunting meanly and with joyous abandon. Mamma hog quickly shunted him around the barn out of sight of the baby pigs, and, with a furious grunt, exclaimed: "What do you mean by making such a human being of yourself before the children?"

And here is another:

Mr. Erastus Pinkley, Negro, was on the streetcar. He approached the conductor, and very politely made the following request: "When we gits to de next street corner, I wants to be procrastinated."

"You want to be *what?*" bellowed the conductor.

Mr. Erastus Pinkley said: "Now don't lose your temper, Boss. I had to look in the dictionary myself before I knew that procrastination means *putting off.*"

When Dr. Lee was teaching school, he had a boy named James Riley on his grade-school football team. Riley was a splendid football player, but he did not like to study. One day, on a surprise quiz, Dr. Lee put this question on the board, to be answered in writing: "Locate and describe the alimentary canal." Jim Riley wrote this as an answer: "The alimentary canal is located between the Mediterranean and Red Sea, is forty miles long, and is owned by Great Britain."

Speaking of how it is not always pleasant work to "rebuke with all authority," as Paul enjoins, Dr. Lee tells how a pastor in so doing is put in the position of the facetious minister at Ocean Grove, who took a little girl on his knee and said: "I don't love you, Nellie."

All the ladies on the breeze-swept veranda laughed, but the little girl frowned and said: "You've got to love me. You've got to."

"Got to? How so?" laughed the minister.

"Because," said Nellie stoutly, "you've got to love them that hate you—and I hate you!"

Once, after preaching twice a day at a Baptist assembly, near San Angelo, Texas, as the thermometer hovered around the one hundred mark every day, Preacher Lee sought to relax and rest by pretending, while he was getting his shoes shined, that he was deaf. The preacher, holding his hand to his ear as though he could not hear, asked the shoe-shine boy many questions. He had the little fellow shouting loudly in attempt to make the "deaf" preacher hear. At every answer the preacher shook his head in puzzlement as though he had not heard. Then he quit asking the boy questions. But he heard the lad talking, and saying: "If your ears were a little longer and I had a saddle, I'd ride you home."

There are many, many more stories that might be told, but we shall conclude this series of little jokes by this one of which Lee is very fond:

Money may not be everything in this world, but it certainly helps out. Some people will do almost anything for a dollar—or a dime. For instance, the minister felt annoyed to find that an old gentleman fell asleep during his sermon on two consecutive Sundays. So, after the service on the second week, he told the boy who accompanied the sleeper that he wished to speak to him in his study. "My boy," asked the preacher when they were closeted together, "who is the elderly gentleman you attend church with?"

"Grandpa," was the reply.

"Well," said the pastor, "if you will keep him awake during my sermon, I'll give you a nickel each week."

The boy fell in with the arrangement and, for the next two weeks the old gentleman listened attentively to the sermon. The third week, however, found him soundly asleep.

The vexed minister sent for the boy and said: "I am angry with you. Your grandpa was asleep again today. Didn't I promise you a nickel to keep him awake?"

"Yes," replied the boy, "but now Grandpa gives me a dime to let him sleep."

Dr. Lee enjoys a joke on himself as well as on anyone else. Not long ago he was preaching at the First Baptist Church (Colored) on Beale Street in Memphis. The occasion was a week of services in connection with the resignation of Dr. Long, the pastor of the church, because he was leaving to accept another pupit in the North. Dr. Long is a very fine, well-educated man, truly devoted to the Lord.

Dr. Lee loves to preach to the Negroes, and his sermon, following a very beautiful number by the choir, was on the subject "Consider Jesus." In the course of the sermon, Dr. Lee told about his old "Mam" Lindy, who attended his mother when some of her babies were born—how, when he himself was born, the old colored woman, holding him in her arms and prancing around the room, exclaimed: "Praise de Lawd! Gawd don' sont a preacher to dis here house!"

Lee went on to tell how he had prayed at her knee, how she had taught him much about God, and finally told of her death, when she said to Mother Lee: "I'se changin' my ole wore out wooden wagon for a chariot of gold."

Many an "Amen" and "Praise Gawd" were heard throughout the audience as Dr. Lee carried on with his sermon and came to his conclusion. After the message, Dr. Long got up to express his appreciation, which he did very beautifully. Among other things, he said: "Dr. Lee is one man that says something all the time he is talking." He added some very complimentary terms about Dr. Lee, concluding with: "I've always known he was the greatest preacher I have ever heard, but never knew *why* until this afternoon; but now I see . . . it's because he had a Negro woman looking after him when he got his start."

Everybody in the audience laughed uproariously, Dr. Lee joining with them in enjoying this very clever word from Dr. Long.

Whenever there is a social gathering at the Bellevue Baptist Church and a little fun is entered into, or in the Lee's home or somewhere, Dr. Lee is quite frequently the life of the party, as it were, keeping people in hearty enjoyment of his humor for a while, but never losing his dignity nor failing to bring the conversation back to a higher and more spiritual plane before the festivities are over. Not long ago the author was talking with Dr. Herbert Lockyer, noted Baptist preacher from England, who related having been at such a gathering when Dr. Lee imitated a colored preacher. The author asked Dr. Lockyer to jot down something about the experience, and here is what Dr. Lockyer wrote:

> Had he not dedicated his unique gifts to the highest end, Dr. Lee could have developed into one of the greatest humorists of our time. And having had the privilege of often ministering in the great Bellevue Church, I know whereof I speak. One has only to hear and watch Dr. Lee at a young people's gathering manipulate a harmonica to realize how entertaining he can be. S. T. Coleridge, in *Table Talks,* remarks, "No mind is thoroughly well organized that is deficient of a sense of humor." Well, Dr. Lee's well-organized mind has an abundance of humor, making him more brilliant still.

Mrs. Robert G. Lee, Memphis, Tenn., 1937

*Bula G. Lee at the Time of Her Graduation from Blue Mountain
College, Blue Mountain, Miss., 1938*

Never shall I forget a party of church friends gathered in my honor, to which Dr. Lee came and at which he gave his marvelous imitation of a Negro preacher. To see him with blackened face, and dressed up as an old-time colored preacher, is a scream. But when he comes to the recital of the preacher's sermon, really one is overcome with hilarity as well as admiration. I laughed and laughed until I cried. What a night! What I admire, though, in Dr. Lee's humor, whether he is entertaining his friends to the dialogs and poems of James Whitcomb Riley and Frank Stanton, playing his harmonica, recounting a rich fund of stories, and the like, is the entire absence of anything coarse or suggestive. Referring to Mark Twain, Ellis Parker Butler says:

"Given his humor ain't refined
Quite enough to suit my mind."

But humor, with Dr. Lee, is ever refined, and suits the best of minds.

Whether Dr. Lee keeps scrapbooks as a hobby, for relaxation, or for utilitarian purposes, he certainly has collected, in seventeen or more of them, the most amazing variety of items that one could possibly imagine. Being, as has been said before, a deep sentimentalist, he seems never to throw anything away that means anything to him. Whatever he has put his hands on, that holds any interest for him and that will go in a scrapbook, will be found in these books. Letters that he has received that he really seems to like, and some that he definitely dislikes, clippings about his own ministry or the churches that he has served, or about couples that he has married, or people that he knows, about his family, about friends, about acquaintances, about famed people, find their way into the scrapbooks at some time or other. There are notices of world events, sporting events, Baptist bulletins, clippings about the Bible, jokes, poems that he loves to read, and more letters, from the governors of various states to the smallest child in his own church. Many of the magazine articles that he has written are pasted in these scrapbooks. Telegrams that he has received, copies of telegrams that he has sent, circulars of Bible conferences where he has spoken, report cards, ticket stubs, and countless other items are all here "filed."

Simply that the varied interests of the man may be seen, and that something as to the working of his mind may be understood, we intend now to pick up one of the scrapbooks at random, and to make a list of just a portion of the diverse items that are found in this one volume:

A quotation from Henry Ward Beecher: "The blossom cannot tell what becomes of its odor; and no man can tell what becomes of his influence as an example."

Dr. Lee invited as principal speaker at the Texas State Convention of the B. Y. P. U.

Letter asking for help, $100.00, written by a stranger and requesting Dr. Lee to have part in sending a boy to college.

Comment of Dr. Lee regarding Dr. E. C. Dargan, written on a church bulletin: "I heard him last Sunday. Oh, how he did magnify Christ! Very fine, he was!"

Letter from Frank Lee.

Letter from Dr. Vollmer.

Letter from Ellis A. Fuller.

Letter from Jolly.

A notice that he paid a pledge to Furman University.

A letter from a man stating that he was honored to have Dr. Lee as a guest, when Dr. Lee could have been the guest of the governor of the state.

A notice that he was to appear in *Who's Who in America.*

A letter from Dr. DeMent.

A clipping from a newspaper, telling about a dog walking from Hollywood, Florida, to Marietta, Ohio.

The quotation of a poem that Dr. Lee likes, by Robert Pollock:

THE SOLITUDE OF NATURE

> Pleasant were many scenes, but most to me
> The solitude of vast extent, untouched
> By hand of art, where Nature showed herself
> And reaped her crops: whose garments were
>   the clouds;
> Whose minstrels, brooks; whose lamps, the
>   moon and stars;
> Whose organ-choir, the voice of many waters;
> Whose banquets, morning dews; whose heroes,
>   storms;
> Whose warriors, mighty winds; whose lovers,
>   flowers;
> Whose orators, the thunderbolts of God;
> Whose palaces, the everlasting hills;
> Whose ceiling, heaven's unfathomable blue;
> And from whose rocky turrets, battled high,
> Prospect immense spread out on all sides round—
> Lost now between the welkin and the main,
> Now walled with hills that slept above the
>   storm.

A picture of the gravestone of his father, David Ayers Lee.

A newspaper picture of Bula G. about to give a recital.

A letter from Brother Ben.

A pass to Russwood Baseball Park, presented by the Memphis Baseball Association.

A clipping about the Lindbergh baby.

A letter from Brother Tom.

A write-up about Brother Tom, known as "Tackhole" Lee, who was for years the champion rifle shot of the world, and even now ranks with champions in trap shooting.

A picture of the Passion Play at Oberammergau.

A notice of royalties received from certain books.

A notice of bills paid by Dr. Lee on certain items.

A letter from Dr. Lee to his Brother Tom.

A picture of Panama.

A picture of the Harmony Church and Dr. Lee's first baptizing.

A pass on the Illinois Central Railroad.

A 1,000,000 Mark Reichesbank note, 1923.

Snapshots.

An article by Charlie Paddock, the runner, regarding Jim Thorpe, the great Indian athlete.

A "Believe It or Not" clipping about Billy Sunday circling the bases, on a baseball diamond, in fourteen seconds.

Railroad ticket stubs.

Baggage checks.

An article saying that "Dizzy" Dean, while a pitcher at Houston, walked three men to fill the bases, and then struck out the batter, Al Todd.

A character sketch of Dr. Lee, appearing in the *Memphis Evening Appeal*.

More poems.

Receipts for money orders mailed from Colon to his mother, when Lee worked on the Panama Canal.

It will be seen what we mean in stating that Dr. Lee keeps everything that he gets his hands on, and places in the scrapbooks anything that is pasteable. All of these items are of vital interest to him. Certainly, many jokes, poems, and epigrams that are in these books are reference material—though strangely filed!—for future sermons or articles that he may write. But, primarily, they are there for sentimental reasons, because of their relation to some person or place or event that he wants to remember or refer to at some future time.

Music, too, has always had a great influence upon

Dr. Lee. Under its lovely ministration he seems utterly to relax. He remembers vividly the banjo picking of the Negroes on the river; the Polk Miller Negro Quartet, who sang at the Town Hall in old Fort Mill—how they thrilled and inspired him; the singing of the village choir; the Hawaiian music in South America; the Whitney Brothers Quartet at college, singers who had performed before Queen Victoria; Madame Schumann-Heink, and Enrico Caruso. Once he traveled all the way to Atlanta simply to hear the great Italian tenor. But above all, Dr. Lee loves the old hymns of the Church and the Gospel songs, when they are rendered well and devoutly by born-again believers in the Lord Jesus Christ. Often, when a choir begins singing oratorios, Dr. Lee squirms, but when they are singing the old songs that the saints of the last generation, and every century, have loved so well, he is caught up into the heavens and is brought very close to God.

We conclude this chapter with the quotation of Frank L. Stanton's poem, *Going Home*, beside which Dr. Lee has written in ink, "Poem I love."

> Adieu, sweet friends—I have waited long
> To hear the message that calls me home.
> And now it comes like a low, sweet song
> Of welcome over the river's foam;
> And my heart shall ache and my feet shall roam
> No more—no more. I am going home!
> Home! Where no storm, where no tempest raves,
> In the light of the calm, eternal day;
> Where no willows weep over lonely graves
> And the tears from our eyelids are kissed away.
> And my soul shall sigh, and my feet shall roam
> No more—no more; I am going home!

Chapter XII

LOVER OF SOULS

FAITHFUL SHEPHERD OF THE SHEEP

It is not a common thing to find a man gifted as a speaker who enjoys pastoral work. It is equally rare to come upon a man who is noted as a shepherd of the flock who will also excel as a preacher. The preacher, if he be faithful to his calling as the pastor of a church will fulfil his duties to his people, but generally he finds pastoral calls and other duties that befall the minister of a church to be very burdensome and boresome, and he longs to be relieved of such responsibilities that he may devote himself fully to the preaching ministry. The pastor, happy in serving the needs of the people whom he loves deeply, generally finds the preparation of the weekly sermons a great and rather unpleasant chore, be he ever so faithful.

In Robert G. Lee the Lord has given the Church a servant with two great gifts. There is nothing in the world that Dr. Lee would rather do than preach the Gospel, but right abreast of his great longing to preach is his desire to be of service to those whom God has put in his charge, and to other needy souls. As busy as Dr. Lee is in study, sermon preparation, writing, and speaking not only in his own church but throughout the whole land, he does not find the

230

pastorship either boring or burdensome, for nothing is humdrum or dull in the life of this man. He is a lover of souls, and thus he preaches the Gospel whenever opportunity arises, both from the pulpit and also to individuals; he is a lover of people, and consequently finds happiness in serving those of God's sheep who have been committed to his care. Whenever Lee is in Memphis, he begins his days early, around 6 a. m., and continues until eleven or twelve o'clock at night. Within these hours there falls across his path the wide variety of daily experiences that any pastor knows. The day will begin, of course, with the reading of God's Word and prayer. It will include office hours, during which he will dispatch the business of the church, attend to his correspondence, and interview any number of people who may have appointments or who may come to see him without pre-arrangements. Usually there are hospital calls, and almost every day there are visits to be made to the homes of members of the church, or others whose names have been given to him or whom he has met either in some of the church services or elsewhere. There may be errands to attend to for some of his people, or visits on personal business matters, but the hours will speed by as this energetic pastor devotes himself to that to which God has called him for that day. During each week there are two or three sermons to be prepared, and Dr. Lee does a thorough and careful job, laying the foundation, gathering material, arranging an outline, and drawing together the finished product.

Perhaps the best way to illustrate the active life

of Pastor Lee will be to examine, at random, a few pages from his diaries.

Thursday, August 20, 1942

7 a. m. Home from vacation via St. Louis. Mother [Mrs. Lee] met me at train. At home, Betty Lee [Bula G.'s daughter] greeted me with hilarious rapture. Went immediately to Spinks home, 1541 Waverly, where death of Mrs. Spinks had come. Back home for breakfast via funeral home for a few minutes. Office at 9. Glad to be back. Talked to Mrs. Koonce a bit. Funeral of Mrs. Spinks at Cosmopolitan Funeral Home. Saw the Gambels on my way to cemetery. Stopped at Mrs. F. G. Crain's on way back. Mrs. Dr. Stanfield, Mr. and Mrs. Parchman, to see new baby, Mrs. F. P. Allen and the Cadens. Visited Mrs. Rother, Mr. Jennings, Mrs. Clampit in Methodist Hospital. Bill Berlin, Juanita Payne, and Mrs. Leland Murphy in Baptist Hospital. (Mrs. Murphy's baby was born dead.) Had conference with Mrs. Holloway. Talked with Lucille Crawford about Woman's Missionary Union presidency. Visited the Hollis family on Poplar. Conference with Wheaton quintette.

Friday, August 28, 1942

Up at 6. Worked on sermon. Prayed. Went to Negro Vacation Bible School. Talked there. Visited in all hospitals—22 visits in all. Talked with Bill McBride about being a Christian. Visited Mrs.— and talked to her about living more for Christ. Talked to Mr. Frank Peltier about lovely memorial honor roll. Had conference with Mrs. Stone, Mrs. Toler, Mrs. Smith about Mrs. Stone's presidency of Homemakers' Bible Class.

Saturday, September 5, 1942

Up at 6 a. m. Study. Prayer. Writing. Phoned Mrs. Sheppard about Dick Morley. Went to office. Phoned Mrs. Carlisle about Mr. Bell. Called on Mrs. Beusse and Mr. Bell in Sterick Building. Mr. Bell will unite with Bellevue. Visited Mr. and Mrs. Bass. Visited Mr. and Mrs. Nestor. He made his confession of faith and will join. She will, by letter, first Sunday possible. He is leaving for Army.

Visited the Coopers on Central. Visited Dick Morley,
Mr. and Mrs. Legg, and others on Marianna. Talked to
little Verna Belle Legg about becoming a Christian. She
will join our church soon. Father leaving for Army. Made
several other visits, missed some. Went to ball game.
Studied my sermon on "God of Jacob, Our Refuge" while
there. Conference with Mrs. Shangle about Juniors. Phoned
Mr. and Mrs. Carter. Phoned Mr. and Mrs. Mayo about
work.

Sunday, September 13, 1942
Up at 6. Prayer. Study. Evangelistic service for Junior
Department. Had 11 to confess faith in Christ. Preached
on "God of Jacob, Our Refuge." Service broadcast. Baptized
2 after morning service. Preached at night—33 additions,
baptized 10 at night. Very tired when went to bed.
Grieved over news of Lt. Perkins' being killed. First in
our church membership to die.

Friday, December 11, 1943
Starting my 16th yr. at Bellevue. Visited Harris and
Buoun family—mother died. Made 10 hospital visits,
6 home visits. Called Mr. S. B. Hollis, Mr. Grady
Harrison, Mrs. Rosalie Brumbelow on telephone. Had fun-
eral for Mrs. Mattie Harris 11a. m. Went hunting in
afternoon for one hour—killed one rabbit, one quail.
Attended Y.W.A. and Business Women's Circle meetings.
Phone message from Marjorie Park saying she had yielded
by faith to Christ and would join church next Sunday.

December 18, 1943
Woke up with severe cold. Wrote a Christmas sermon.
Came to office. Talked at a P.T.A. meeting on the subject
"Courage in the Crisis." Visited four families in their
homes. Conference with Mr.—about marital trouble.
Told Roy good-bye. Married Henry V. Bolten, Jr., and
Martha Geraldine Hawks (led him to Christ in 1937).
Ate lunch at the Toddle House. Paid for Dorothy Linden-
mayer's and her brother's and two sailors' supper. Married
Miss Della Houston and Mr. Winston Moore. Home.
To bed not feeling well. Wrote Mrs. Hathorn.

December 23, 1943
Dr. McCutchen died. Ate supper with teachers. Taught
S. S. lesson to teachers. Conducted prayer meeting. Had
Lord's Supper. Church beautifuly decorated for Christmas,
soft candlelight. Went to funeral home for Mrs. Mc-
Cutchen.: Went to McC home and spent a while. Home
and, to bed.

December 24, 1943—*Christmas Eve*
Up early. Prayed. Read Hillis on David Livingstone.
Wrote an article. Went to Press Club. Went to tailor
to get trousers fixed. Went to hardware store. Bought gas
logs for "Mother's" Christmas present. Fixed up several
Christmas presents. Made 14 visits—hospital and home.
Conference with Mr.—about son. Dr. McCutchen's fun-
eral. Married Mr. Samuel Miller and Miss Florence
Wilkerson. Stayed home for Christmas Eve with Betty
Lee.

January 2, 1944
Up early. Boogie's [Bula G.'s] birthday. My engagement
day, 1913, 30 years ago. Conferences with several folks,
Conference with Negro Welfare Committee. Two
funerals. Made 12 visits. Wrote an article. Had birthday
supper with Bula G., Betty Lee, and Mother. Married a
lovely young couple from Nashville. Visited Mrs. Cleveland in Baptist Hospital, new baby. Home, to bed.

January 5, 1944
Up at 5 a.m. Wrote, prayed, studied. To office. Funeral of Mrs. Swindell. Wrote 12 letters by hand to sick
folks. Visited several in Baptist Hospital. Went to airport,
Mother taking me. Boogie and Betty Lee came to see me
off. Betty Lee such a joy. Flew to Nashville, 1 hr. 18 min.
Went to Sam Davis Hotel. Called Mr. Ingraham. Called
several others. Attended meeting of steering committee
of Payment of Debts on Tenn. Institutes. Took 11 p.m.
train for Memphis. Arrived Lennox Station at 6:35 a.m.
Mother met me.

January 8, 1944
Up early. Wrote, prayed, studied. Went to office. Had

conference with gentlemen who gave $8,000.00 in bonds
to the church on conditions. Made 9 hospital visits. Wrote
a number of letters. Home for supper. Drank glass of
milk, no time for more. Forgot later to eat. Attended
Finance Committee meeting. Had "battle" over debt payment matter in Tennessee. Went home at 11:10. Could
not sleep. Was waked up at 2:50. Call about Mrs. King's
illness. Bula G. and I rushed over there. She died a few
minutes after our arrival. I stayed there until 7. Went
home and rested a while. Made funeral arrangements for
2:30 Sunday. Went to church office. Wrote many letters
by hand. Cleared up my desk. Found it comforting to
keep busy.

January 17, 1944, Grand Rapids, Michigan
6 a.m. No taxi in sight. Got one after so long. Arrived
Morton Hotel. Bath, then breakfast in cafeteria. Took nap
afterwards. Dr. Hammontree called on me. Ate lunch at
1. Mission at 3 p.m., good crowd. Offering for mission over
$6,000. Preached on "Upon One Stone, Seven Eyes."
Homer Rodeheaver led singing. Back to hotel after meeting
many friends. At 5:30, bath, rest, supper. Back to Mission.
Great congregation. Preached on "To Whom Shall We
Go?" Snowing. Homer Rodeheaver sang lovely song,
"After Awhile." To bed at 10 p.m. I remember the offer-
ing today at Mission was $8,000.00.

Monday, January 18, 1944
Up early. Wrote and studied and prayed. Lunch with
Pat and Bernie Zondervan. Preached at 2:30 on "Adorn
the Doctrine." Snow and still snowing. Supper with Dr.
Ironside of Moody Church. Preaching on "John the
Baptist" by Dr. Ironside. Song service led by Rode-
heaver. I preached on "Sorrows of Jesus." Big crowds.
John Shy took me to the train at 10 p.m. on my way
to Cincinnati.

February 3, 1944
Up early. Betty Lee sick. Breakfast. Wrote some. Prayed.
Prepared prayer-meeting talk on "Bones of Joseph." Ad-
dressed Cotton Farmers' Assoc. of Shelby County. Made

14 visits. Visited Judge Camille Kelly's Court. Went to teachers' meeting supper. Talked to teachers of Adult Department. Conducted prayer meeting. Talked on "Bones of Joseph"—such a large, attentive, attendance. Had conferences afterwards with 4 people. Left so many things undone—so much put on me today. I wonder if I can hold up. O Lord, help me to serve, and give me strength and wisdom. Good night Lord, we are on the same good terms, You and I. Please help me. I am "exceeding sorrowful unto death" about my people. Went home at 11:30, greatly in need of comfort.

The key to Dr. Lee's being a good and greatly beloved pastor can be summed up in a few words— abounding love toward his people, and thoughtfulness, not only in the big things, but in the little things as well. Children almost worship him, and not from afar; young people adore and admire him; and hosts of the middle-aged and old folks love him sincerely. Many are the times that the pastor has come home at night almost exhausted, but aglow on account of the fact that he has won a young couple to the Lord Jesus Christ, or because some good news, let us say from a hospital, comes to the effect that one of his beloved flock is getting well.

One of the workers at the Bellevue Baptist Church overheard, one day, two boys in conversation as they walked past the church offices. One of them said, among other things: "That's a good guy in there. He keeps candy on his desk." And, in truth, Dr. Lee does always have some candy at his desk to hand to the youngsters who come into his office to see him.

A nurse at the Baptist Hospital tells of a lonely ten-year-old lad from Arkansas who was quite ill in the hospital. She telephoned to Dr. Lee, whom she knows well, and asked him if he would endeavor to stop in to see the little boy. Of course Dr. Lee gladly consented to come, and did so at the first opportunity. It happened to be snowing when he arrived at the hospital, and as he sat by the boy's bed, the youngster looked out the window and noticed the beautiful white world, blanketed in three inches of snow, a rare sight to him. One of the first things the youngster said was: "Oh, boy, I wish I had a snowball! I love to eat snowballs."

Dr. Lee answered immediately: "I'll go down and make you one." And so he did. In fact, he made two large, round snowballs and carried them up to the little boy, and left him a happy lad, with a grin on his face, chewing the cold, white, icy substance. This is the sort of kind thing that almost anyone *could* do, but that very few men as busy as Dr. Lee would take the trouble to do. Would that there were more of us like him!

Thus it is that when a youngster, observing Dr. Lee leaving the platform to dress for the baptismal service, calls out from the front row, "Hello, Dr. Lee!" the pastor does not rebuff the child but, rather, replies, "Hello, Bill," making the boy feel at home, and holding his friendship and devotion in that way. Another young chap was heard to remark one time, upon Dr. Lee's return to the pulpit after an absence of several weeks: "Now we don't *have* to have that other preacher any more. Dr. Lee has come home."

And this is the way young people generally feel about their pastor. When Lee was in New Orleans, among a large number whom he led to Christ were a young man and his girl, who later became man and wife. Years passed, and then the path of this couple, not quite as young now as they were at one time, crossed Dr. Lee's again. They had moved from New Orleans because of the fact that the firm that employed the husband had transferred him to Memphis. At a new-member banquet held in the Bellevue Baptist Church some few weeks later, he arose and made this little speech: "I did not feel that I was coming to a strange city when I transferred to Memphis, because I knew Dr. Lee was here. Although I was born and reared in New Orleans, I looked forward to coming here to live, so that I might be near him again. For I believe that Dr. Lee is the greatest man in the world today. He led me and my wife to know Christ as Saviour, and we both feel that God has been so good to bring us here, so that we can serve Him under Dr. Lee's leadership."

Dr. Lee's interest in and influence upon young people is evident by the multitude of letters and clippings that are to be found in his scrapbooks. Thumbing through them, we find a letter from a young lady of Memphis, to whom Dr. Lee had sacrificially given around $600.00 to help her through college, one of many expenditures that he makes in that direction and which he calls "investing in human lives and leaving the results to God." There is another letter, this one from Columbia, South Carolina, dated 1947, as is the former, from a young man whom Dr. Lee helped through school. Still another letter, dated three weeks later than the one just mentioned, is from a young preacher whom Lee had helped financially and who planned, at the time the letter was written, to enter Louisville Seminary. More than one

hundred boys and girls owe their opportunity to go
to college to the generosity of Robert G. Lee. Most of
them have turned out well—85 or 90 per cent have
repaid him, and others, while they may not have
repaid all of the money loaned, have done well
since graduating from colleges. Only one or two
stand out as having failed, either in college or in
repaying their benefactor for his assistance. Dr. Lee
is frequently asked, by young men who are to be ordained into the ministry, to have a part in the ordination service, generally to give the charge to the new
pastor. Such invitations are not issued to those whom
the young men do not respect and love.

Lee's office is always open to any visitor, though
he is sometimes driven almost to the point of dis-
traction by callers who stay for from forty-five minutes to an hour repeating and repeating their problems and complaints and ailments. He wants them to
tell these things to him, and he longs to be of help
to them; however, the pastor is not slow of mind
and does not need to have something repeated many
times for him to understand it. There is so much
work to be done that he feels the time is wasted,
once the need has been made known and he has
sought to deal with the problem and has prayed with
his callers.

He is grateful for every visit, and receives many
kinds, seeking to give everyone his utmost attention
while they are there. One morning a little girl knocked
at his door. She said: "Dr. Lee, I am Glenda Kay
Lynch. Here is a stick of gum for you." The pastor
accepted it, and that very day wrote her a letter by
hand to thank her for it. A gentleman gave him a

check for $500.00 for the building fund, on that very day. He wrote and thanked the man for his generous gift, but not with any more care or courtesy or enthusiasm than to the little lady who had presented him with the chewing gum.

With what care and attention and love this busy man ministers to his people! He received a notice of the birth of a little girl to a young couple in his church. When this baby was three days old, he wrote her the following letter:

March 27,1937

Dear Little Lady:

I received your sweet letter—the first you ever wrote.

I see how wise you are in the parents you chose. They are so fine and sweet.

And I hope you will always be a joy to them in every way.

May God enrich you and them with the growth of body, with the wealth of health, and with the sweetness of joy.

I hope I'll live long enough to baptize you when you are born again by the Spirit.

Judging from your voice as I heard it the other night, you are going to be an alto.

God bless you, darling lassie—you and those to whom you are so dear.

ROBERT G. LEE

This young lady recently made a public confession of Christ at Bellevue.

And this is the kind of letter that the pastor receives from the children of the church:

July 9, 1947
Gardena, California

Dear Dr. Lee:

I got your picture and I loved it so much I am going to have it framed. Tell Miss Ruth [Miss Ruth Calvert, Dr. Lee's secretary] I thank her for sending your picture. I am

Dr. Lee, Commencement Speaker, with Dr. Lawrence T. Lowry, President of Blue Mountain College, in June, 1938, when Bula G. Lee Graduated

Bellevue Baptist Church, Memphis, Tenn.

Robert G. Lee,
Memphis, 1938

going to keep your letter because I like your letter very, very much it is so nice. I wish I was back with Bellevue Baptist Church. Tell every men and ladies that I know hello for me, will you, please? I will hold you in my heart in love and prayer. Be a sweet and loving pastor for me.

God bless you in all ways, and always.

Love and prayers, your loving

JUNE A. SPENCER

The "all ways, and always" of June's letter is copied from Dr. Lee's usual wish to those to whom he writes.

Another way in which Dr. Lee endears himself to his people is by the very personal interest that he takes in the matters of weddings and funerals. These are not considered by the pastor to be simply other tasks which must be done and gotten over with, but as opportunities to serve Christ and to make Him known in speech and in manner.

He is asked to conduct a great many weddings. His service is longer than the average, but he seeks to make it both reverent and meaningful. No matter who the couple may be, even though they may come from very poor families, Dr. Lee makes it his business to dress formally. If the ceremony is in the autumn, winter, or spring, he wears his Prince Albert coat and striped trousers. If the wedding should be in the summer-time, he dreses in an immaculate white double-breasted gabardine suit. He strives to make every ceremony rich with beauty and to sweeten it with a personal touch. He may say something of this kind: "I held this boy [or this girl, or both] in my arms when he was a tiny baby. My hands had the honor of lowering him into the waters of Holy Baptism, and now I have the pleasure of uniting him

in sacred matrimony with his beloved." And because of his very warm-hearted attitude toward the
young people, it is not an unusual thing at all for a
couple to postpone a wedding for a week, or several weeks, in order to suit Dr. Lee's convenience.

Dr. Lee says that largest fee that he ever received
for performing the wedding ceremony was $25.00,
and the least he ever received was two match-heads,
presented by an insolent young man, a Roman
Catholic who married a Baptist girl who, although
not a member of the Bellevue Baptist Church, in-
sisted that Dr. Lee must conduct the wedding or there
would be no marriage. So arrangements were made
to have the wedding in the Lees' home on Peach
Street. Mrs. Lee went out and bought flowers, to
make the living room as attractive as possible. The
couple were due at seven in the evening. But instead
of arriving at that time, they telephoned, saying that
they were running a little bit late. Another hour
passed, and another telephone message came. Finally
the young people arrived, and while the girl was
polite and gracious, the young man was exceedingly
rude, and added insult to churlishness by handing
the pastor the two match-heads as a "fee."

Until recent years, when Dr. Lee was out of the
city as well as when he was at home, he used to make
the time—for he would not have had it otherwise—to
send birthday and anniversary cards, in his own hand
and with a personal word on each card, to the
members of his church upon the occasions of their
celebrating these events. He was especially careful to
send anniversary cards to elderly couples, and congratulatory messages to friends on important days in

their lives. Of late years, because of the tremendous schedule he has undertaken, he has had to abandon this practice. Yet here is an illustration of his thoughtfulness. It was our privilege on one occasion, to preach at the Bellevue Baptist Church in Memphis while Dr. Lee was in another city. It was the only time in our experience that we ever received a telegram from the man whose pulpit we were supplying, telling us of prayerful interest in the ministry and asking God's blessing upon us and the Word that we would give. This was the message of the wire:

HOLDING YOU IN MY HEART IN PRAYER AND APPRECIATION. I THESSALONIANS 5:23 AND HEBREWS 13:20-21.*

At funerals Dr. Lee seeks to be helpful and comforting to the bereaved, and to preach a Gospel message at the same time. He does not have one "set" funeral sermon, or even several such, but makes the discourse very personal in appreciation of the deceased and also for the comfort of the loved ones who are gathered there. He may follow some such method as this one that we have noted in his files: to use the letters in the name of the deceased, as an acrostic, as a basis for Scripture portions or personal comments about the one who has gone Home. Then he will be careful to recall some kindly deeds that the deceased has done and speak of them, or the Christian characteristics that made the life lovely. When the deceased was not a Christian, then

---

* I Thessalonians 5:23: "And the very God of peace sanctify you wholly; and I pray God your whole spirit and soul and body be preserved blameless unto the coming of our Lord Jesus Christ." Hebrews 13:20-21: "Now the God of peace, that brought again from the dead our Lord Jesus, that great shepherd of the sheep, through the blood of the everlasting covenant, make you perfect in every good work to do His will, working in you that which is wellpleasing in His sight, through Jesus Christ; to whom be glory for ever and ever. Amen."

the pastor goes out of his way to make the plan of salvation clear so that others there will not be lost, too. Some have professed to believe in Christ following such services.

Dr. Lee had been visiting in the Methodist Hospital one day when, coming out to get into his car, he saw an old Negro "mammy" trudging along, heavily burdened with bundles and packages. She was holding a scrap of paper in one hand, murmuring to herself, and she looked so forlorn and so weary that the pastor asked her whether she was in trouble, and whether he might be of some help to her.

"I'se lookin' for McNeil Street, and I'se walked and walked and can't find it nowhere," she said.

Lee asked her if he might look at the scrap of paper that she was holding, so as to see what number she sought on McNeil Street. When he had seen the paper, he said: "Why, Auntie, you are at least two or three miles away from this address. You'll never find it walking around here. Hop in my car, and I'll drive you over there in a few minutes."

The old gray-haired "mammy" tried to get inside the car and after a great deal of awkward twisting about, she finally made it. Just before she closed the door, a certain realization of the "chance" she was taking came upon her! Looking up into Dr. Lee's face, she asked, in a half fearful voice: "You ain't fixin' to take me no place where you ain't got no business, is you?"

Dr. Lee indentified himself, and then she joyfully recalled having heard him preach once at her own church. "It was the time," she said, "when we laid the chief cornerstone." Still a little bit embarrassed

that she had been so overly cautious and had misjudged Dr. Lee, she remarked later: "But you can't
be too careful these days with so much devilment
going on."

On June 15, 1947, a brilliant young college student,
Allan Skiles, walked down the aisle of the Bellevue
Baptist Church and gave his heart to the Lord Jesus
Christ. A little more than a month previous to this
occasion, Dr. Lee had driven sixty miles into the
country to bury the grandmother of this young
man, at the request of Allan's mother, Mrs. Louise
Skiles, a member of Bellevue. It so happened that
the day of the funeral was the first Sunday in May,
the annual occasion when Dr. Lee preaches his
famous "Pay Day—Some Day" sermon in his own
pulpit.

Although Dr. Lee was to leave for St. Louis that
night after the service to attend the Southern Baptist
Convention, he had scheduled himself for a busy day,
teaching his Bible class in the morning and preaching
at the morning service. A phone call came to the
church directly following the morning service,
bringing an urgent and tragic message to a mother
in the membership—that her son had just been killed
in an airplane crash. When Dr. Lee heard the sad
news, before eating the lunch that Mrs. Lee had
prepared and brought to the church so that he might
make the trip into the country for the Skiles funeral,
the pastor rushed to see the mother of the victim of
the plane accident. Then, getting a hasty bite, he drove
over into Mississippi for the funeral of Grandmother
Skiles.

Allan Skiles listened attentively to the preacher's

message. The Holy Spirit spoke to his heart then and he received the Lord Jesus Christ as his Saviour. A few weeks later he united with the Bellevue Baptist Church.

Many of Dr. Lee's friends had urged him, on that first Sunday of May, to think of himself and not to overdo. But suppose he had refused the funeral service in Mississippi! A young man might never have come to know Christ as Saviour. Or assume that he had not gone to the home of the victim of the plane crash! Then an opportunity to express the comfort of the Lord would have been missed.

In the South it is not customary to give thank offerings to the ministers who conduct funerals, although occasionally appreciation of service of this kind is expressed with a monetary gift. Mrs. Skiles sent Dr. Lee the largest check that he has ever received for conducting a funeral—$50.00; but he returned the check, saying it was too much and that he could not accept it. She sent, then, one for $25.00, begging him to take it, which he did. On the other hand, he has, upon rare occasions, supplied funds to purchase coffins or to buy burial ground, when those who have died have been from families of limited means, unable to take care of the normal funeral expenses.

Lee is not mealy-mouthed in the matter of speaking to those whose deaths are evidently approaching. If he knows the sufferers, and is sure that they are Christians, he usually says something to the effect that they realize, of course, that they are going Home soon to be with the Lord Jesus, and tells them of some of the joys that await them in the new Home,

thanking them for their kindness, or faithfulness, or
loyalty as members of the Bellevue Baptist Church.
If he learns that the sufferer is not a Christian, he
endeavors, of course, to lead such a one to the
Lord, so that the afflicted may be assured of his eternal salvation. In no case, whether the visit be in a
hospital or in a home, whether the people whom
Lee visits are old or young, if they are Christians,
he prays with them, and if they are not Christians, he
does the same, if they will permit it, asking the
Lord to touch their hearts. They may refuse to
participate in prayer; but they cannot keep Lee
himself from praying that God will reveal to them
their need and His provision in the Lord Jesus Christ.

Although Dr. Lee cherishes the affection in which
many people hold him, he is not afraid to offend if,
by so doing, he feels that ultimately he can be
of help to the offended party.

Some years ago he married a young couple. For
a while they seemed to be happy, but then one day
Dr. Lee met the husband in the center of the city,
and the expression on the man's face caused Lee to
ask a question: "Are you happy?" The man said that
he was, and this called forth from Dr. Lee further
comment: "Boy, that statement is as bad as the
statement of Ananias. Nobody with a face as long as
you have can claim to be happy."

Upon hearing his friend's confession that, to tell
the truth, he was not happy, the pastor pursued the
inquiry: "Excuse me and my long nose," he said, "but
is your wife extravagant?"

The man said that he owed so much money that he
was only a little bit ahead of the sheriff, and that he

had an idea that the sheriff was moving at the rate of a mile a minute, while he himself was going at only about half that speed. Dr. Lee then told him that he happened to know what his salary was, that he noticed the kind of car he drove and that he lived in an expensive apartment, and the pastor added that he observed that his companion's wife "dressed in tiger-skin clothes on a possum-skin income."

The harassed man admitted all this to be so. He said that he was delighted with his wife, but that he was terribly bothered by the debts that were being incurred. So Dr. Lee went over to the home of this couple that night. The wife did not know that he was coming and welcomed him with gracious courtesy. After a while Dr. Lee asked for a drink of water. When the lady went back into the kitchen to get the water, Lee asked if he might see the refrigerator, and she assented. He spoke of its size and beauty, and asked, with nonchalant impoliteness: "Is this paid for?"

His hostess told him that all of their furniture had been bought on the instalment plan. Observing her fur coat hanging on a chair across the room, the pastor asked if that was paid for. His hostess was beginning to become angry. She admitted that the coat was not paid for, and then, when Dr. Lee inquired about the rental of the apartment, and the husband informed him what it was, he asked, with the impertinence of a jaybird invading the mockingbird's nest, whether the car was paid for.

By that time, says Lee, the lady was "sizzling" in her fury. So he addressed her: "Now, don't get angry with me. I led you and your husband to faith in

Christ. I baptized you both. I married you. I have asked these questions because you are getting into financial difficulties on a salary not equal to expenditures." Some husbands, he told her, are tempted to dip into their employer's till or make unwise financial investments in order to try to make money to get relief under the weight of debts. And he added: "Your husband might never get into trouble, but it would be better to sell your car, have a cheaper apartment, and dress less beautifully, and have him happy and unworried, than to come to the place where you will be asking for a permit to talk to him through a screen on Sunday afternoon."

After this comment and a few that followed, and following a season of prayer, Lee left the apartment. The couple took his advice and now are a happy and loving pair, having a sense as to money values, loyalty in love, devotion toward their children, and a joy in marital and church relationships.

No earnest Christian who has upon his heart a burden for the souls of lost men and women can be satisfied to bear witness only among his own acquaintances, and no zealous minister can possibly be content to preach the Gospel of Christ only in his own pulpit, or from the public platform alone. No less can Dr. Lee confine his testimony to the saving grace of the Lord Jesus Christ to Bellevue and its congregations. Opportunities come to him to speak to individuals about the Saviour because he prays that he will have them, and he believes that his prayers are heard and answered.

Apropos of this, a perfect illustration may be seen in an experience that Dr. Lee had, on one occasion.

He was out of the city one week, and during his absence he was unable to get out of his mind two men whom he had intended calling upon before leaving Memphis, but had lacked opportunity. One of these men was a member of a Methodist church, but was a regular attendant at Bellevue, while the other was a Baptist whose membership was in a church in a distant city. These men had strayed far away from the Lord, and Dr. Lee wanted to reach them. Arriving home on Saturday, Lee prayed that, in some way, the Lord would make it possible for him to speak to these men *soon*. One lived in the northeast section of the city, and the other on the southeast side. To call upon both of them would take considerable time, and Lee was weighed down with a great deal of work. That evening the pastor had to go down to the tailor shop to get a suit that had been pressed, and there, miles away from their homes, were both of these men, at the same stand getting their shoes shined. Such a definite answer to his prayer gave Lee holy boldness to speak to them immediately, and within a short time both united with the Bellevue Baptist Church, assured of their salvation through the Lord Jesus Christ, and ready and eager to serve Him. One of them is a deacon at Bellevue at the present time.

Suitable occasions to present Christ also come because Lee looks for them and makes them. Thus, taking the grandchildren out to dinner at a near-by hotel opens the way for this servant of God to speak to a waitress about Christ. The result of this word of testimony was that Dr. Lee drove some miles from his home into South Memphis at a later time, and there explained fully the way of forgiveness and salvation to this girl, winning her to the Lord. Or again, while in the city of Birmingham, Alabama, for a meeting at Howard College, a time of refreshment with some friends in a drug store presents an opportunity for Dr. Lee to ask the young lady serving them there whether she is a Christian. Upon her admission that she hardly knew what the inside of a church looked like, Lee's heart reached out to her. He excused himself from his friends after a few moments, and went over to where the girl was busy wiping off some tables with a damp cloth. "Listen, my dear," he said, "you have missed the biggest thing in life, not being a Christian."

With a shrug of the shoulders the young lady admitted that she guessed this was so.

"Would you let me tell you how to be a Christian?" asked the preacher.

"I guess I would," she replied.

"Well, put your rag down now, and listen to me. Here is what God says you must do to be saved"— and then Lee quoted Scripture after Scripture to her to show her the way of life. Finally he put the question to her personally as to whether she would put her trust in Christ, and she said that she would. Leaving the young lady, after she had given him her hand as a taken of her sincerity, Lee prayed with her saying: "Lord, help this little girl to do what she ought to do." He says that he expects to see her in Heaven.

Several years ago Dr. Lee wrote a series of articles for *The Sunday School Builder*. The title of the whole series was "Among the Ten Thousand," and in these articles Lee told of personal experiences in winning to Christ some of the ten thousand who had united with the Bellevue Baptist Church up to that time. Every one of the incidents would be interesting and profitable, did we have space to reprint them. We have been obliged to select two only.

The first contains the account of how the busy pastor of Bellevue took the time and made the effort to witness of Christ to a little man who had a newspaper route in Memphis during the days of the great depression. But let Dr. Lee tell us in his own words:*

"He is such a good man."

"He loves the Lord."

"He is as honest as a man can be."

"He loves the Bellevue Baptist Church."

"He thinks the Bible class is wonderful."

"He always has something good to say about his pastor and church."

"He is certainly a different man from what he once was."

These are comments I recently heard about a man who is a member of our church. I was in his home the other day—visiting for the purpose of giving any encouragement I could and of adding my prayer to the work of the doctors to help this good man get well. On leaving the house, I began to think of his life as a Christian— of how it began when he was born again, of how he grew in grace, of how—humbly and with little or no notice—he faithfully served.

And I recall now when first I saw him. One cold day in winter it was—when Memphis was receiving the lash of a northwestern blizzard. He was a grayish little man, with shoulders slightly stooped, who moved in a hurry without seeming to hurry. And later, when I saw him

---

* This article is reprinted through the gracious permission of the Sunday School Board of the Southern Baptist Convention, Nashville, Tenn.

face to face, I found that he had a bright twinkle
in his eyes, and his firm lips carried the faint suggestion
of a constant smile.

It was back in the days when strong men, sometimes scantily clothed, were selling apples on street corners
—the days when old men, poorly clad, were carrying
newspapers—when I met him. This attractive man was
walking several miles each day in his work of delivering
newspapers, and "walking lots slower when I return home
than when I leave home," as he afterward expressed it.
His "paper route" brought him by our church. I decided one day that I would introduce myself to him and
ask him if he were a Christian. This I did—in this
manner.

I went down on the corner of Court and Montgomery
one afternoon at about the hour he usually appeared on
the street. In a little while I saw him hurrying, criss-
crossly, back and forth across the street—delivering his
papers. As he drew near to me, I greeted him. He spoke
pleasantly to me but did not seem inclined to stop. I introduced myself, saying, among other things, "I am
the pastor of the church right in this block."

He laughed. "Oh, yes, I know you; heard you once—
went to sleep. But my wife hears you every Sunday
—an' she says you're the doings." He chuckled merrily
and seemed about to hurry away.

I asked him his name. "Baker—without much to bake,"
he said. "See you again!" He was on his way—hurrying
without seeming to hurry.

He did see me again, but not of his own determination,
but of mine. I took my stand on the corner again several
days later. As he came along, I said, "Mr. Baker, any
good news in your papers today?"

"Yes, plenty good news—along with much crime," he
said quickly.

I said: "I know some good news—and better news than
any news in your papers, along with much sin."

He asked me what the good news was. I said: "The

good news is that Christ died for our sins according to the Scriptures, and Christ died for the ungodly." Then I said: "Would you let me talk with you about being a Christian?"

He said: "Yes, if you can make me understand it. But let's sit down while you talk; my legs ain't what they used to be." We sat down on the curb. I told him the plan of salvation—quoting verses from John's Gospel. I urged him to accept Christ. He did. He came before the church the next Sunday, confessing his faith. I baptized him, his wife rejoicing greatly, even as he, in the salvation that came by the grace of God through his faith in Christ Jesus.

That was ten years ago. He says that the good news I mentioned to him when I urged upon him the necessity of being a Christian is still the best news in the world. Of him and to him the Master says: "Well done, thou good and faithful servant." And when I visit S. H. Baker at 1418 Madison Avenue, Memphis, I think of how he is ready for the Father's home of many mansions.

What a tremendous privilege God has given to us to be the messengers of the Gospel of redemption in His Son! He could have told the story of salvation through the sun, or the moon, or the planets; through the stars that brighten the darkest night; through the raging of the seas or through the songs of the birds. But He did not. He could have given the message of redeeming love through the angels, or He could write it across the sky in letters of fire. But He did not and does not. Rather, He has called upon us who are His own to be witnesses to the Lord Jesus Christ. And, if we are serious in our responsibilities as Christians, we shall pray that doors will be opened for effectual testimony. He who means business with God will not lack opportunity and response. Robert G. Lee means business with God, and consequently he seeks, whenever he can find time so to do, to bear a word of personal testimony to some soul outside of Christ and prays to God that He will open the way. One of his experiences of this nature is told in *The Sunday School Builder* for February, 1947, another true story written by Robert G. Lee, entitled "A Visit in the Rain."*

I saw them at the midweek prayer service the other night. I saw them at Sunday school and at the preaching services last Sunday. And, seeing them—singing joyfully from the same hymn book—seeing them as they looked earnestly up into my face while I preached, feeling the kindly pressure of their young hands as they came by and shook hands with me after the benediction, I thought of the first time I had seen them.

I saw her first. It was a rainy day that had drenched the dawn and nullified the brightness of the noon and was threatening to make the afternoon a dread thing as the day hurried toward the mid afternoon. That day, busy with writing, trying to think, I had not spoken to anyone who was a Christian about any Christian duty. Nor had I put on the heart of any unsaved sinner the claims of Christ for his soul and life. I decided that I would.

I put on my raincoat, went down to a little eat shop, ordered lunch, and prayed that I would have opportunity successfully to guide some Christian to higher ground or to lead some sinner to faith in Christ—or to do both.

After I had eaten, I went into an office building across the street. I found no one there that I had not already spoken to. I went into a drug store. I saw an attractive young woman serving at the cosmetic counter. I went up to the counter and began to look over its plenteous profusion of prefumes and powders.

The young woman took note of me and asked me what I wanted. I said I would like to buy some talcum powder.

* Used by the kind permission of the Sunday School Board of the Southern Baptist Convention, Nashville, Tenn.

She got it. I asked her whether it were white or flesh-colored. She poured some out in the palm of her hand to prove its whiteness. Then she wrapped it up.

When I handed her the price in money, I said: "Are you a Christian, young woman?" She told me that she was but, in substance, was not doing much about it. Then she recognized me and said that she had heard me preach.

I asked her where she held church membership. She said in a country church near Grenada, Mississippi. I then said something about the fact that she was not practicing what I had preached about church membership. "No, I guess not,"she said with a smile, "but my husband and I hear you preach."

I asked her if her husband was a Christian. She said he was a Catholic, but he himself did not think he was saved. "But the other Sunday night," she said, with elation in her eyes, "he said when you preached and gave the invitation, something he could not explain took place in his heart. He should be talked to."

I asked: "Do you think he would talk with me?"

"Yes."

"Tonight?"

"No, because we are going out with some friends."

I told her to tell her husband I had talked with her and would like to meet him.

The next day I dropped by to ask whether her Catholic husband would talk with me. With gladness she said: "Yes, on Saturday. We eat lunch together in the drug store. Meet us there about twelve o'clock, and I will introduce him to you."

On Saturday I found them eating at a little table in the drug store. She introduced him to me and me to him. They had just finished eating. I told him there were so many people around that perhaps he would like to talk in my office. Courteously, he said he preferred that. I took him in my car, brought him to my office, talked with him on the plan of salvation, and let him ask me

Pulpit, Choir, and Organ of the Bellevue Baptist Church,
Memphis, Tenn.

Dr. Lee Addressing Congregation before Baptismal Service at Bellevue

Dr. and Mrs. Lee at their Twenty Fifth Wedding Anniversary, 1938, Celebrated in the Bellevue Baptist Church The Church Auditorium Was Decorated to Simulate a Garden, and the Congregation Presented the Lees with a Set of Sterling Silver

The Lee Home at 1668 Peach St., Memphis, Tenn.

any questions about what Baptists believe, about the Bible, about the plan of salvation.

To give a volume in a line, I say he accepted Christ there in my office. The light on his face testified to the new birth in his heart. He thanked me for what I had done for him in showing him the way. He asked prayer—"because." he said, "I come from a long line of staunch Catholics."

The following Sunday morning he confessed his faith publicly before a great congregation, and his wife came forward with tears and smiles on promise of letter from her home church.

And that is the young couple I see at the midweek service, in Sunday school and Training Union, in the church worship services—the young couple I had not seen until I visited her in the drug store.

Several years ago, interested friends of a successful businessman in the city of Memphis asked Dr. Lee if he would be kind enough to call upon their friend, with the view of trying to point him to Christ. They said that they had tried to bring this man to the place of faith in the Lord, but had been unsuccessful, and warned Lee that he might have rather a hard case on his hands, as the man in question had sown many wild oats in his younger days and was still living the way of all flesh. He was not, they said, at all receptive to anything that pertained to Christianity.

Within a few days Dr. Lee called on this man at his business office. In the reception room, the girl at the information desk asked the pastor if he had an appointment, and Lee admitted that he did not have one, but stated that the matter concerning which he wished to see Mr. So-and-so was an extremely urgent one.

The young lady replied that she was afraid that Dr. Lee would not be able to see her employer without an appointment, but no more had she said this than the door of the inner office opened and the man himself came out, saying: "Oh, yes, he can." Then, turning to Dr. Lee, he inquired: "What did you want to see me about?"

Lee did not want to undertake the conversation in such a public place, with many of the office force listening in, and so he replied with a remark that he hoped might cause the man to invite him into his private office, saying: "I want to talk to you about the biggest proposition on earth."

"What is it?" the man asked abruptly.

Dr. Lee, since he was obliged to speak his piece in such a public place, answered quietly and very deliberately: "I came to talk to you about being a Christian."

"No, I *will not* talk with you about that," the man shouted. "Take away your salary and you will quit preaching tomorrow!"

Quick as a flash, yet in a soft voice, Dr. Lee replied: "That's a lie."

Of course, others who were in the office could not help overhearing some of the conversation. There seemed to be tense excitement among them, none of them knowing exactly what to expect, with their boss being told so candidly that he was a liar! Doubtless to their utter astonishment, the "boss" changed his attitude entirely, and in a very cordial voice said: "Come in! I like you."

So Dr. Lee finally got into the private office, where he sat down and had opportunity for testimony when his brusque host told him that he did not believe in hell, adding that God was not just, who would let people go to such a place.

In response to these remarks, Dr. Lee asked a question: "Do you sell cars?" The man replied in the affirmative, and Lee posed another: "If I bought a car from you, would you make me pay for it twice?"

Emphatically the man replied: "No, of course not!"

"I agree," countered Dr. Lee, "because you are a just businessman. You do not require two payments for one debt. So also is God just. He never demands two payments for one debt. Jesus paid your sin-debt on the Cross, and that payment avails for your salvation the moment you receive Him as your Saviour. *You* accept *Christ,* and *God* accepts *you* as righteous, in Christ."

The man pleaded that he was very busy and could give no more time to Dr. Lee then. He did promise, however, that some time he would call the preacher up and invite him to come and speak with him again. "But," he added with considerable emphasis, "don't you come to see me any more, and don't you call me up. *I'll* call you when *I want to see you.*" So Dr. Lee departed.

Some weeks went by, so that Lee hardly expected that he would hear from this man again. But one night, somewhere between 12:30 and 1:30 a. m., Dr. Lee's telephone rang and a voice, the voice of this businessman, asked him if he would come over to his house and talk with him. The man explained that his family was away and that he was terribly disturbed. Lee dressed very hurriedly and drove over to the address that was given to him. Upon entering the house, very abruptly this now earnest man said to Lee: "Preacher, I have committed every sin in the world. I have broken every commandment, except to kill a man."

Dr. Lee answered: "You are wrong there, for you have also killed a man."

"No, I have never done that!" the man ejaculated.

"Oh, yes you have," said Lee, "and I helped you do it!" Observing the genuine astonishment on the face of his host, Dr. Lee continued: "We killed Jesus; and yet, even though we have done that, He is willing and eager to save us, to save you."

The man became more serious. "Do you mean to tell me, man to man, face to face," he asked, "knowing all this about me, that He is willing to blot the record out and forgive me, and save me?"

"That is what I've been preaching these many years," Dr. Lee answered. "They are God's promises. God's honor in His Word is at stake, and so is every promise that He has ever made." Then the pastor quoted many Scriptures to him—John 3:18; John 3:36; John 5:24; and many others.

The two sat there silently for a little while, and then this man arose, putting out his hand to Dr. Lee, and said: "All right, here goes." The two of them knelt and prayed together.

On the following Sunday this erstwhile cynic walked down the aisle of the Bellevue Baptist Church and made a public profession of Christ, uniting with the church. On the night that he was baptized, he went back to Dr. Lee's office and gave the pastor a check for $1,000.00 to be used for the Lord's glory, he said, adding: "I've got to make up for lost time."

Several years later this businessman left the city

of Memphis to make his home in another metropolis.
Before leaving Memphis, however, he called on Dr.
Lee and, shaking his hand in farewell, said: "The
biggest regret I have in leaving is in leaving you."
Friends report that although he has stumbled several
times during his Christian experience, he has gotten
up again on each occasion, and today is living out
and out for the Lord, a good testimony to Christ in
the city of his abode.

The pastor is ever fearful lest someone, because
Lee has failed to make a visit or to get in touch with
him in one way or another, may die without his
name having been written in the Lamb's Book of
Life. He recalls a little, old, wrinkled lady of about
eighty years of age who was received into the
Bellevue Baptist Church by letter, although Dr. Lee
had not seen her. But a young preacher in the
Bellevue Church had visited this lady, who was dying
of cancer, and knew that she was a born-again
believer. So, on November 2, 1947, Dr. Lee, reading
her letter before the congregation, received her as
a member of Bellevue. The letter that he read to the
church that Sunday was dated "the Saturday before
the second Sabbath in November, 1902." For forty-five
years this lady had kept this letter in her trunk, not
uniting with any church on earth! Three days after
the letter was read at Bellevue, she went to be with
Christ. It impresses Dr. Lee that there are far, far too
many who have put off coming to a personal relationship with the Lord as this old lady put off
uniting with a church, and that thus they have
neglected a far more important thing—that their
names should be written in the Lamb's Book of Life.

Chapter XIII
LOVER OF TRUTH AND RIGHTEOUSNESS
CONVICTIONS AND CRITICISMS

Dr. Lee had just finished an address in the stadium of Louisiana University some few years ago, where he had spoken to about 5,000 people on the subject "Jesus." Into his message he had put all his great devotion to the Saviour, all the ability which God has given him, and all the strength of his virile body. After speaking with a few people following the message, the preacher went into the locker room of the gymnasium to wash up and to get his brief case and other belongings, and he heard two professors, in another aisle of lockers, discussing the message that he had just given. In the course of their remarks, one of the men said to the other: "I do not believe everything Dr. Lee said, but I have no doubts about *His* believing it all."

There can be no doubt in anyone's mind that Dr. Lee is wholly sincere in all that he preaches. He has very strong convictions, convictions of the heart as well as the head, and he cannot dilute them in any way, no matter to whom he is speaking or with whom he is dealing. If his expressions of his persuasions cause offense or enmity, then he feels that he must endure such consequences for his faith.

As to the Bible, he is a cover-to-cover believer in it as the inerrant Word of God, and he preaches accordingly. If the Bible records miracles, then miracles are true. If the Bible says that man is a sinner, then man is a sinner. If the Bible speaks of a Heaven and a hell, then there is a Heaven and there is a hell. If the Bible tells of a personal devil, then there is a personal devil. If the Bible reveals redemption through the Lord Jesus Christ, then such redemption is assured. If the Bible teaches Christian baptism, then Christian baptism should be observed. If the Bible teaches that Balaam's ass talked, then Balaam's ass talked. If the Bible prophesies that Christ is coming again, then Christ is coming again. There are no reservations about the Word of God with Robert G. Lee. Consequently, some of the more liberal theologians are rather critical of him, saying that he is too fundamental in his doctrinal position. But criticism is not new to Dr. Lee; he has broad shoulders to bear it, and more, he has the Lord Jesus Christ upon whom he can roll the burden. Non-Baptists sometimes accuse Lee of being too baptistic; Baptists sometimes accuse Lee of not being sufficiently baptistic. No man can please everyone at all times if he has any firm convictions in his own heart, and Lee understands this and goes about his business of serving the Lord with a full heart.

Dr. Lee subscribes to all of the articles of faith of a true Baptist church, which are, briefly: (1) Belief that the Scriptures of the Old and New Testaments are the Word of God and the infallible and sufficient rule of religious faith and practice; (2) that there is only one true and living God, an infinite and intelligent Spirit, existing and revealed to us as the Father, the Son, and the Holy Spirit, equal in every divine perfection, and executing distinct but harmonious offices in the great work of redemption; (3) that man was created in the image of God but, by violating the law of his Maker, fell from that holy and happy state, and that by his apostasy man is so affected that he is by nature a sinner, and as such is exposed to judgment; (4) that Jesus Christ is the Son of God, the Second Person in the Godhead, being very and eternal God, who, when the fulness of time was come, took upon Himself man's nature with all the essential properties and infirmities thereof, apart from sin, and that in this one Person He is very God and very man; (5) that salvation is wholly by grace and only through the merits and mediation of the Son of God, who was made sin for us, that we might be made the righteousness of God in Him; (6) that Christ has secured justification for such as believe on Him, a justification which includes the pardon of sin and the promise of eternal life on principles of righteousness, and that thus justification is bestowed, not in consideration of any works of righteousness which we have done, but solely through faith in the precious blood of the Lord Jesus Christ; (7) that regeneration is the work of the Holy Spirit within the believer whereby he becomes a new creation and has imparted unto him a new life, which manifests itself in repentance and faith and holy obedience; (8) that true believers never fall finally from a state of grace but that, although they may walk in darkness at some times and be chastened for their sins,

they are the objects of the special care of God and
are saved in accordance with the promises of God's
Word; (9) that full assurance of salvation may be
had in this life; (10) that God, by His infinite power
and wisdom, upholds, directs, disposes, and governs
all things from the greatest even to the least, and
that He causes all things to work together for good
to them that love Him, according to His purpose, and
that He hears and answers the prayers of the saints
and gives special grace to them in times of need;
(11) that the soul of man is immortal, that there
will be a resurrection of the body, both of the just
and unjust, the just to eternal blessedness with God,
and those who have died in their sins to judgment
and eternal separation from God; (12) that the
universal Church, which with respect to the internal
work of the Spirit and the truth of grace may be
called invisible, consists of the whole number of the
elect that have been, or shall be, gathered together
into one under Christ, the Head thereof, and is His
body and bride; (13) that baptism is the immersion
in water of a believer into the name of the Father
and the Son and the Holy Spirit, and is a prerequisite to participation in the Lord's Supper, as
is also membership in a Gospel church; (14) that
the first day of the week is the Lord's Day, to be
sacredly devoted to religious purposes and preparation for the rest that remaineth for the people
of God; and (15) that civil government is of divine
appointment for the interests of society, and that
magistrates are to be prayed for and conscientiously
honored, except only in things opposed to the will
of God and of His Son, our Lord Jesus Christ, who

is the only Lord of the conscience and the Prince of the kings of the earth.

Dr. Lee has himself set forth what he believes a scriptural Baptist church to be in eighteen terse sentences, which we list below:

This is a Baptist church, and as such, our church membership believes:

(1) In the rights of the individual, not close ecclesiastical rights;

(2) In personal faith, not proxy faith;

(3) In the priesthood of all believers, not the priesthood of a class;

(4) In free grace, not sacramental grace;

(5) In the direct approach to God, not in the indirect;

(6) In believer's baptism, not in infant baptism;

(7) In the voluntary principle, not the coercive principle, in religion;

(8) In the unity, sufficiency, and sole authority of Scripture, as the rule both of doctrine and polity;

(9) In the credible evidence of regeneration and conversion as prerequisite to church membership;

(10) In immersion only, as answering to Christ's command of baptism and to the symbolic meaning of the ordinance;

(11) In the order of the ordinances, baptism and the Lord's Supper, as of divine appointment, as well as the ordinances themselves;

(12) In the right of each member of the church to a voice in the government and discipline;

(13) In each church, while holding fellowship with other churches, solely responsible to Jesus Christ;

(14) In the freedom of individual conscience, and the total independence of church and state.

(15) We believe that in religion we have no priest but Christ.

(16) We believe that in sin there is no sacrifice but Calvary.

(17) We believe that in all things we have no authority but the Bible.

(18) We believe in only one confessional, and that confessional the throne of grace.

Further, Dr. Lee is a premillennialist, and for this faith he has his critics. But he is convinced that it is the teaching of the Scriptures that the Lord Jesus Christ will return—first, to take His Church to Himself, and second, to the earth to establish His kingdom upon the earth, as predicted in Old Testament Scriptures; that this coming will be before the Millennium, and that it will be the Lord Himself who will set up the millennial government. He believes that the return of the Lord is a bodily, visible coming back of the One who ascended from earth after His resurrection, to the right hand of the throne of the Majesty on High.

It is frequently said that the baptismal service, as it is conducted by Dr. Lee, is one of the most reverent and beautiful to be seen in our day. Certainly it is no fault of his if it is not, for he approaches it prayerfully and with the sense of its divine institution and its holy meaning. He looks back to the Cross and all that the death of Christ means to us, and stands in the baptismal waters as upon holy ground. Lee insists that every candidate for baptism appear before him for a face-to-face talk as to the symbolism of the ordinance, so that the applicant will understand why he enters into the waters and will do it in sincerity, and also as to how he is to act during it. The pastor always wears a freshly laundered white robe and sees to it that all the candidates are furnished with clean white clothes for the occasion, as an emphasis upon the homage due to God; He also quotes Scripture passages and gives a message on the meaning and value of obedience in the matter of this ordinance, making it clear that water baptism has no part in anyone's salvation, but that it is an act of submissiveness that ought to be observed by every believer in the Lord Jesus Christ.

There are still other convictions, apart from doctrinal issues, to which Dr. Lee holds very strongly. He cannot abide people's leaving a church service before its conclusion, and he makes this clear in his own church almost every Sunday. A great deal of prayer and preparation is behind each sermon delivered. Usually the whole sermon, and the whole service also, have been focused upon the concluding few minutes of the sermon. An invitation is then given, or the message is applied personally to those in the audience. People who, unthinkingly, rise from their seats at any point in the concluding portion of the service are, whether they like it or not, the devil's instruments in diverting the attention of the hearers from the message that God has for them. Consequently, Dr. Lee occasionally publishes in his church bulletin, or announces from the platform, the following statement:

> If I were your dinner guest, and left before the meal was over, without asking to be excused, you would think I was discourteous. And I would be! That's what I think of people who leave just as the invitation is being given for people to accept Christ.
>
> If I walked into the operating room and slapped the arm of the surgeon who was operating on your loved one to save him from physical death, you would think that I was

cruel. So do I think that those who attend our services and hinder the effort to enlist Christians in service, to urge those who are lost to accept the Saviour, by leaving as the Invitation Hymn begins.

In this church every visitor is an honored guest. This does not mean that you have the liberty to leave during the invitation or before the benediction. Let these words to the wise be sufficient.

This statement, by the way, has been copied and published in multitudes of church bulletins throughout the nation.

As to those who hold office in the Bellevue Baptist Church, Lee requires of his deacons that they be tithers, that they renounce card playing, dancing, the use of alcoholic beverages, participation in any form of worldliness, and that they promise to attend all services of the church unless unavoidably hindered. Of Sunday school teachers it is required that they refrain from worldly practices that would militate against their Christian testimony, and they must sign a covenant card pledging themselves to attend the prayer meetings and the weekly teachers' meeting. It is expected of them, of course, to be present at the services on the Lord's Day.

Robert G. Lee, as the under-shepherd of the flock of God at the Bellevue Baptist Church, is convinced that his leadership has been divinely appointed. As a shepherd, he feels that it is his mission to direct the program of the church and to see that that program is carried out. Consequently he is sometimes accused of "riding rough" over the desires and feelings of some of the membership, but that does not deter him. If his is a God-appointed place, then he must please God rather than men.

However, it must be said of him that he does not willingly offend his fellow workers, and time and again, as his diaries show, he has risen early in the morning gone to individuals whom he has hurt, and apologized and asked forgiveness of them. But above all, he marches forward, with the help of God, to the goal that God Himself has laid upon his heart.

Outside of the activities of the church, Dr. Lee is positive in his convictions, too. He is a great defender of the sanctity of the home, and is a strong opponent of all that he considers to be evil, whether in the individual habits of the membership of his church, or in social vices, or in civic unrighteousness. Lee hates tobacco in any form. He particularly abhors seeing women smoke, especially those with babies, or old ladies. And when he feels he has a right to rebuke those who participate in this habit, he does not hesitate to do so. Against liquor all the righteous fire of his righteous being is kindled. He denounces gamblers whenever the opportunity comes to him so to do. And he is fearless in expressing himself when he feels that there has been civic injustice of one kind or another.

The result is that Dr. Lee has enemies. He is in good company, for what great man does not have them? Concerning this matter, he often says; quoting another:

> No enemy? The boast is poor!
> You've hit no traitor on the hip!
> You've dashed no cup from perjured lip!
> You've never turned a wrong to right;
> You've been a coward in the fight.

For he who has no enemy will be one who is not very positive in his beliefs or actions. It was the Lord Jesus who said: "Woe unto you, when all men shall speak well of you! for so did their fathers to the prophets" (Luke 6:26). And Dr. Lee puts it this way: "If, when I die, some man gets up and says in some sort of dreary voice, or any sort of voice: 'Dear old Dr. Lee, he never made an enemy in his life,' I hope God will raise me to life long enough to kick the coffin lid off, and to say: 'That's not so!' "

Yes, Lee has his enemies. Some preachers have been enemies of his, perhaps through misunderstanding or because he will not give a commendation to some in whose practices he does not believe. One preacher wrote him a letter accusing him of preaching "one thing up North where there is liberalism, and another thing down South." Lee does no such thing; he preaches the revealed truth of God wherever he may be.

There are others who are inimical to him, such as a few college professors, for his stand against evolution and liberalism. He has also made enemies of those to whom he has loaned money, who have not repaid it. Some of these, when reminded by him that the debt was due, have turned against him, calling him "a money grabber."

He has been criticized by others who say: "Dr. Lee always has his way." And certain choir directors, with whom he has worked in the past, say that he is hard to work with, or that he does not know music. But Dr. Lee is convinced that God's message is carried "by the foolishness of preaching, and not by the singing of cantatas." Then, among false beliefs Lee has raised enemies—Christian Scientists, Seventh Day Adventists, and the like.

It is not surprising to know that dealers in alcoholic beverages are enemies of Dr. Lee, who frankly says that "only a fool will make liquor, only a fool will sell it, and only a fool will drink it." As to the gamblers, they fear him and are uncomfortable in his presence; for he opposes the only thing that is their life's blood. Once a young friend of Dr. Lee, a minister, accompanied the pastor to a night baseball game at the ball park in Memphis. The two preachers sat down to find themselves surrounded by a group of professional gamblers. These gamblers recognized Dr. Lee, for almost everyone in Memphis knows who he is even if they do not know him personally. The older man and his younger companion had not been in their seats very long before, one by one, the gamblers got up and moved away to another section in the grandstand. In due course all of them had departed, and as a consequence the two ministers enjoyed the game tremendously, having plenty of room to move around and no obstruction to their view of the ball game!

The Memphis pastor has certainly received tremendous criticism from his theological opponents, the liberals, who do not like the Gospel of our Lord Jesus Christ, as it is presented in the Word of God.

While most of the letters that Dr. Lee receives are complimentary to the nth degree, they are not all that way. Ordinarily he pays little attention to anonymous letters, but occasionally he reads them carefully and tries to learn from them. Here is one that we find in his files. It is dated May 20, 1943, written from a hotel in the city of Memphis:

Dear Dr. Lee:

Twice now I have gone to your church seeking spiritual comfort and help, and twice have I been denied. Perhaps it is that I did not seek earnestly, but let me tell you my story. My parents were Baptists, steadfast and true in their faith in God, and they sent me to Sunday school and church each Sunday. I suppose the teaching I received there, and also of my parents, passed lightly over my head. At least I never took them very seriously, as many children do. When I grew to teen age and struck out for myself I quit going to church. I tried to find happiness in other ways. Not that I ever did any bad crimes. I always tried to be honest and tried to treat my fellow man as I'd like to be treated, but in a way, I guess my life has been a rather sordid one. Some drinking, a few women and various things for amusement. Somehow lately I can't seem to enjoy these as I once did. Not that I'm much older; I am still in my early thirties. Still I don't get the same satisfaction I once did. So I thought perhaps if I turned back to the church, indeed I had a longing to be a better man.

I had heard of the brilliant Dr. Lee, who had the largest congregation of any church in town. So one Sunday I gathered my courage and went to your church. Frankly, Dr., I was disappointed. You indeed were brilliant, your delivery superb, but somehow I did not gain anything. You didn't show me the way back at all. I rather wondered even at your sincerity. I went back Mother's Day evening. You were in fine fettle that night. Remember? You interspersed your talk with stale jokes and a series of gymnastics that surpassed even Billy Sunday's. You condemned smoking mothers, and you had an attentive audience which laughed at your jokes—but, Dr. Lee, your sermon left me cold. I still wonder at your sincerity, and how can I do otherwise? I'm still groping in the dark, even worse than before. I try to pray but can't somehow. There seems to be a barrier that if I could just break down but I haven't found a way.

I shall be in your audience Sunday night again. Shall I be thrice denied?
A Lost Soul

Several months later, a young man whom Dr. Lee did not know came to him after a Sunday morning service in the church and said: "I have misjudged you, and I want to ask your forgiveness." The pastor assured the man that he forgave him, although to this day he does not know with certainty what it is that he forgave. He has an idea, however, that it was this young man who wrote him the letter signed "A Lost Soul."

One who was opposed to Dr. Lee's building program at the First Baptist Church, New Orleans, wrote him an anonymous letter, after Lee announced that he was leaving for Charleston. He simply signed the letter "A Member." But the handwriting was familiar to Dr. Lee. This person was certainly both a critic and an enemy:

Dr. Lee

Since your resignation, I have found out the debt you are leaving us with. This debt was made for your sake, to please you. I hope your heart will feel this heavy burden when you get in your new field. You are a good man, but you love that dollar above your God and above your church. We have lost faith in you. It's best you go.
A Member

Beside this letter, in one of Dr. Lee's scrapbooks, is a notation written in Lee's own hand:

When Henry Ward Beecher unrolled a big fold of paper found on his desk, when he appeared before his morning congregation, one April 1, he found only this

written on it—"April Fool." He made this comment:
"I have gotten letters without signature, but this is the
first time I have gotten a signature without a letter."
That is my attitude toward the letter opposite, and I recognize the handwriting of the "member."

Other criticisms have come more directly, and
with them have come a heavy heart and a searching
mind, lest the criticisms be justified and he be
out of the Lord's will. The censure that bothers
Dr. Lee most is that which impugns his motives, for,
after all, others do not know his heart nor can
they be aware of the prayer behind his decisions.

Over against such discouragements are the en-
couragements from the hand of God—evident results in the winning of souls and the growth of the
church, blessing upon the outside ministry, and
answers to prayer innumerable. We have mentioned
not a few of these in this volume, but here is one
that we have run across as we write this chapter, and
while this prayer has not to do with Memphis but
New Orleans, the answer came in its finality during
Lee's pastorship at the Bellevue Baptist Church.

In one of the scrapbooks, filled with events of
New Orleans days, is to be found a Prayer List, and
on that list are twenty names to be prayed for, in
addition to Robert G. Lee himself. Of the twenty
names, one is crossed out because of death. Of
the nineteen remaining names, there are three beside
which Dr. Lee has written "Prayer answered," and
the date of the answer. The sixteen others were
mostly Roman Catholics, and Lee was praying for
their salvation. On a recent visit to New Orleans,
Dr. Lee discovered that every one of those people for

whom he prayed in New Orleans days, and had continued to pray for since from time to time, has been saved and is now an active worker in his own Protestant church, for the most part Baptist.

One source of inspiration to Dr. Lee was Dr. George W. Truett of Dallas. The first time Lee ever heard Truett preach was in Greenville, South Carolina, at the First Baptist Church, while Lee was still a student at the Furman Fitting School. The first public personal work that the young man ever did was during Dr. Truett's meetings at that time. The Dallas preacher concluded a message with an invitation to the lost, asking the Christians in the audience to seek out the unsaved about them, and young Lee approached an unsaved man dressed in a hickory shirt and wearing red suspenders and no coat, and urged him to go forward to the platform with him, and to tell Dr. Truett of his desire to receive Christ as his Saviour. So Lee led the man forward. Truett shook hands with the two of them, whispering a very solemn "God bless you." When young Lee got back to his room that Sunday night he wept for an hour, thinking upon the great Christ proclaimed by a great preacher, and wondered whether God would ever let him preach as Dr. Truett preached.

In 1927, Dr. Lee was invited to hold a series of meetings at Baylor College, Belton, Texas. Upon his arrival at the college, he found a letter from Dr. Truett, written in his own hand, dated October 26, 1927, as follows:

My dear Dr. Lee:
This is just to express my deeply grateful joy that you are to lead the noble Baylor College in a series of

meetings. I pray and shall pray that great and gracious blessings may attend your visit to Belton. You will find there one of the most inspiring college situations to be found in all the world.

Just know that the hearts of our Texas people are ever deeply warmed when you come this way. The oftener you will come, the better we shall like it.

More and more and more, may God bless you and make you a blessing—is and shall be the prayer of

> Ever yours in the best bonds,
> GEORGE W. TRUETT

In reply to this gracious letter of confidence and commendation to God, Dr. Lee wrote, also in longhand, as follows, on a letterhead of the President of Baylor College:

Dear Dr. Truett:

Your letter of recent date greatly cheered my heart and strengthened me for the responsibilities and opportunities of the great task at Baylor College.

It was so fine of you and so like you to write me as you did. And words are inadequate to express my appreciation of your kind letter—a letter which helped me so, a letter which I shall treasure through the years.

The meeting starts well. Several of the girls were saved last night. Please ask your people to pray for us daily.

God continue His mighty use of you through every hour of every day of every year for many, many years.

> Gratefully and lovingly,
> ROBERT G. LEE

In 1929 Dr. Lee was in communication with the First Baptist Church of Lubbock, Texas, pertaining to a call that the church was prayerfully contemplating issuing to him to be its pastor. During the time that this correspondence was active, Dr. Lee received a telegram from Dr. Truett, dated at Dallas on December 13, 1929, and reading as follows:

DR. ROBERT G. LEE
BELLEVUE BAPTIST CHURCH
MEMPHIS, TENN.
MY BEST THOUGHTS AND MOST FERVENT PRAYERS ARE WITH YOU AS YOU GIVE CONSIDERATION TO LUBBOCK'S CALL. CERTAINLY IT IS ONE OF OUR GREATEST AND MOST CHALLENGING FIELDS AND OUR WHOLE STATE WOULD GIVE YOU WHOLEHEARTED WELCOME. MAY YOU FIND AND FOLLOW GOD'S WILL IN THE MATTER.

GEORGE W. TRUETT

Another letter from Dr. Truett, which is not dated, is in Lee's files. It was sent in connection with the Southern Baptist Convention, held in Ft. Worth. Dr. Lee was Chairman of the Program Committee, and when the convention was over, Dr. Truett wrote him as follows:

My dear Dr. Lee:

Let me express my most cordial and grateful appreciation of the great service you rendered at our Ft. Worth convention, as Chairman of the Program Committee. My feeling is that you steered the program in a notably remarkable way, for the best interest of the convention.

It is my feeling also that the recent convention was one of the best we have had in years. Surely God's people received new heart and hope because of the spirit of such a convention.

I thank God for you, upon every thought of you, and fervent is, and shall be, my prayer that your great ministry may be crowned with ever enlarging service and usefulness!

Faithfully yours,
GEORGE W. TRUETT

Precious memories flooded Lee's heart when Dr. W. A. Criswell, a sound, gifted, and influential young

man, whom God is using widely as the successor to
Dr. Truett at Dallas's First Baptist Church, invited Dr.
Lee to be a guest speaker in his church for eight days
in 1945. Dr. Criswell preached the Convention Sermon
in St. Louis in May, 1947, and Dr. Lee wrote him
a note of appreciation for his message. In response,
Criswell wrote, under date of May 26, 1947:

> My dear Friend:
> How you did cheer my heart with your kind words of
> appreciation for the sermon in St. Louis. You cannot
> know how delighted I am in a word of commendation
> from the great preacher that you are. Truly I "thank my
> God upon every remembrance of you."
> You know my prayer? "Lord, make me one tenth of one
> per cent the preacher that Robert G. Lee is."
> Sincerely yours,
W. A. CRISWELL

The place that Dr. Truett held in Lee's heart
is authenticated by what the Memphis preacher said
at a memorial service for George W. Truett, held
in connection with a meeting of the Tennessee
Alumni of Southwestern Baptist Theological Seminary, Nashville, in 1944. We publish Dr. Lee's sermon
in full.

TRUETT—PEERLESS PREACHER
By Robert Greene Lee

A woeful sense of inadequacy oppressed me when first
I began to think upon this subject. That sense of inadequacy is still upon me. When so many pens have written
in wisdom of Dr. George W. Truett, when so many
tongues have spoken in praise of him, when so many
minds have thought in adoration of him, when so many
millions of hearts have throbbed in bowing assent to
all that has been written and to all that has been printed
and to all that has been spoken of him—how can I

plant another noticeable flower of tribute? It seems as though one were asking me to repeat a great musical triumph of a thousand-instrument orchestra on one feeble flute—as though one were requesting me to play Beethoven's *Ninth Symphony* on a tin whistle. Will not all I say be as water from a garden hose upon rain-soaked lawn?—as the pouring out of one small vial of incense in an out-pouring reservoir of perfume?—as striking with fumbling fingers a thousand-stringed harp played so skillfully by others?—as lighting a feebly-flickering candle amid the splendors of five hundred flaming incandescent chandeliers? Maybe so. Yet, because you have honored me by asking me to speak some words about him who in greatness matched our mountains and our plains, who in humility was like unto Moses, who in preaching power stood above many preachers as a great palm tree in a desert of mediocrity, I have pitched my mental tent upon him—hoping that out of the abundance of the heart my mouth shall speak, hoping that I shall not spoil with man's mean paint God's fair lily.

Consider first some—

I—PERTINENT PANEGYRICS

There are panegyrics as to some other preachers.

About *John the Baptist*: "He descended upon the iniquities of his day with a torch in one hand and a sword in the other. He spoke with a judicial tone."

About *Gunsaulus*: "He was the center from which the stuff of redemptive goodness radiated to the circumference of human well-being."

Of one preacher, Cowper wrote: "He that negotiates between God and man, as God's ambassador, the grand concerns of judgment and mercy should beware of lightness in his speech. 'Tis pitiful to court a grin when you should woo a soul—to break a jest when pity would inspire exhortation."

Senator Carmack about *Sam Jones*: "His own will bound his limbs to the stake of duty and his spirit kindled the flame in which his body was consumed."

About *John A. Broadus* one wrote: "He could preach as wonderfully to a congregation of twenty as to a congregation of two thousand."

About *Spurgeon* it was written: "In his marvelous success and distinguished commendations there is mingled the biography of a great many humbler individuals who stood by him with a heroism that was wonderful and with a devoutness that was sacred. His words were accepted with authority, many of his mistakes overlooked, many magnificent gifts presented."

About *Moody* it was written: "The one-time bootstore clerk took one continent in one hand and another continent in another hand and rocked them both toward God. His twofold message was forgiveness for the past and strength for the future."

About *Paul*, the great apostle, one wrote: "He left a trail of glory across the Gentile world."

About *Samuel*, the prophet of old, one wrote: "He washed the heart of Israel with the snow of high ideals."

About *Isaiah*, the Old Testament evangelist, one said: "In his preaching were the thunders and lightnings of Sinai and the foregleams of Calvary."

About *Beecher* it was written: "All the bells in his belfry rang out the truth of God."

About *Talmadge*. "Millions were blessed by his marvelous ministry."

But put together all tributes paid all great preachers and take something from each one—and you will secure an adequate appraisal of Truett, peerless preacher.

Consider the—

II—Pall of the Peerless Preacher's Passing

When he went from us it was as though the sun were in darkness veiled, as though the moon hid behind the blue draperies of her sky boudoir, as though the starlit sky had less of brightness, as though the birds had voices of wailing only, as though the winds sighed and sobbed and brought little comfort, as though all silences were vocal with sadness, as though all light was in struggle against darkness.

As one said of Lincoln:
"He went down
As when a kingly cedar green with boughs
Goes down with a great shout upon the hills
And leaves a lonesome place against the sky."
His last days were—not as Robert Toomes—tottering with feeble mind. His last days were—not as Marlborough in his dotage—miserably melancholy. His last days were— not as Sir Walter Scott—all the fire of his creative genius gone. His last days were—not as Napoleon in captivity— garrulously holding forth upon the glories of the past.

He went from us as a soldier oft in battle comes home from hard and victorious warfare. He went as a sailor comes home from wide stretches of the seas—seas sometimes calm, seas sometimes stormy. As a hunter home from the hills, he went from us. As a harvester of souls carrying his sheaves, he went away. As one whose worn-out wooden wagon was changed to a chariot of gold, he passed through the gates that open inward to the glories of Heaven. Trite, yet true, to say he lived a great life. To a glorious deathbed, watered all around by the tears of millions, fearlessly he fared forth to stand in the presence of the Christ. And the shadow of his death fell like a pall upon hundreds of thousands of homes and tens of thousands of churches and millions of human hearts the world over.

With his going, consider the—

III—People's Pronouncements

Anthony said of Caesar:
"He was the noblest Roman of them all. His life was gentle—and the elements so mixed in him that all the world might stand up and say, 'This was a man.'"
Since this tribute paid a conqueror in the distant days gone forever into the tomb of Time, more beautiful pronouncements have hardly been made concerning any man—pronouncements on the part of people as to his modest greatness, as to his far-reaching life, as to his

unselfish service, as to his compassionate love, as to his world-wide ministry.

The greatest of men pronounced him great. The excellent pronounced him most excellent; the most refined pronounced him most refined; the most cultured pronounced him cultured; the most earnest pronounced him earnest; the greatest preachers pronounced him great among the greatest. The most wicked pronounced him devout. The mental giants pronounced him a great mind. Great-hearted men pronounced him a great heart. Many people pronounced him possessed of popular prestige. The prominent pronounced him prominent. The pre-eminent pronounced him pre-eminent. Giants among men pronounced him a giant. The tenderest pronounced him tender. The humble pronounced him humblest in sweet humility. All agreed that he was one of the most remarkable, unique, and gifted preachers Baptists have ever had and that God has ever used.

You do not need to be reminded that as a preacher he was a—

IV—Perfervid Preacher

He was ardent—assiduously ardent. He was glowing—gloriously glowing. He was not just a single flame, but a conflagration—not a meteor, but a sun—not a flash of celestial lightning, but the North Star. He was not just a single ember, but a hearthstone aflame. He was not just a strong breeze; he was a wooing cyclone. It is a marvelous achievement, as a sculptor, to "raise children unto God from the sterile womb of stone"—as Michelangelo did—to carve a block of marble into an image so perfect that you can almost see the muscles move, the nerves quiver, and the heart beat. It is a marvelous achievement to be able, in the realm of music, to make "surging seas of tone subservient to your rod"—as Beethoven did. It is splendid achievement to be able so to weave words together in the expression of human thought as to sway an audience and cause them to listen to you like slaves to an emancipation proclamation or like children frightened at the roar of a storm. It is a nobler achievement, a holier accomplishment, and a diviner art to adorn the Gospel in the daily life, and to give the teachings of Jesus a new incarnation. This Dr. Truett did. His perfervid preaching was not that of debating difficulties, or of speculating, or considering philosophies, but that of proclaiming the Word of God! Never did he preach as one in subdued discussions in an academic grove. Never did he preach with the piping voice, but with trumpet tones. Never did he preach as an epicure in philosophies. Never did he preach as a feeder of inflamed popular appetite for amusement. Never did he preach as an administrator of laughing gas for the painless extraction of sin. Never did he preach as a dainty taster of intellectual subtleties. Never did he preach as an expert in speculative cleverness dealing in the abstraction of an up-to-date gospel. Never did he preach as a dealer in fine-spun metaphysical disquisitions—but with wooing urgency that lifted up the crucified, risen, reigning Lord Jesus. Positively perfervid, he spoke the language of certainty in the pulpit. He went into the pulpit with his heart burning. Then he shared that fire with the friend in the pew. He let his heart catch on fire and then he used all his God-given powers to setting other hearts on fire.

Dr. Truett was a preacher with—

V—PENITENCE-PRODUCING PATHOS

Who that ever heard him can forget the range of the wonderful voice? Just as there was power in his posture, so there was greater power in his voice. Just as there was beauty in his gesture, so there was greater beauty in his voice. Just as there was might in the co-operation of his tongue and person, so his voice was like an orchestra. With the reach of an eagle's wings and as low, at times, as a lion's tone, at every intermediate point it possessed some peculiar quality. It had in it the mother's whisper and the father's command. It had in it wooing and warning. It had in it a minimum of mirth and a maximum of mourning. It had in it the mother's lullaby and the judge's severity of death sentence. It ranged high, intermediate, or low in obedience to his will—and men listened through the long hour, wondering that it was so short, and "unaware that they were bewitched out of their weariness by the charm of a voice—not artificial"—but a voice that answered to the soul and its beating. Concerning Beecher's voice this is written: "As a lad he could not make himself understood in ordinary talk. As a minister he toiled under a master coach. In time he learned how to whisper as a cooing dove, or soar like a storm at sea. Whatever the volume of his pitch, he made himself easily audible. As a master of public speech, he knew how to play on all the pipes of the majestic organ."

Who that ever heard him can forget the pathos that was in Truett's voice? It made tender hard hearts. It made dry and stony eyes gush with tears. The God who floated His navies of deliverance into Egypt in the tears on a baby's cheeks, did, using Truett's voice, cause human hearts to shift scenes of riot for penitential tears. It makes one think of what Lincoln wrote after hearing Alexander Stephens speak. "I heard Stephens speak some hours ago—and my old dry eyes are still wet with tears."

The world will never forget even for a moment that Truett was a—

VI—Preacher of Personal Piety

That simply means he was a man of God. "*There was a man sent from God whose name was George Truett.*" What the widow of Zarephath said to Elijah the wide world could say of Truett: "I know that thou art a man of God." He did not preach cream and live skim milk. He "adorned the doctrine of God our Saviour in all things." He was "always bearing about in the body the dying of the Lord Jesus, that the life of Jesus might be made manifest in the body."

To be pronounced proficient in any science, art, or laudable pursuit is a desirable compliment. To be pronounced a finished scholar, a consistent philosopher, a profound metaphysician, a learned theologian, a skillful surgeon, a logical and elocutionary preacher, a successful lawyer, a master musician, a great physician, a consummate statesman and diplomatist are indeed high compliments. But to be pronounced a man of God is higher than all of them. I am not speaking of professional piety, but of personal purity. Without this personal purity as a path in which the preacher must walk, his life will be like distant fire to the cold, like painted water to the thirsty, like rubber fruit to the hungry. Whatever light he makes will be as gaudy stage lights rather than the light of a rising sun. As to his words—no corrupt communication proceeding out of his mouth. As to his association with women—no playing with fire, giving no occasion to the gossiper. As to his achievements—not thinking of himself more highly than he ought to think. As to his relations with others—having a conscience void of offense toward God and men. As to himself, the one with whom he must sleep and eat and walk and live—keeping no secrets on the closet shelf, not standing with the setting sun and hating himself for things he has done. This Dr. Truett did. Thinking of him and the audience before which he stood, I think of old Samuel at Gilgal:

> "Behold, here I am: witness against me before the Lord, and before His anointed: whose ox have I taken? or whose ass have I taken? or whom have I defrauded? whom have I oppressed? or of whose hand have I received any bribe to blind mine eyes therewith? and I will restore it you. And they said, Thou hast not defrauded us, nor oppressed us, neither has thou taken ought of any man's hand" (I Sam. 12:3-4).

A preacher was Dr. Truett who was—

VII—PERSISTENT IN PRAYER PATH

A preacher who does not pray and keep out of his life the things that hinder prayer is as foolish as the athlete who would keep strong without eating, as the soldier who would fight without weapons, as the teacher who would teach mathematics by dispensing with the multiplication table or figures.

There are two commands God gave Elijah that every preacher needs to obey "Go hide thyself" (I Kings 17:3) and "Go show thyself" (I Kings 18:1). These two simple and powerful commands show us the need of separation before service. Meaning that we ought to go to the private place *with* God before we go to the public place *for* God. Meaning every preacher needs to hide by the brook Cherith before he meets the antagonists on Carmel. Meaning that we need the discipline of the private place to know how to prepare for victory in the public place. Meaning that we need to know aloneness with God before we meet and mingle with people. We need the solitary place in order to have the sanctifying place. We need to hide ourselves in the prayer closet before we show ourselves in the pulpit.

Jacob went alone with God upon the heights of Bethel, and he came forth from his solitude as a prince of Jehovah. Paul went alone with God into the desert of Arabia, and came forth with a tongue of flame and with an heart of fire. John the Baptist went alone with God in the wilderness, and came forth as an evangelistic voice to pioneer the way for the Messiah. Luther went alone with God, and came forth as the knight errant of the Reformation. Lincoln and Lee went alone with God amid the pelting hailstorms of the Civil War, and came forth with tranquil hearts.

Next we find that Washington went alone with God at Valley Forge, and came forth with the luster of a new patriotism upon his brow, and with the breath of the Eternal upon his spirit.

Elijah went alone with God; he hid himself and came forth with a torch of light in his bosom. Let us notice the prayer path of Elijah. The whole land was pining under the most fearful of judgments. Every brook, save that lonely rill of Cherith, had failed. No dewdrops spangled the forest with their crystal jewels. No rain torrents answered the silent inarticulate cry of the gasping earth.

The ground upturned by the ploughshare had become rigid furrows of iron. The dust lay thick upon the highways. The heavens above were a blazing furnace. All day long, from the chariot of the sun, there seemed to be discharged bolts of scorching fire. Nature lay prostrate helpless under the withering curse. How was all this? James 5:17 tells us: Elijah "prayed earnestly that it might not rain: and it rained not on the earth by the space of three years and six months."

It was by prayer Jacob wrestled and prevailed. It was by prayer that Joshua arrested the fiery wheels of the sun's chariot, and it was by prayer that Daniel shut the lions' mouths, and cheated death of its prey. It was prayer —the prayer of good King Hezekiah and the pious remnant among those who owned his scepter, that saved Jerusalem from utter destruction and the people from captivity. He carried his desperate case and cause; he spread the railing letter of the Assyrian invader before God in an agony of prayer. Next morning before the hushed tents of Sennacherib, the grounds were covered with his dead; this was the divinely renewed testimony that "the effectual, fervent prayer of a righteous man availeth much."

Prayer had much part in the ministry of Dr. Truett. To deny this would be to deny that the sun has brightness, that flowers have fragrance, that fire has heat, that music has melody.

But we would cheat ourselves of wisdom we need to have and to hold if we did not remember that as a preacher, potent and peerless, Dr. Truett was—

VIII—PLENTIFULLY PERTURBED.

Truett is described as to this by the truth that the preacher proceeds from the fundamental assumption, based upon the Scripture, human history, and contemporary observation, that something is radically wrong with men, to which is added the conviction that he must do something about it. His only proper beginning is a painful, personal perturbation because of the needs and the

Dr. Robert G. Lee Greeting Governor J. Strom Thurmond of South Carolina upon the Occasion of the Preacher's Return to Edgefield to Speak in First Baptist Church in 1946

Mrs. Robert G. Lee in 1945

distresses of his fellowmen. This emergency makes him a voluntary exile from all of the shady groves of philosophic pondering and peace, and he goes out into the market places and factories and battlefields of men with a burden upon his back, tears flowing down his face, and a fire burning in his heart. He is characteristically and chronically a troubled man, and he first gets the ear of men by the arresting power of his anxieties and agonies. Perturbed about sinners who heard but would not heed. Perturbed about followers who followed but afar off. Perturbed about churches which were "drifting sepulchers manned by frozen crews." Perturbed about denominational causes under attack. Perturbed by "wild boars in God's garden." Perturbed by small congregations. Perturbed by men and women who were participants in the degradation of human love. Perturbed by men whose pocketbooks grew fat while their souls became lean.

Consider now—

IX—PERPETUAL PERMANENCY

He preached often on "Thy Will Be Done." He practiced what he preached with beautiful constancy. As of Abel we can say: "Being dead he yet speaketh." Believing with John, we say: "He that doeth the will of God abideth for ever." Reaffirming Daniel Webster's dying words and applying them to Dr. Truett: "I still live."

There is so much about a good and great man you cannot wrap in a shroud. There is so much about a good and great man you cannot enclose in a coffin. There is much about a good and great man you cannot haul off in a hearse. There is so much about a good and great man you cannot bury in a grave—so much about a good and great man you cannot entomb in a marble vault. He will live in the hearts and homes and councils of men long after his photograph has faded; long after his grave has sunk to the level of the earth; long after the street on which he lived is forgotten; long after all who knew him in the flesh are themselves dead. For he knew and did the will

of God, and God's promise is: "He that doeth the will
of God abideth for ever." And for this, even as for him,
this great ambassador of God, we give thanks—praying
that "the God of peace, that brought again from the
dead our Lord Jesus, that great shepherd of the sheep,
through the blood of the everlasting covenant," will make
us "perfect in every good work to do His will," working in
us "that which is wellpleasing in His sight."

Chapter XIV
LOVER OF WORDS

Words are the vehicle of expression. By a man's words we are able to determine his thoughts. They are, as Henry Ward Beecher put it, "pegs to hang ideas on." How are our thoughts to be clothed apart from words? If any man doubts the value and power of words, let him go to a foreign land, unacquainted with its language, and try to express himself; or let him try to speak in his own tongue to an audience, to present a great cause, if he has a limited vocabulary. It is not the quantity of words that a man uses that governs his listeners, but the quality of them. As Job said to Eliphaz: "How forcible are *right* words!" (Job 6:25). Thus it is that he who would proclaim in an adequate way the greatest message of the universe—the love, mercy, and grace of God toward men, as presented in His Word—should make it his business to master words, so that he may employ them for the purpose of bringing those in darkness into God's marvelous light, and of exhorting those who are in the light to walk according to it.

Lee, impelled from the moment of his conversion by an irresistible power to be a preacher of the Gospel of Christ, early recognized the value of words and set himself to acquire a large vocabulary and to become proficient in its use. A well-placed word is of more value than a multitude of ill-used utterances, and is, in addition, a thing of beauty. As Lord Chesterfield writes, in his *Letters*: "Words are the dress of thoughts; which should no more be presented in rags, tatters, and dirt, than your person should." But Bob Lee did not begin to study words simply out of duty; he had a love of words. That love never died, but as the years have passed, he has found ecstatic delight in the usage of them. His calls upon the dictionary become visits; his excursions, camping trips. As a result, he has at the tip of his tongue the proper word for each occasion—the adjective which will throw brightest light on the noun, the verb that will give greatest strength to the clause, and the phrase that will most brightly illumine the thought. Among the outstanding characteristics of Lee's great oratory is his exercise of words, by which he paints candid portraits for his audiences, wherein righteousness becomes a thing of symmetry and beauty, while evil shows itself in the full enormity of depravity and sin.

Lee's excursions with words lead him into many channels, but ultimately to the harbor of his desire— effective preaching of the Gospel. As a musician experiments with melodies and harmonies, or as a philatelist fondles his stamps, so Lee finds his pleasure and does his daily stint of mental gymnastics by toying with words and phrases. These exercises may issue into an acrostic or some humorous jotting, into a poem of one verse or several stanzas, into an expressive clause denoting its author's love of justice or hatred of evil, or into a sermon outline. But in the end they contribute toward making him a better preacher. Witness this excerpt from Lee's sermon "The Curse of Conjecture" in his book *Be Ye Also Ready**:

> I speak of God's inspired, infallible, inerrant Word, and the conjectures concerning that Word.
>
> Today when critics know little of what they criticize, having no sympathy and touch with what they judge, like the unimaginative and unemotional horse traders of the village backlot—utterly unqualified to sit in judgment upon Tennyson or Browning—are those who pillory in unhidden doubt and ridicule many narratives of the Bible.
>
> At the sound of their conjectural comets, their faith-flaunting flutes, their hypercritical harps, their spurious sackbuts, their perversely phantasmal psalteries, their deceptive dulcimers, their flippant fifes, their presumptuous piccolos, in a conjubilant chorus of erroneous assumptions, many bow down and worship, giving ear to that which gives the heart no rest, and the soul no peace, and life no anchor in time of storm.
>
> With baskets full of guesses they go forth, like the "enemy [who] came and sowed tares among the wheat and went his way," swaggeringly sowing surmises, proudly planting probabilities and perhapses, making maybes mighty in many minds by misinterpretation, giving quaquaversal quips where guidance should be guaranteed.

Dr. Lee may be scheduled to deliver the charge at the ordination of a young Baptist preacher. Driving in his car, or riding in a train or plane, he begins to assemble alliterative words that ought to apply to a minister of the Lord. Out of this will come an outline composed of such words as: "Preach," "Pray,"

---

*Published by Zondervan Publishing House.

"Preparation," "Patience," "Purity," "Personal appearance," "Paying debts," and "Practice."

On another journey, while resting his eyes from reading, he may begin to mull over the names of the members of his church, and catalog those names. Here are a few groupings, made in an hour of relaxation, which stimulated the mind of the preacher as he arranged them:

Animals

Kidd (S. E., Jr.)
Campbell (Mrs. James M.)
Lamb (T. A., Jr.)
Stagg (E. L.)
Veall (Mrs. L. P.)
Lyons (Dan F.)
Koonce (Mr. C. S.)
No cats, but we have a Kitts (D.D.)

Locations

Field (Larry G.)
Meadows (Robert R.)
Lea (Miss Elizabeth)
Park (Miss Mary)
Marsh (Mrs. C. I.)
Greenhill (Mr. Joseph E.)
Harber (Harold F.)
Hill (Miss Woodine)
Tunnell (Mrs. Cora)
Street (Mrs. J. L.)
Lane (Gilbert)
Via (Mr. Duell C.)

Courtship

Love (Mrs. S. T., Jr.)
Huggins (Miss Ada Ellen)

Parts of a House

House (E. J.)
Lott (Otis)
Holmes (Miss G.)
Garrett (Mr. D. W.)
Kitchen (Mrs. Effie)
Wall (Mrs. R. G.)
Sink (Miss Leta)
Davenport (Mrs. S. V.)
Frame (Austin C.)
Furniss (John T.)
Gates (Mr. J. F.)
Hall (T. Ward)
Fones (H. D.)
Locke (Alvin)

Food

Bacon (Mrs. N. T.)
Burger (Willard)
Coffey (Mrs. D. C.)
Pease (Mrs. Robt. W., Jr.)
Pepper (Walter M.)
Wiener (Mrs. L. C.)
Berry (Bob)
Lemman (Mrs. M. S.)
Simmons (Mrs. J. D.)
also Cooke (Mrs. Bess)
Frye (George M.)

Moods

Gay (Mrs. M. J.)
Jolly (Mrs. C. M., Jr.)
Fears (R. E., Jr.)
Cross (Mrs. K. P.)
Joyce (Mrs. W. A.)
Moody (Mrs. Julia)

Music

Sharp (Keith)
Flatt (Miss Frances)
Medley (Mrs. C. C.)
Birdsong (E. S.)

Crime and Punishment

Crook (Miss Cornelia)
Skinner (Mrs. E. W.)
Rooker (L. A.)
Lynch (C. S.)

Justice (Mrs. T. E.)
Gamble (Mrs. P. T.)

Parts of the Body

Cheek (Mrs. L. M.)
Legg (Clifford)
Haire (Mrs. Jessie)
Wiggs (Mr. Walter E.)
Wrinkle (Mrs. V. C.)
Curle (E. L.)
Nohse (Mrs. S. C.)

Birds

Parrotte (Mrs. Billie)
Hawkes (Earl)
Peacock (Mrs. J. D.)
Pidgeon (Mrs. James)
Drake (Miss Hazel)
Crowe (Mrs. J. L.)
Crain (F. G.)

We might go on, if space permitted, with other classifications of the Bellevue membership, as under *Months and Seasons, Plants, Directions, Cities, Distances and Quantities, Values, Speed, Countries, Troubles, Weather, Time,* and *Implements of War.* But the examples given will serve sufficiently to illustrate such mental exercises as Dr. Lee enters into for relaxation and stimulus of thought.

On a sheet of paper in Dr. Lee's files, we find a memorandum that seems to contain jottings resulting from a week's ministry in Allentown, Pennsylvania. Evidently Lee was not the only speaker at the conference, as will be observed. Here are some of the things that stamped themselves upon his mind during the week:

(1) Cherry pie in Allentown—never ceases to be a rarity;
(2) One service nobody came in late;
(3) One meeting at Waldheim—130 "at the altar," 61 upon confession of faith;
(4) Flowers on the light posts of Allentown;
(5) Sentences from sermons heard:

"We hunt for eggs in youth—for spectacles in old age."

"We regret the letter we did not write—and the forgiveness we did not ask."

"The rain is a string around God's finger to remind Him not to drown the world."

"The life of self is death; the death of self is life."

"Lamps do not talk—they shine."

"Jesus did not come from Heaven to take our part, but to take our place."

"Anybody old enough to be lost is old enough to be saved."

Dr. Lee may be in an idyllic mood. Out of such an occasion there will come forth verses of poetry. These are not great poems perhaps, but we must remember that they were written in moments of relaxation, time that others might waste, and they are not the productions of one whose energies can be devoted to poetry. They do, however, reveal the poetic sense of their author, Robert G. Lee.

MOONLIGHT

(Written when Robert Lee was 16 years of age)

Jewels tonight, moon—jewels tonight,
Are sparkling somewhere in thy silvery light—
Are glimmering in thy magic light:
Gems, dear moon, like the soul of a child—
Snow-white, resplendent, pure, undefiled.

Loving tonight, moon—loving tonight,
Goes on somewhere in thy tender light;
Yes, is felt in thy enfolding light:
Love comforting the soul oppressed,
As a dove its brood in the dear home-nest.

People tonight, moon—people tonight
Are dying somewhere in thy solemn light—
Dying *lost*, in thy tremulous light;
On land and on the wild, wailing sea,
And knowing not, moon, Him who made thee.

Songs tonight, moon—sweet songs tonight
Are sung somewhere in thy mellow light,
Are heard in thy pale but potent light:
Songs sad or glad, soft, low, and sweet—
Victorious songs and dirges of defeat.

Souls tonight, moon—great souls tonight
Are sinking somewhere in thy silent light,
Sinking sadly in thy silken light:
Sinking, O moon, to the depths of hell,
Suffering horrors no tongue can tell.

Yea, souls tonight, moon—white souls tonight
Are lifted *up* in thy crystalline light,
Are lifted above thy glorious light,
Are borne away from earth's clammy sod,
To commune forever with their God.

Prayers tonight, moon—true prayers tonight
Are prayed somewhere in thy peaceful light,
Are wafted through thy celestial light,
Are heard above the starry skies,
And are *answered* by *Him* in Paradise.

Prisoners tonight, moon—prisoners tonight
Are shut from thy dear, enchanting light,
Though longing to bathe in thy luminous light:

Prisoners, O moon, by man unforgiven,
But loved alway by the King of Heaven.

Angels tonight, moon—angels tonight
Disport themselves in thy golden light,
With garments brighter e'en than thy brilliant light—
With shouts of joy make Heaven resound:
For a soul that was lost at last is found!

HAPPY PAPPY

By Robert G. Lee

Good mawnin', suh, my little son,
Yo' life on earth is jes begun;
You busted my o'd heart with joy
When doctor folks said, "It's a boy!"
An' if you want to know whose happy,
I'm tellin' you I is—yer pappy

Yes, suh, big man, you sho is sweet,
Yo' face so wee, yo' pinkish feet,
An' little bitsy chubby fists,
A-buddin' on them tiny wrists,
An' folks, they know the man who's happy
By jes a-watchin' me—yer pappy.

I sees you bundled up at rest,
Yo' head against yo' mammy's breast;
My heart goes swellin' up wid pride,
An' I jes knows this world so wide
Ain't got a man could be so happy
As him that neighbors call—yer pappy.

You're welcome as a glad surprise;
That truth shines out in all our eyes;
An' all the folks, they're glad you're here,
Glad that you brought our home good cheer;
An' I'm jes hoppin', laughin' happy,
So proud to call myself—yer pappy.

SPRINGTIME

By Robert G. Lee

The peach trees bare and trim,
In valley boudoirs dim,
Are putting on their petticoats of pink;
And maples unabashed,
By Winter's hand unsashed,
Half-naked shiver by the river brink;
Sing, my heart, sing:
It's Spring—it's Spring.

The crane, to line her nest,
Plucks feathers from her breast,
While close her golden-crested mate his watch is
And snowy scarf and shawl   (keeping;
From mountain shoulders fall,
And budding vines o'er trellis frames are creeping—
Sing, my heart, sing:
It's Spring—it's Spring.

In holy twilight hush,
The voice of hermit thrush,
Wren, cardinal, and whippoorwill are calling;
And under greening oaks,
The marsh frogs' raucous croaks
Give weirdness to the warm soft rains a-falling—
Sing, my heart, sing:
It's Spring—it's Spring.

A jasmine-scented breeze
Is moving where the trees
Are robing in their bright and new-green dresses;
And, as sweet maidens fair,
In sunshine dry their hair,
The meadow willows toss abundant tresses—
Sing, my heart, sing:
It's Spring—it's Spring.

Tulips and daffodils
Nestle among the hills,

In scented sunshine blankets sweet and soft;
God weaves a mystic skein
O'er cragmoor, hill, and plain,
O'er verdant fields and arches far aloft—
Sing, my heart, sing:
It's Spring— it's Spring.

Stream, vale, and furrowed sod,
Show fingerprints of God,
Who fringes with His glory all the flowers,
Holds sea and springtime nest
In hand that needs no rest;
Shows mercy through Life's swift allotted hours—
Sing, my heart, sing:
It's Spring—it's Spring.

RED CHERRY PIE

By Robert G. Lee

They talk to me of nectar rare
Politely served with cake to spare;
They serve me cabbage from the pot,
And honey sweet with biscuits hot—
But that for which I often sigh
Is luscious, sweet, good cherry pie!

They serve me apple pies, and peach,
And other things for which I reach;
I like to swallow cracklin' bread
And country ham with gravy red—
But still, the thing I can't pass by
Is *one* more piece of cherry pie.

I eat fried eggs and toasted cheese,
And *always* just the things I please;
Fried chicken, and the dressing too,
Preserves made of the berries blue—
But always that for which I cry
Is plenty of sweet cherry pie.

I want squash and turnip greens,
Good sausage meat and Boston beans,
The biscuits hot with butter spread,
And custard cream and jellies red—
But give me oft, until I die,
That blessed, juicy cherry pie.

For turkey, duck, and ham I pine,
And often on baked fish I dine;
I eat all kinds of sugared cake
And other dainties that cooks bake—
But there's *one* thing I don't deny:
I'd rather have red cherry pie.

I SAW GOD LIGHT THIS HOUSE

By Robert G. Lee

I saw God light this big world-house last night
With planet lamps and star flambeaux on high;
For where deep darkness dwelt in depth and height
He swung His net of stars across the sky.

The moon, a monstrous yellow cameo,
I saw Him pin upon the sky's full breast,
While close around white stars were all aglow,
Like strings of pearls against black velvet pressed.

Red comets fled adown the dome's steep place
Where once the stars fought Sisera of old;
From hand of Him who hangs the earth in space
They fell, like jewels, down stairways of gold.

Swift meteors ablaze sped on their way,
Archangels they, it seemed, full clothed in flame,
Commanded by the Light of light, today
And yesterday, forever more the same.

I saw the moon, like a huge jonquil bloom
Within the spacious garden of the stars,
While like tall tapers in cathedral gloom
Blazed forth full strong Orion's gleaming bars.

The slender tops of ancient, tall pine trees
Stood on hill rims, me and the moon between;
And while His glory flamed in Pleiades
These tossed like purple plumes 'gainst silver screen.

I saw God light this big world-house last night
With stars, like burning coals, on hearthstones green;
I would that me He had made, in His sight,
As starlight sweet, as moonbeams white—so clean.

The longest of Dr. Lee's printed poems is entitled "War Again?" It was published in 1939, when the Second World War broke out.

WAR AGAIN?

War?
Shall shriek of hissing, bursting shell
Announce approach of heartless hell
In village street, where children play,
In churches where our women pray?

Shall ripping, dripping bayonet
Make war's promiscuous ditches wet
With brains and blood of slaughtered sons
Who bravely die beside hot guns?
Shall armpits stink with bloody sweat
In dugout tombs where men forget
The fragrance of the mignonette—
The privet hedge and violet?

Shall cannon thunder boom once more
In homeland or on foreign shore—
As nations see their streams turn red
With blood of murdered millions shed?
Shall nations of our tortured earth
Forget the joys of peaceful mirth?

Shall millions of our fairest sons
Go down before the belching guns
And leave our world as drear and dark,

As dumb and dazed and sad and stark,
As distant worlds without their suns?

Shall men all drunk with war's mad wine
Find joy in deadly bullet's whine?
Find music in the war drum's moan—
Find music in the wounded's groan?
Find beauty in each ghastly face—
All crushed and marred in every place?
Shall men whose homes wish their return
Let hearts with deadly hatred burn?

Shall millions brave in tortures writhe—
Cut down before war's cruel scythe?
Shall hillside cove become a grave
And death ditch for ten thousand brave?
Shall men make plains their slaughter floors
And tie black crepe on many doors?

Shall motor drone of bomber's flight
Mean death that stalks abroad at night?
Shall midnight find us crouched in dread,
And morning count our mangled dead
In streets all splotched with ghastly red?
Shall virgins to man's lust be fed,
And garden fair with bones be spread,
While men find sewers welcome bed?

Shall garden plots be butcher pits
For men by bombs blown into bits?
Shall many sobs like cyclones rise?
Shall love light die in human eyes,
Whiles curses drown man's bitter sighs?

Shall wombs of women barren be
Because of lovers lost at sea—
While men, like maniacs who rave,
Make shrouds for men of rolling wave?
Shall sweethearts die in mud and muck,
Some women's breasts never give suck
To child by him who comes no more,
But called her name in battle's roar?

Shall damp suspicion hang again
Upon the councils of all men?
Shall waving fields of golden grain
Be torture racks of awful pain—
All soaked with gruesome, crimson rain?

Shall marching millions gaily tread,
And soon become our vanished dead?
Shall skeletons and skulls be fence
To circle world in strife forlorn,
And altars offer war's incense
While countless millions mourn?

Shall crimson bubbles cover seas?
Shall poison breath ride every breeze?
Shall minds of many men be crazed?
Shall cities by man's bombs be razed,
And altars desecrated be—
Where men in peacetime bend the knee?

Shall men make widows of men's brides,
And let death ride on rolling tides?
Shall men in madness of war's claims
Forget the millions that war maims?
Shall men find fragrance in war's stench
While faces stare in mud-filled trench?
O God, forbid!

Robert G. Lee is the author of about twoscore published volumes, the first of which was published in 1912, *Bothersome Families,* and the last in 1948, *Pulpit Pleadings.* His three most widely-known works, perhaps, are *Lord, I Believe* (1927), *A Greater Than Solomon* (1935), and *The Name Above Every Name* (1938). These are all books of sermons, revised for the appearance of the messages in print. In addition to the many volumes of his sermons, Dr. Lee contributed to several other books, upon invitation, which include great sermons by such famed men as

G. Campbell Morgan, J. H. Jowett, Clovis G. Chappel, etc. His writings* have been read by many thousands, some having all of Dr. Lee's works, and others having only one title, or several titles.

The value of the writing ministry of any man cannot be measured accurately, for one hardly knows, generally speaking, who reads his writings or where his books are read. But occasionally letters come— sometimes from far out-of-the-way places—to encourage the heart as to the usefulness of putting one's thoughts on paper and having them published. Lee receives multitudes of communications from all parts of the world as to how much his sermons in print have meant to their readers. And sometimes the communications come from close at hand. These two letters will suffice to illustrate the point.

Chincoteague, Virginia
July 21, 1946

My dear Rev. Lee:

An ex-serviceman from Florida placed in my hands a copy of your book *Lord, I Believe*— and I believe that the Lord Himself has placed in my heart the desire to say the kind of "thank you" that will be heard all the way up to the Throne.

Doubtless you have had much acclaim. But I received the impression (from the seventeenth chapter of the Gospel of Luke) that Christ Himself was evidently left with a letdown feeling, after He had healed the lepers, and only one, a stranger, returned to give Him thanks.

So—I do not want one of His servants today to have silence from me when that servant is entitled to as large a "thank you" as you are entitled to for the benefit your book has brought me . . .

RACHEL MARVEL

*For complete list of Dr. Lee's published volumes, see Appendix.

Memphis, Tennessee
September 24, 1948

Dear Dr. Lee:

I want to express to you my deepest appreciation for the gift of your book *The Name Above Every Name*. I have read some of the sermons and I believe they are among the greatest I have ever known. I count it a great privilege to be associated with you in the work of our Lord and my prayer is that I may prove worthy of such an honor.

Without any flattery whatsoever I would like to write with the pen of an angel just how much you have meant to me. Your love for the Lord Jesus and your passionate preaching of His gracious Gospel have been a means of bringing into my life an inspiration that will help me to be a more faithful servant of our Saviour . . .

Yours in His Name,
BROOKS RAMSEY

This young man, by the way, was helped by Lee to find a pastorate, where he now serves the Lord faithfully.

From Dr. Lee's sermons, as they appear in print and from stenographic jottings taken down by listeners in his audiences, we record statements on a variety of subjects so as to illustrate the working of the man's mind and to evaluate his years of study of words. All of his expressions are transparently descriptive of that which Lee is seeking to say, which is, after all, the purpose of language.

Of course, these utterances were first made by a gifted orator speaking to large audiences, and therefore the praise, or derision, or pathos, or humor, or whatever characteristic or mood is described, was made more real and vital, by attitude and tone of voice, than cold type can possibly make it.

Some Christians are dying of spiritual diabetes—too much sugar.

I do not read some books, because I do not want to swim through fifty yards of sewage to get one teaspoonful of truth.

I will not sacrifice truth for popularity or praise.

All criminals do not wear stripes.

The Bible travels more highways and walks more by-paths and knocks at more doors and speaks to more people in their mother tongues than any book the world has ever known or can know.

If some fed their bodies as carelessly as they read and study the Bible, they would soon become emaciated.

Entirely too many who claim to be Christian go a-round with faces long enough to eat ice cream out of the bottom of the churn.

The habits of some animals are more to be desired than the habits of some folk—at least, I never saw a hog get drunk, nor a horse chewing tobacco, nor a billy goat smoking; nor have I heard a cow mooing profanity nor a dog barking vulgarity.

The farther the planets are from the sun, the slower they move; the farther we get from Jesus, the slower we move.

When we magnify self, we minimize our office.

When public opinion is on the side of vices, I refuse conformity, though it is to incur ostracism. Rather ostracism among men than to be odious before God.

A Christian optimist is one who makes lemonade out of the lemons handed him along life.

Reason never would have let my wife marry me, but *Faith* did.

Some evolutionists tell us that deer got their horns by rubbing their heads together. If this were true, some young "dears" I know ought to have horns on their heads by this time.

It is as impossible to play with sin and not get burnt, and not cause hurt, as it is to stop bullets on the way to their target with a tennis racket.

I have more respect for the burglar who puts a jimmy under my window and steals my wife's wedding ring than I have for any Ph. D. college professor who, wielding the piratical cutlass of criticism against the Bible, breaks into the house of faith of my boys and girls.

Some people *remember* themselves into obscurity, while others *forget* themselves into immortality.

I am willing for a preacher to hack grammar to pieces, if he will let God use him in preaching to break the hearts of sinners.

The hardest instrument for any Christian to play is second fiddle.

Modernism mutilates the Bible, minimizes sin, humanizes Jesus, and deifies man.

If I had one hair in my head that was in favor of liquor, any time, I'd pull it out.

John the Baptist could not get a call to any Baptist church today, because of the way he dressed; and the women would not invite him into their homes, because they would not know how to make grasshopper salad.

It's better to care for what God knows about you than for what men think about you.

Ingersoll strutted to and fro—somewhat as the devil goes to and fro, up and down the earth. He was as a windmill running furiously but pumping no water to refresh the thirsty.

There are so many *isms* that should be made *wasms*

An empty wagon makes the most noise.

If some young ladies spent more time on their knees

and less time before their mirrors, this would be a better world, and the devil would have a holiday now and again.

Don't wiggle in your seats. I can hit a moving target just as easy as I can one that is sitting still.

Self-labeled scholars who gag on a rib and swallow a live monkey—head, hair, tail, and all.

God floated into Egypt His navy of deliverance on the tears on a baby's cheek.

When men have burned martyrs at the stake, God has picked up a handful of the hot ashes and has thrown them across countries and continents, and wherever these ashes have fallen, rivivals have come.

Be careful that you don't grow proud because you are not proud. Humility departs when we get proud over being humble.

The lost accord in churches is more tragic than the Lost Chord in music.

Not one brick but many bricks make a wall; not one soldier but many soldiers make an army.

Real religion does not go along with a self-centered and pusillanimous life.

Defining the Christian religion from the human side, not the divine side, is like telling people the value of a diamond by quoting the price of pewter.

If a pecan tree has as many fruitless branches as some churches have absent members on Sunday night, it would not feed one squirrel for a week.

An iceberg and a rose are both pure—the iceberg is pure repellently, while the rose is pure attractively.

Grace is the unmerited and unlimited favor of God upon the utterly undeserving.

Worship is being wholly occupied with God.

God makes our bodies human channels through which His divine will becomes articulate.

Heaven's choir came down to sing when Heaven's Son came down to save.

Take Jesus out of the Bible! It would be like taking heat out of fire, melody out of music, or fact out of history.

Like a yellow jonquil in the sky.

Some churches are like drifting sepulchres, manned by frozen crews.

Jesus conquered death by dying, which is in antithesis of what the world thinks about death.

Heaven is a place as beautiful as the mind of God can conceive, and the power of God can create.

Yet all these statements, terse and definitive as they may be, are not to be compared with the language that falls from Lee's lips or runs from his pen as he proclaims the matchless virtues of Jesus. Thus does he write, for example, in *The Rose of Sharon!**

No voice can compass, no pen include, the full statement of Christ's character. The world over, architects striving to build cathedrals worthy of Him, fall short of their high objectives. A sense of inadequacy falls oppressively upon musicians who try to create music sweet enough for His hymns of praise. Sculptors, searching all quarries, nowhere find marble white enough for His forehead. Orators, whose sentences are flights of golden arrows, express only a meager measure of the honor due Him. Writers, words dropping from their pens like golden pollen from stems of shaken lilies, feel the inadequacy of all words to set Him forth in His beauty. Devout poets, reaching from pole to pole with wings of their poetic genius, struggle for some metaphor by which to express Him. Profound scholars, rushing with archangelic splendor

*Published by Zondervan Publishing House, Grand Rapids, Mich. 1947.

through mysterious realms of thought, light their brightest torches at His altar fires.

Or again, on another page in the same volume:

Jesus never struck a jarring note, never made a misstep. On Him circumstances left no fingerprints. Popularity, never caused Him to hasten a footstep. Hostility never caused Him to falter. Temptations never loosened a moral fiber. As all the rivers are gathered into the ocean, so Christ is the ocean in which all moral excellencies and spiritual pleasures meet. Even His enemies said they could find no fault in Him. Even His worst foe proclaimed Him innocent. He challenged them with this question: "Which of you convinceth Me of sin? And if I say the truth, why do ye not believe Me?" (John 8:46). God found no blemish in Him: "And lo a voice from Heaven, saying, This is My beloved Son, in whom I am well pleased" (Matt. 3:17). Christ Himself said: "I do always those things that please Him." Christ is a sea of sweetness without one drop of gall. Things that shine as single stars with a particular glory all meet in Christ as a glorious constellation. "For it pleased the Father that in Him should all fulness dwell" (Col. 1:19). All loveliness is derivative and secondary, but the loveliness of Christ is original and primary. His is the beauty of holiness. Holiness is glory internal. Glory is holiness shining forth outwardly. He is the Lord of Glory. And if you see no beauty in Him that you should desire Him, it is because the god of this world has blinded your mind— and you are a victim of dawdling ditties, missing life's central melody. The eyes of your understanding have not been enlightened.

Chapter XV

PREACHER OF RIGHTEOUSNESS

PREPARATION AND PREACHING: A FAMOUS SERMON

Whatever gifts Robert G. Lee has, and he is blessed with many of them, beyond and above all others is the gift of preaching that God has given him. He who, as a lad, saw between the ears of his plough-mule, as if in letters of fire written in the sky, God's call to preach; who, as a young man, working in ditches and on docks, strove with every fiber of his being to get an education so that he could become a preacher; who, in student years and early ministry, read everything that he could lay his hands upon, prayed incessantly, and labored assiduously to improve his knowledge and ability, in manhood and now at three-score and more years of age, is first and last a preacher of the Gospel of Christ. When one thinks of Robert G. Lee, one thinks of preaching; when one thinks of preachers, one thinks of Robert G. Lee.

It is told that George Pentecost was accosted once, when he preached in the city of Edinburgh, by Horatios Bonar, who had heard him make his address. Mr. Bonar, putting his hand upon Pentecost's shoulder, said to him: "You love to preach to men, don't you?"

"Yes," responded Pentecost.

"But," asked Bonar, "do you love the men you preach to?"

It can truthfully be said of Dr. Lee that he not only loves to preach, but he bears in his heart a great love for those to whom he proclaims the Gospel. And let it be remembered, in all his preaching, Robert G. Lee is a Gospel preacher. He has both the heart and the message of an evangelist, and this is evident whatever the subject matter of his sermon.

We have said that Lee is primarily a preacher. And as a preacher he is primarily an orator. He does not lack the gift of teaching, and some of his own people think that he is at his best in assemblies of three hundred people or less, as in his Sunday school class for businessmen, when he teaches certain portions or doctrines of the Bible. Lee's fame, however, is as a preacher and his greatest gift is that of preaching to throngs. When he sees before him, not hundreds but thousands—five thousand, ten thousand, fifteen thousand—he is at his best. Nor does he ever reach greater heights than when he talks on the Name and Person of "Jesus." Filled with love for the Saviour, emotional, sentimental, histrionic to his finger tips, with the mind and speech of an orator and the heart of an evangelist, Lee rings all the changes of oratory and of personal appeal and emotion as he warms up to his subject and presents Him who is above all others in kind and degree. It is for this that he worked himself to the bone and suffered privation of many kinds, and prayed far into the night. It is to this that God called him, and he is faithful in answering the call and delivering the message.

Let it not be thought that Lee does not have his

discouragements. There are times when this man, like other men, feels that he has failed miserably— not himself, but the Lord. Once he said to Mrs. Lee, after preaching what she considered to be a great sermon: "I twittered as a sparrow, when I should have sung as a nightingale." Various circumstances may enter into such judgment of himself: it may be true that, upon such and such an occasion, he has not been at his best; or, on the other hand, it may be that he has done well in the Spirit and power of the Lord, but that his own mental condition is such that he does not think he has done well. Or something else may enter into a disappointment of this kind.

Going to a small city in the South, on one occasion, Dr. Lee addressed a full church on his famed sermon "Pay Day—Some Day." His audience was very passive, and there seemed to be much less response at the conclusion of the message than he felt he had a right to expect when he preached the truth of the Gospel of Christ. He could not understand the reason for it until he learned, after the service, that the pastor of the church in which he was speaking had himself, about a week before Lee's coming there, preached Dr. Lee's sermon. It is not to be wondered at, then, that the audience was unresponsive, since most of them undoubtedly thought that Lee was using their own pastor's material!

While Lee was pastor of the First Baptist Church of New Orleans, he preached one Sunday, using as his theme the adverb, "nevertheless." He had run through about all of the "neverthelesses" in the Bible, building himself a solid foundation for the burden of the message and its application. But

somehow he did not seem to be able to "get going."
He had gotten into a situation and did not quite know
how to get out of it. About halfway through his message he suddenly stopped and announced the invitation hymn. Then he said: "I realize that I have
made a complete flop of these 'neverthelesses,' but
nevertheless I have a Saviour who never fails. I
invite you to receive Him." Then Lee quoted from
Charles Haddon Spurgeon when he had said: "Lord,
Thou canst make something out of nothing. Therefore, bless this sermon." Five people came forward
and united with the church after that message, two
upon first confession of faith in Christ.

Lee stood at the door, following the closing of
the service, to shake hands, as was his custom, with
those who had been in church that day. One of the
deacons, a very close personal friend of the pastor,
shook his hand in a friendly way and asked: "Preacher, do you want to go for a little ride?" When
Lee answered in the affirmative, the deacon inquired:
"How far do you want to go?"

"You cannot take me as far as I want to go," was
the pastor's reply.

So Lee got in his friend's car and the two of them
rode for about three miles before a single word was
spoken. At last Lee broke the silence, inquiring of
his friend: "Beloved, what was the matter with me
this morning?"

It was perhaps three miles farther on before
the answer came: "Dr. Lee, you laid a skyscraper
foundation and built a chicken coop on top of it."

"If there had been a capsule on that platform,"
the pastor said, "I could have crawled into it and

mailed myself to the dead-letter office with a one-cent stamp."

Almost every speaker has had such experiences, and, if he has any humility and alertness, will learn from them. There have been other times when speakers have thought that they were at their best, and yet they have seen no visible results. On one occasion when Bob Lee was a student in Furman University, he experienced such a thing. He had been invited to conduct a revival meeting at Cross Hill, South Carolina, and, after he had preached every night and twice on Sundays for a full week, he did not see one single conversion, nor one addition to the church by transfer. He was not only disheartened and embarrassed, he was sick over this matter. When the committee of the church offered him forty dollars for the week's ministry, he refused it, telling them that he had not earned it and that he wanted the church to keep it. And keep it they did. Such an experience drove the young man to his knees and to a heart-searching analysis of his spiritual life and his style of preaching.

Although influenced in youth by Dr. Edwin Poteat in the matter of style, and by Prof. Ben E. Greer as to the mastery of any subject to be dealt with, Lee's style is, nevertheless, all his own. He imitates no one but follows a mode of expression that is distinctively his and no other man's. Lee is Lee.

When he is ready to preach, he is taut as a spring, and spiritually, if not physically, leaps to the pulpit when his moment comes. The audience sees him walk to the rostrum, gracefully and with great dignity, but within there is a burning fire of passion to

preach to lost and needy souls. Because of this
inner tenseness, little things, such as movements of
the audience, or scraps of paper, or petals of flowers,
or hymn books falling, or people arriving late, upset
him terribly. But again he is master of the situation,
and he alone is conscious that these things are an-
noying to him.

When Lee preaches he proclaims that which he
believes to be the truth and will do so even if by
such outspokenness he loses favor with many. There
seem to be two parts to most of Lee's sermons:
one into which the preacher deposits all of his
study, preparation, discrimination, lore, and experience; and another wherein these things are forgotten under the powerful sway of the Holy Spirit
reaching out through this servant of God to lost
souls, careless Christians, and devoted believers
in the Lord Jesus Christ. It is into the early part
of his message that Dr. Lee pours his vast vocabulary, so that one sits in awe and admiration of the
orator; in the latter half of the message the servant
is forgotten in the impact of the evangel, as God
is seen in all His glory and His Son in all His beauty.
Lee does not try to be eloquent; he *is* eloquent, and
throws his whole being into the cardinal truths of the
faith that he proclaims. To hear Lee is to observe
sin in its blackness and the ultimate perdition of
the sinner, and to know God in His love and mercy,
and the glorious hope of the child of God through
faith in Christ. And when Lee inveighs against
opponents of Christianity and the Bible, he is like
a volcano overflowing with its vicious lava. In re-
porting a message of this character that Lee gave at

the Florida State Baptist Convention, *The Florida Baptist Witness* states:

> The first afternoon Dr. R. G. Lee of Memphis, Tennessee, spoke with marvelous power. You might as well try to describe the Atlantic Ocean. There was nothing calm and soothing about that address. It was stormy, piercing, and terrific. It was atomic, explosive, and destructive. The modernist and the critics of the Bible not only had nothing to stand on but they were annihilated. There was neither hide nor hair left of them.

Some have criticized Dr. Lee—how easy it is to criticize others!—because he uses too many adjectives in his sermons, particularly in the introductory portions of them. To such censure he replies: "Jesus is worthy of all the adjectives we can use. No astronomer enraptured by a starry night ever accused the night of having too many stars. No man seeking shade in the heat of the day ever said that the tree had too many leaves. The Christ, once in the grave and now on the throne, once in the place of humiliation and now in the place of exaltation, once in the place of wrath and now in the place of worship, once in the place of curse and now in the place of the crown, once in the place of horror and now in the place of honor, is deserving of the best language of men—and the best is as man's mean paint on God's fair lily. It is as impossible to use too many adjectives in describing Jesus as it is to separate arithmetic from figures or grammar from words."

And when some rebuke him for being too sharp in his reproof of others, he replies: "We only use whips on horses that do not pull."

The subject matter of Lee's sermons varies. First of all, he talks about the Lord Jesus as He is seen

in the Scriptures from the first of Genesis to the
last of Revelation. Second, he talks about the Bible
itself. Third, he preaches about sin and its effect
upon men's lives and their utter ruin in its grip.
Fourth, he often discourses on the limitations of
science to meet humanity's needs. Fifth, he sometimes chooses certain chapters from the Bible, as
Isaiah 53 or John 20, and gives expositions of these
chapters. Sixth, he selects single words in the Scriptures—connectives, or nouns, or verbs: the word
"if" or "and"; mountains of the Bible; trees of the
Bible; rivers of the Bible; miracles; or parables.
Seventh, he may take some subject that he calls
"Love Trails of the Word of God," or give biographical sermons on Bible characters, as Moses, Samuel,
David, Peter, Paul, John, etc. Eighth, he may pick
out of the Scriptures certain habits or actions that
men may have had in common: David *ran,* John *ran,*
and Peter *ran.* Ninth, he frequently uses alliteration,
making up a sermon of such words as "worthy,"
"winsome," "working," "wisdom," and "worship."
Dr. Lee looks with disfavor on the choice of flashy
subjects, such as "Open the Door, Richard," or "The
Downfall of a Suspender." Yet he himself will
select something that is quite colorful, though it may
be Biblical, to wit, "Chasing Fleas and Dead Dogs!"
This message has a text, namely, I Samuel 24:14:
"After whom is the king of Israel come out? after
whom dost thou pursue? after a dead dog, after a
flea."

One can hardly tell when the preparation of any
single sermon begins, for there is constant groundwork laid in Lee's wide reading of the Bible and

other literature, in observance of his fellow men, and in his meditations. Strictly speaking, however, while part of each morning is spent in study, Wednesday morning is used to prepare his sermon for the Sunday morning service, and Thursday morning to prepare the message for Sunday night. Lee writes his messages out entirely by hand, for he feels that he can think better through his pen. He hates mediocrity and despises laziness. Consequently, there have been times when he has felt it necessary to write a sermon five or six times, changing it again and again, before it suits him. On other occasions he has prepared and preached a sermon without writing a single word. When he is through, he turns his written messages over to his secretary, Miss Ruth Calvert, for typing on Saturday.

Once a sermon has been prepared, Lee does what he calls "picturizing" the message. We asked him to describe in his own words what he means by "picturizing," and here it is:

> I hardly know how to explain what I mean by "picturizing" my sermons. In a sense it is a sort of memorizing, and yet not really memorizing. I write out my sermons. When I have them typed I read them over a few times, sometimes as many as six times, and as I do, I form pictures of what I have written.
>
> For example, when I talk of the Cross casting its shadow and light from Calvary's hill to Pilate's court, and from Pilate's court to the meeting of the Sanhedrin with Caiaphas, and from there to Gethsemane, and from Gethsemane to the Upper Room, and from the Upper Room in Jerusalem to the Jordan River where He was baptized, and from the Jordan to Nazareth where He was brought up to Bethlehem, and from Bethlehem across the three dumb centuries, and from the three centuries,

Dr. Lee Enjoying a Joke at His Birthday Party at Bellevue Baptist Church, November 11, 1946

At Pinebrook Bible Conference, E. Stroudsburg, Pa. (L. to R.) Dr. Percy B. Crawford, Director of the Young People's Church of the Air, and the Conference; the Author; and Dr. Lee, in 1947

Dr. Lee Baptising Miss Beverlay Patton of the First Baptist Church of Nashville, Tenn.

when no prophet's voice was lifted, to the Temple on Mt.
Moriah, and from there to the Tabernacle in the wilder-
ness, and from there to the bloody doorposts of the
Passover night, and from there to Eden, where Despair
had pitched his black pavilions on man's sterile and
blasted estate—I turn what I have written into Calvary's hill
on one end and the Cross on the other, with its head on
Calvary's hill and its foot in Eden. Underneath this hor-
izontal Cross I picture Pilate, and then the Jewish
Sanhedrin with Caiaphas presiding, and then the Upper
Room with the full moon above, in a house in the city of
Jerusalem; next the Garden of Gethsemane, and then the
Jordan River, and John baptizing Jesus; then Bethlehem
with all the folks related to our Lord. Then I picture
a long bridge, three hundred miles long, across a chasm
marked at the bottom with word "s-i-l-e-n-c-e." From one
end of this bridge a long finger points to the glorious
Temple on Mt. Moriah. Then from Mt. Moriah an
angel flies with a bucket of blood and puts it on the
lintels and posts of one hundred doors. From the Passover
doorposts there is a winding road with a finger pointing
"To Eden," and this road ends where black tents are
pitched in a desert.

As I preach, pictures I have created as I read over
my sermons, roll in upon me. Sometimes I have had to
create two thousand different pictures for one sermon.
I turn my language into pictures, and preach through
pictures, which roll in upon me, and by me, and around
me, by the hundreds as I preach.

This is the best I can describe "picturizing." I never
have a memorized typed page in my mind as I preach,
but always pictures, always.

The test or any man's preaching is its results. Of
what value intellect, knowledge, groundwork, the
finished sermon, oratorical genius, and crowd appeal
if these gifts do not accomplish anything for God?
The greatest speaker on earth, unless he be an instrument of the Holy Spirit of God, will effect

nothing for Him. Lee has marked ability, God-given, but behind all his preparation and all his skill are prayer and submissiveness to the mind and will of God. And the results of his ministry are evident. We are not speaking, particularly, of the counting of heads after a Gospel invitation is given, although the numbers who come forward under Lee's ministry are astonishing. Not every man who makes public profession of faith, however, is a genuine convert, sad to say. It is possible to influence people to rise to their feet and to kneel at the altar on emotional appeal alone. What are the lasting results, in regenerated lives and dedicated hearts? The years have revealed multitudes thus affected under Dr. Lee's preaching. And what is the result in the preacher's own life? The years have disclosed a man increasing in spiritual stature and in favor with God.

Perhaps the most famous sermon in the annals of American Protestantism is Dr. Russell H. Conwell's "Acres of Diamonds." Dr. Conwell, between the years 1870 and 1925, preached this message more than six thousand times, and, through the earnings from it, founded Temple University in Philadelphia. God permitting, we have no doubt that Robert G. Lee's famed message "Pay Day—Some Day" will surpass "Acres of Diamonds," not in the number of times that it is delivered, but in public esteem. Already, midway through the year 1949, "Pay Day—Some Day" has been given nearly four hundred times, and hardly a day goes by that the Memphis pastor does not receive an invitation to preach it in some city or town throughout the United States. Without meaning to disparage Dr. Conwell in any way whatever, it is our own conviction that Dr. Lee's celebrated sermon greatly surpasses "Acres of Diamonds" in its message and in its results, for in "Pay Day—Some Day" the sure judgment of God is clearly told and the Gospel of our Lord Jesus Christ is presented in all its gracious invitation. Many myriads of people —including gamblers, infidels, drunkards, even some who were planning murder, and we make this statement guardedly—have been brought to the place of faith in Jesus Christ as their Saviour, and of making public confession of Him, through the Word proclaimed in "Pay Day—Some Day."

This famous sermon was first presented as a brief talk at a prayer meeting in Edgefield, South Carolina, one Wednesday night in 1919. When the service was over, Mr. E. J. Norris, one of the members of the First Baptist Church in Edgefield, said to Dr. Lee: "You've got something there, my boy. Why don't you make a full-length sermon out of it? I think it is wonderful."

That very night the young pastor went home and sat up until two o'clock the following morning enlarging and polishing the message. It has been revised a little bit from time to time throughout the thirty years that it has been used, but basically it is the same message that it was when it was first delivered.

In addition to preaching "Pay Day—Some Day" throughout various states in the Union, Dr. Lee, ever since he has been in Memphis, has given this message from his own pulpit on the first Sunday of May each year. It is not a short message, for it requires one hour and fifteen minutes for delivery. One might suppose that after some twenty hearings the audiences at the Bellevue Church might fall off. But on the contrary, each year the crowd is larger than the year before, and in the last two years, 1948 and 1949, it has become necessary for the Bellevue Baptist Church to hire Ellis Auditorium, the civic assembly hall, in order to accommodate those who have come to listen to this famous sermon. But even then it was wise to get to the auditorium by 6:30 in the evening to have any assurance whatever of obtaining a good seat. By 7:15 there was standing room only. In 1949, although the two halls of Ellis Auditorium will accommodate 8,650 people, 2,000 were turned away. When more than 10,000 come out to hear—some for the twenty-second time—a message that has been delivered in that city twenty-two times, it is worth hearing.

"Pay Day—Some Day" has recently been filmed as a sound motion picture in technicolor, and thus the famed sermon will reach thousands upon thousands of people who might never hear it otherwise. It is estimated that Dr. Lee has preached this message to approximately 1,000,000 persons. But he is not ubiquitous, and there are many localities that he cannot possibly reach in person, so that this film ought to have a ministry in itself.

The film was shown for the first time at Dr. Lee's home church, Bellevue, on December 7, 1948. The pastor was there with members of his family. The screen replica of Lee's preaching was seen and heard by 1,000 people on that first night, and by full houses at Bellevue on the next three nights. It takes about ninety minutes to show it, and is a very natural reproduction of Dr. Lee's supernatural message.

"Pay Day—Some Day" has never appeared in print to this time, for Dr. Lee has felt that he wanted it to come fresh from his own lips to all those hearing it for the first time. However, he has been persuaded that it may have an even wider ministry in print, and so has consented to its publication in this volume. It is published in full in the chapter that follows. Concerning this message, we quote the words of a dear friend, Dr. Homer A. Hammontree, spoken soon after he heard Dr. Lee give "Pay Day—Some Day": "I do not see how anyone can listen to that message and not be saved!"

Chapter XVI

PAY DAY—SOME DAY

By Robert G. Lee

Arise, go down to meet Ahab king of Israel, which
is in Samaria: behold, he is in the vineyard of
Naboth, whither he is gone down to possess it. And
thou shalt speak unto him, saying, Thus saith the
Lord, Hast thou killed, and also taken possession?
And thou shalt speak unto him, saying, Thus saith
the Lord, In the place where dogs licked the
blood of Naboth shall dogs lick thy blood, even thine.
And of Jezebel also spake the Lord, saying, The dogs
shall eat Jezebel by the wall of Jezreel (I Kings 21:
18, 19, 23).

I introduce to you Naboth. Naboth was a devout
Israelite who lived in the foothill village of Jezreel.
Naboth was a good man. He abhorred that which is
evil and clave to that which is good. In spite
of the persecution of the prophets he did not
shrink from making it known that he was a worshipper of Jehovah. He was an example of one who
had not bowed the knee nor given a kiss to Baal.
Naboth would not change his heavenly principles for
loose expediencies. He would not dilute the stringency
of his personal righteousness for questionable com-

326

promises. Now Naboth had a vineyard surrounding
his house. This little vineyard, fragrant with blossoms
in the days of the budding branch and freighted
with fruit in the days of the vintage, was a cherished
ancestral possession. This vineyard was near the
summer palace of Ahab—situated about twenty miles
from Samaria—a palace unique in its splendor as
the first palace inlaid with ivory.

I introduce to you Ahab—the vile, egotistical,
covetous toad who squatted upon the throne of
Israel—the worst of Israel's evil kings. King Ahab
had command of a nation's wealth and a nation's
army, but he had no command of his lusts and
appetites. Ahab wore rich robes, but he had a
sinning and wicked and troubled heart beneath them.
Ahab ate the finest food the world could supply—
and this food was served to him in dishes splendid
by servants obedient to his every beck and nod—
but he had a starved soul. Ahab lived in palaces
sumptuous within and without, yet he tormented himself for one bit of land more. Ahab was a king, with
a throne and a crown and a scepter, yet he lived
nearly all of his life under the thumb of a wicked woman—a tool in her hands. Ahab has pilloried himself
in the contempt of all right-thinking, right-living,
God-fearing men as a mean and selfish rascal who
was the curse of his country. The Bible introduces
him to us in words more appropriate than these when
it says:

> But there was none like unto Ahab, which did sell
> himself to work wickedness in the sight of the Lord,
> whom Jezebel his wife stirred up. And he did very

abominably in following idols, according to all
things as did the Amorites, whom the Lord cast
out before the children of Israel (I Kings 21;
25-26).

and

And Ahab made a grove; and Ahab did more to
provoke the Lord God of Israel to anger than all
the kings of Israel that were before him (I Kings
16:33).

I introduce to you Jezebel, daughter of Ethbaal,
King of Tyre (I Kings 16:31), and wife of Ahab,
the King of Israel—a king's daughter and a king's
wife, the evil genius at once of her dynasty and of
her country. Infinitely more daring and reckless was
she in her wickedness than was her wicked
husband. Masterful, indomitable, implacable, the in-
stigator and supporter of religious persecution, called
"the authentic author of priestly inquisitions," a
devout worshipper of Baal, she hated anybody and
everybody who spoke against or refused to worship
her false and helpless god. As blunt in her wickedness and as brazen in her lewdness was she as
Cleopatra, fair sorceress of the Nile. She had all the
subtle and successful scheming of Lady Macbeth,
all the adulterous desire and treachery of Potiphar's
wife (Gen. 39:7-20), all the boldness of Mary Queen
of Scots, all the cruelty and whimsical imperiousness
of Katherine of Russia, all the devilish infamy of a
Madame Pompadour, and, doubtless, all the fascination of personality of a Josephine of France. Most
of that which is bad in all evil women found expression through this painted viper of Israel. She
had that rich endowment of nature which a good
woman ought always to dedicate to the service of

her day and generation. But—alas!—this idolatrous
daughter of an idolatrous king of an idolatrous people
engaging with her maidens in worship unto Ashtoreth
—the personification of the most forbidding obscenity,
uncleanness, and sensuality—became the evil genius
who wrought wreck, brought blight, and devised
death. She was the beautiful and malicious adder
coiled upon the throne of the nation.

I introduce to you Elijah, the Tishbite, prophet
of God at a time when by tens of thousands the
people had forsaken God's covenants, thrown down
God's altars, slain God's prophets with the sword
(I Kings 19:10). The young prophet, knowing much
of the glorious past of the now apostate nation,
must have been filled with horror when he learned of
the rank heathenism, fierce cruelties, and reeking
licentiousness of Ahab's idolatrous capital— at a time
when Jezebel "set herself, with Ahab's tacit consent, to extirpate the religion of Jehovah from the
land of Israel." Holy anger burned within him like
an unquenchable Vesuvius or the flames of Marti-
nique. Elijah! Heir to the infinite riches of God he!
Elijah! Attended by the hosts of Heaven he! Little
human companionship he had! But he was not
lonely—because God was with him, and he was
sometimes attended by the hosts of Heaven. He wore
a rough sheepskin cloak, but there was a peaceful,
confident heart beneath it. He ate bird's food and
widow's fare, but was a physical and spiritual
athlete. He had no lease of office or authority, yet
everyone obeyed him. He grieved only when God's
cause seemed tottering. He passed from earth without
dying—into celestial glory. Everywhere where cour-

age is admired and manhood honored and service appreciated he is honored as one of earth's heroes and one of Heaven's saints. He was "a seer, and saw clearly; a hero, and dared valiantly; a great heart, and felt deeply."

And now with these four persons introduced we want to turn to God's Word and see the tragedy of pay day some day! We will see the corn they put into the hopper and then behold the grist that came out the spout.

The first scene in this tragedy of "pay day—some day" is—

I—THE REAL ESTATE REQUEST—"Give me thy vineyard."

> And it came to pass after these things, that Naboth the Jezreelite had a vineyard, which was in Jezreel, hard by the palace of Ahab king of Samaria. And Ahab spake unto Naboth, saying, Give me thy vineyard, that I may have it for a garden of herbs, because it is near unto my house: and I will give thee for it a better vineyard than it; or, if it seem good to thee, I will give thee the worth of it in money (I Kings 21:1-2).

Thus far Ahab was quite within his rights. No intention had he of cheating Naboth out of his vineyard or of killing him to get it. Honestly did he offer to give him its worth in money. Honestly did he offer him a better vineyard for it. Perfectly fair and square was Ahab in this request and, under circumstances ordinary, one would have expected Naboth to put away any mere sentimental attachment which he had for his ancestral inheritance in order that he might please the king of his nation—especially when the king's aim was not to defraud or

rob him. Ahab had not, however, counted upon the
reluctance of all Jews to part with their inheritance
of land. By peculiar tenure every Israelite held his
land, and to all land-holding transactions there was
another party, even God, "who made the heavens and
the earth." Throughout Judah and Israel, Jehovah
was the real owner of the soil; and every tribe
received its territory and every family its inheritance
by lot from Him, with the added condition that the
land should not be sold forever. "The land shall not
be sold for ever: for the land is Mine; for ye are
strangers and sojourners with Me" (Lev. 25:23).
"So shall not the inheritance of the children of
Israel remove from tribe to tribe: for every one of
the children of Israel shall keep himself to the
inheritance of the tribe of his fathers . . . But every
one of the tribes of the children of Israel shall keep
himself to his own inheritance" (Num. 36:7-9).
Thus we see that the permanent sale of the paternal
inheritance was forbidden by law. Ahab forgot—
if he had ever really known it—that for Naboth to
sell for money or to swap for a better vineyard his
little vineyard would seem to that good man like a
denial of his allegiance to the true religion to sell it
when jubilee restoration was neglected in such
idolatrous times.

So, though he was Ahab's nearest neighbor, Naboth, with religious scruples blended with the pride
of ancestry, stood firmly on his rights—and, with
an expression of horror on his face and with tones of
terror in his words, refused to sell or swap his vineyard to the king. Feeling that he must prefer the
duty he owed to God to any danger that might arise

from man, he made firm refusal. Fearing God most
and man least, and obeying the One whom he feared
the most and loved the most, he said: "The Lord forbid it me, that I should give the inheritance of my
fathers unto thee" (I Kings 21:3). True to the
religious teachings of his father with real-hearted loyalty to the covenant God of Israel, he believed that
he held the land in fee simple from God. His father
and grandfather, and doubtless grandfather's father,
had owned the land before him. All the memories of
childhood were tangled in its grapevines. His father's hands, folded now in the dust of death, had
used the pruning blade among the branches, and
because of this every branch and vine were dear. His
mother's hands, now doubtless wrapped in a dust-
stained shroud, had gathered purple clusters from
those bunch-laden boughs, and for this reason he
loved every spot in his vineyard and every branch
on his vines. The ties of sentiment, of religion, and
of family pride bound and endeared him to the place.
So his refusal to sell was quick, firm, final, and
courteous. Then, too, doubtless working or resting
or strolling as he often did in his vineyard hard by
the king's castle, Naboth had had glimpses of strange
and alien sights in that palace. He had seen with
his own eyes what orgies idolatry led to when the
queen was at home in her palace in Jezreel; and
Naboth, deeply pious, felt smirched and hurt at
the very request. He felt that his little plot of ground,
so rich in prayer and fellowship, so sanctified with
sweet and holy memories, would be tainted and be-
fouled and cursed forever if it came into the hands
of Jezebel. So with "the courage of a bird that dares

the wild sea," he took his stand against the king's proposal.

And that brings us to the second scene in this tragedy. It is—

II—THE POUTING POTENTATE—He came "into his house heavy and displeased."

Naboth's quick, firm, courteous, final refusal took all the spokes from the wheels of Ahab's desires and plans. Naboth's refusal was a barrier that turned aside the stream of Ahab's desire and changed it into a foiled and foaming whirlpool of sullen sulks.

> And Ahab came into his house heavy and displeased because of the word which Naboth the Jezreelite had spoken to him: for he had said, I will not give thee the inheritance of my fathers. And he laid him down upon his bed, and turned away his face, and would eat no bread (I Kings 21:4).

What a ridiculous picture! A king acting like a spoiled and sullen child—impotent in disappointment and ugly in petty rage! A king, whose victories over the Syrians have rung through many lands— a conquerer, a slave to himself—whining like a sick hound! A king, rejecting all converse with others, pouting like a spoiled and petulant child that has been denied one trinket in the midst of one thousand playthings! A king, in a chamber "cieled with cedar, and painted with vermillion" (Jer. 22:14), prostituting genius to theatrical trumpery.

Ahab went into his ivory house, while the sun was shining and the matters of the daytime were all astir, and went to bed and "turned his face to the wall"—his lips swollen with his mulish moping, his eyes burning with cheap anger-fire, his wicked heart

stubborn in perverse rebellion. Servants brought him
his meal, plenteously prepared on platters beautiful:
but he "would eat no bread." Doubtless, musicians
came to play skilfully on stringed instruments, but
he drove them all away with imperious gestures and
impatient growlings. He turned from his victuals as
one turns from garbage and refuse. The conqueror
of the Syrians is a low slave to dirt cheap trivialities.
His spirit, now devilishly sullen, is in bondage to
sordid objectives. The giant is bound to earth by
cheap cobwebs.

What an ancient picture we have of great powers
dedicated to mean, ugly, petty things. Think of it!
In the middle of the day, the commander-in-chief of
an army seized by Sergeant Sensitive. General Ahab
made prisoner by Private Pouts! The leader an
army laid low by Corporal Mopishness! A monarch
moaning and blubbering and growlingly refusing to
eat because a man, a good man, because of the commandments of God and because of religious principles, would not sell or swap a little vineyard which
was his by inheritance from his forefathers. Ahab
had lost nothing—had gained nothing. No one had
injured him. No one had made attempt on his life.
Yet he, a king with a great army and a fat treasury,
was acting like a blubbering baby. Cannon ability was
expressing itself in popgun achievement. A massive
giant sprawling on the bed like a dwarf punily pee-
vish! A big whale wallowing and spouting angrily
about because he is denied minnow food! A bear
growling sulkily because he cannot lick a spoon
in which is a bit of honey! An eagle shrieking and
beating his wings in the dust of his own dis-

pleasure like a quarreling sparrow fussily fighting
with other sparrows for the crumbs in the dust of
a village street! A lion sulkily roaring because he
was not granted the cheese in a mouse trap! A
battleship cruising for a sham battle!

What an ancient picture of great powers and
talents prostituted to base and purposeless ends
and withheld from the service of God! What an
ancient spectacle! And how modern and up-to-date,
in this respect, was Ahab, king of Israel. What a
likeness to him in conduct today are many talented
men and women. I know men and women—you know
men and women—with diamond and ruby abilities
who are worth no more to God through the churches
than a punctured Japanese nickel in a Chinese
bazaar! So many there are who, like Ahab, withhold their talents from God—using them in the
service of the devil. People there are, not a few, who
have pipe-organ abilities and make no more music
for the causes of Christ than a wheezy saxophone
in an idiot's hands. People there are, many of them,
who have incandescent-light powers who make no
more light for God than a smoky barn lantern, with
smoke-blackened globe, on a stormy night. People
there are—I know them and you know them—with
locomotive powers doing pushcart work for God.
People there are—and how sad 'tis true—who have
steam-shovel abilities who are doing teaspoon work
for God. Yes! Now look at this overfed bull bellowing
for a little spot of grass outside his own vast
pasture lands—and, if you are withholding talents
and powers from the service of God, receive the rebuke of the tragic and ludicrous picture.

And now, consider the third scene in this tragedy of "pay day—some day." It is—
III—THE WICKED WIFE—"And Jezebel his wife."

When Ahab would "eat no bread," the servants went and told Jezebel. What she said to them, we do not know. Something of what she said to Ahab we *do* know. Puzzled and provoked at the news that her husband would not eat—that he had gone to bed when it was not bedtime—Jezebel went to investigate. She found him in bed with his face turned to the wall, his lips swollen with mulish moping, his eyes burning with cheap anger-fire, his heart stubborn in wicked rebellion. He was groaningly mournful and peevishly petulant—having, up to the moment when she stood by his bedside, refused to eat or cheer up in the least.

At first, in a voice of solicitousness, she sought the reason of his choler. In "sweet" and anxious concern she said: "Why is thy spirit so sad, that thou eatest no bread?" (I Kings 21:5). And then, as the manner of women is unto this day, she doubtless put her hand on his forehead to see if he had temperature. He had temperature all right. Like the tongue of the wicked, he was set on fire of hell. Then he told her, every word full of petulance and mopish peevishness as he spoke: "Because I spake unto Naboth the Jezreelite, and said unto him, Give me thy vineyard for money; or else, if it please thee, I will give thee another vineyard for it: and he answered, I will not give thee my vineyard!" (I Kings 21:6).

Every word he said stung like a whip upon a naked back this wickedly unscrupulous woman who had never had any regard of the welfare of anyone who did not worship her god, Baal—who never had any conscientious regard for the rights of others, or for others who did not yield to her whimsical imperiousness.

Hear her derisive laugh as it rings out in the palace like the shrill cackle of a wild fowl that has returned to its nest and has found a serpent therein! With her tongue, sharp like a razor, she prods Ahab as an ox driver prods with sharp goad the ox which does not want to press his neck into the yoke, or as one whips with a rawhide a stubborn mule. With profuse and harsh laughter this old gay and gaudy guinea of Satan derided this king of hers for a cowardly buffoon and sordid jester. What hornet-like sting in her sarcasm! What wolf-mouth fierceness in her every reproach! What tiger-fang cruelty in her expressed displeasure! What fury in the shricking of her rebuke! What bitter bitterness in the teasing taunts she hurled at him for his scrupulous timidity! Her bosom with anger was heaving! Her eyes were flashing with rage under the surge of hot anger that swept over her.

"Are you not the king of this country?" she chides bitingly, her tongue sharp like a butcher's blade. "Can not you command and have it done?" she scolds as a common village hag who has more noise than wisdom in her words. "Can you not seize and keep?" she cries with reproach. "I thought you told me you were king in these parts! And here you are crying like a baby and will not eat anything because you do not have courage to take a bit of land. You! Ha! Ha! Ha! Ha! You the king of Israel, and allow yourself to be disobeyed and defied by a common clodhopper from the country. You are more courteous and considerate of him than you are of your queen! Shame on you! But you leave it to me! I will get the vineyard for you, and all that I require is that you ask no questions. Leave it to me, Ahab!"

> And Jezebel his wife said unto him, Dost thou now govern the kingdom of Israel? arise, and eat bread, and let thine heart be merry: I will give thee the vineyard of Naboth the Jezreelite! (I Kings 21:7).

Her rejoinder to his weakness reminds us so much of Lady Macbeth's rebuke to Macbeth on the night of King Duncan's murder, when he came back with the dagger in his hand, trembling all over, and she asked him to take the daggers back to the murder spot and "smear the sleepy grooms with blood." "Infirm of purpose; give me the daggers!" Or her words make us to think of other words Lady Macbeth spoke when she was working to get Macbeth's courage to the "sticking place":

> Was the hope drunk
> Wherein you dressed yourself? hath it slept since?
> And wakes it now to look so green and pale
> At what it did so freely? . . . Art thou afraid
> To be the same in thine own act and valour
> As thou art in desire? Wouldst thou have that
> Which thou esteemest the ornament of life,
> And live a coward in thine own esteem?

Ahab knew Jezebel well enough to know assuredly that she would do her best, or her devil's worst, to do what she said she would do. So slowly, as a turtle crawls out of the cold mud when the hot sunshine hits it, he came out of his sulks, somewhat as a snake arouses and uncoils from winter sleep. He doubtless asked her, with a show of reluctant eagerness, how she was going to get Naboth's vineyard. She, if she acted as human nature naturally expresses itself, tickled him under the chin with her lily white and bejewelled fingers, or kissed him peckingly on the cheeks with her lips screwed in a tight knot, and said something akin to these words: "That's my secret just now; just leave it to me!"

Now, let us ask, who can so inspire a man to noble purposes as a noble woman? And who can so thoroughly degrade a man as a wife of unworthy tendencies? Back of the statement, "And Ahab the son of Omri did evil in the sight of the Lord above all that were before him" (I Kings 16:30) and back of what Elijah spoke, "Thou hast sold thyself to work evil in the sight of the Lord" (I Kings 21:25), is the statement explaining both the other statements: "Whom Jezebel his wife stirred up." She was the polluted reservoir from which the streams of his own iniquity found mighty increase. She was the poisonous pocket from which his cruel fangs fed. She was the sulphurous pit wherein the fires of his own iniquity found fuel for intenser burning. She was the devil's grindstone which furnished sharpening for his weapons of wickedness.

I suppose Ahab considered himself the master of his wife. But it was her mastery over him that stirred him up to more and mightier wickedness than his own heart was capable of conceiving, than his own mind was capable of planning, than his own will was capable of executing.

Yes—we ask again—who can so degrade a man as a woman of wicked tendencies and purposes? Is not a woman without spiritual religion and love of God in her heart like a rainbow without color?— like a strong chlorinized well from which the thirsty drink?—like a heated stove whose heat is infection? —like kissing lips with deadly poison spread?

What a tragedy when any woman thinks more of paint than purity, of vulgarity than virtue, of pearls than principles, of adornment than righteous adoration, of hose and hats than holiness, of dress than duty, of mirrors than manners! What a tragedy when any woman sacrifices decency on the altar of degradation—visualizing the slimy, the tawdry, the tinseled! Know ye not yet, ye women, that the degeneracy of womanhood helps the decay of manhood? Know ye not that when woman is lame morally man limps morally?—that when woman slips morally man slumps morally?—when woman fags in spiritual ideals man sags in spiritual ideals? Study history as much as you please and read the Bible as often as you will, and you will see that the moral and spiritual life of no nation, no community, no city, no village, no countryside, no home, no school, no church ever rises any higher or flows any stronger than the spiritual life of the women.

Who was it dominated the papacy in its most shameful days? Lucretia Borgia—a woman. Who was it really ordered the massacre of Saint Bartholomew's day? Catherine de Medici—a woman. Who was it breathed fury through Robespierre in those dark and bloody days in France when the guillotine was chopping off the heads of the royalty? A woman

—determined, devilish, dominant! Who was it who caused Samson to have his eyes punched out and to be a prisoner of the Philistines, after he had been judge in Israel for twenty years? Delilah— a woman! Who was it caused David to stake his crown for a caress? Bathsheba—a woman. Who was it danced Herod into hell? Herodias—a woman! Who was it who was like a heavy chain around the neck of Governor Felix for life or death, for time and eternity? Drusilla—a woman! Who was it, by lying and diabolical stratagem, sent the spotless Joseph to jail because he refused her dirty, improper proposal? Potiphar's wife. Who was it suggested to Haman that he build a high gallows on which to hang Mordecai, the Jew? Zeresh—a woman—his wife! Who was it told Job in the midst of his calamities, financial and physical, to curse God and die? A woman—his wife. Who was it ruined the career of Charles Stewart Parnell and delayed Home Rule for Ireland in the good days of good Queen Victoria? Kitty O'Shea—a woman. Who was it caused Anthony to throw away the world at the battle of Actium and follow the enchantress of the Nile back to Egypt? The enchantress herself, Cleopatra,—a woman —the lovely serpent coiled on the throne of the Ptolemies.

So also it was a woman, a passionate and ambitious idolatress, even Jezebel, who mastered Ahab. Take the stirring crimes of any age, and at the bottom more or less consciously concerned, the world, almost invariably, finds a woman. Only God Almighty knows the full story of the foul plots hatched by women. This was true, as we shall presently see, with the two under discussion now. But let me say, incidentally, if women have mastered men for evil, they have also mastered them for good—and we gladly make declaration that some of the fairest and most fragrant flowers that grow in the garden of God and some of the sweetest and most luscious fruit that ripens in God's spiritual orchards are there because of woman's faith, woman's love, woman's prayer, woman's virtue, woman's tears, woman's devotion to Christ. But we must not depart further from the objective of this message to discuss that. Let us come to the next terrible scene in this tragedy of sin.

The next scene is—

IV—A MESSAGE MEANING MURDER—"She wrote letters."

Jezebel wrote letters to the elders of Jezreel. And in these letters she made definite and subtle declaration that some terrible sin had been committed in their city, for which it was needful that a fast should be proclaimed in order to avert the wrath of Heaven.

> She wrote letters in Ahab's name, and sealed them with his seal, and sent the letters unto the elders and to the nobles that were in his city, dwelling with Naboth. And she wrote in the letters, saying, Proclaim a fast, and set Naboth on high among the people: and set two men, sons of Belial, before him, to bear witness against him, saying, Thou didst blaspheme God and the king. And then carry him out, and stone him, that he may die (I Kings 21:8-10).

This letter, with cynical disregard of decency, was a hideous mockery in the name of religion. Once get the recusant citizen accused of blasphemy,

and, by a divine law, the property of the blasphemer
and rebel went to the crown. "Justice! How many
traitors to sacred truth have dragged the innocent
to destruction!"

Surely black ink never wrote a fouler plot or
death scheme on white paper since writing was
known among men. Every drop had in it the adder's
poison. Every syllable of every word of every line
of every sentence was full of hate toward him who
had done only good continually. Every letter of
every syllable was but the thread which, united
with other threads, made the hangman's noose for
him who had not changed his righteous principles
for the whim of a king. The whole letter was a
diabolical death-warrant.

The letters being written, they must be sealed;
and the sealing was done, as all these matters of
letter writing and sealing were done, by rubbing ink
on the seal, moistening the paper, and pressing the
seal thereon. And when Jezebel had finished with
her iniquitous pen, she asked Ahab for his signet
ring; with that ring she affixed the royal seal. She
sealed them with Ahab's ring! (I Kings 21:8). When
Ahab gave it to her he knew it meant crime of some
sort, but he asked no questions. Moreover, Jezebel's
deeds showed that when she went down to market,
as it were, she would have in her basket a nice vineyard for her husband when she returned. She said
to herself: "This man Naboth has refused my honorable lord on religious grounds, and by all the gods
of Baal, I will get him yet on these very same
grounds." She understood perfectly the passion of a
devout Jew for a public fast; and she knew that

nothing would keep the Jews away. Every Jew and every member of his household would be there.

"Proclaim a fast"! Fasting has ever been a sign of humiliation before God, of humbling one's self in the dust before the "high and lofty One that inhabiteth eternity." The idea in calling for a fast was clearly to declare that the community was under the anger of God on account of a grave crime committed by one of its members, which crime is to be exposed and punished. Then, too, the fast involved a cessation of work, a holiday, so that the citizens would have time to attend the public gathering.

"Set Naboth on high!" "On high" meant before the bar of justice, not in the seat of honor. "On high" meant in the seat of the accused, and not in the seat to be desired. "On high" meant that Naboth was put where every eye could watch him closely and keenly observe his bearing under the accusation. "And set two men, base fellows, before him." How illegal she was in bringing about his death in a legal way! For the law required two witnesses in all cases where the punishment was death. "At the mouth of two witnesses, or three witnesses, shall he . . . be put to death" (Deut. 17:6). The witnesses required by Jezebel were men of no character, men who would take bribes and swear to any lie for gain.

And let them "bear witness against him"! In other words, put him out of the way by judicial murder, not by private assassination. "And then carry him out, and stone him, that he may die"! A criminal was not to be executed within a city, as that would defile it! Thus Christ was crucified outside the walls

of Jerusalem! We see that Jezebel took it for granted
that Naboth would be condemned.

And so one day, while Naboth worked in his
vineyard, the letters came down to Jezreel. And one
evening, while Naboth talked at the cottage door
with his sons or neighbors, the message meaning
murder was known to the elders of the city. And that
night, while he slept with the wife of his bosom, the
hounds of death let loose from the kennels of hell
by the jewel-adorned fingers of a king's daughter
and a king's wife were close on his heels. The message meaning murder was known to many but not
to him, until they came and told him that a fast had
been proclaimed—proclaimed because God had been
offended at some crime and that His wrath must be
appeased and the threatening anger turned away,
and he himself, all unconscious of any offense toward God or the king, set in the place of the accused,
even "on high among the people," to be tried as a
conspicuous criminal.

Consider now—

V—THE FATAL FAST— "They proclaimed a fast."

And what concern they must have created in the
household of Naboth, when they knew that Naboth
was to be "set on high," even in the "seat of the accused," even before the bar of "justice," because of
a ferocious message calling religion in to attest a
lie. And what excitement there was in the city when,
with fawning readiness to carry out her vile commands, the elders and nobles "fastened the minds"
of the people upon the fast—proclaimed as if some
great calamity were overhanging the city for their
sins like a black cloud portending a storm, and pro-

claimed as if something must be done at once to avert the doom. Curious throngs hurried to the fast to see him who had been accused of the crime which made necessary the appeasing of the threatening wrath of an angered God.

Yes, the rulers of Jezreel, "either in dread of offending one whose revenge they knew was terrible, or eager to do a service to one to whom in temporal matters they were so largely indebted, or moved with envy against their own iniquity, carried out her instructions to the letter." They were ready and efficient tools in her hands. No doubt she had tested their character as her "butcher boys" in the slaughter of the prophets of the Lord (I Kings 18:4,13).

And they did! "And there came in two men, children of Belial, and sat before him" (I Kings 21:13). Satan's hawks ready to bring death to God's harmless sparrow! Satan's eagles ready to bury their cruel talons in God's innocent dove. Satan's bloody wolves ready to kill God's lamb! Satan's boars ready with keen tusks to rip God's stag to shreds! Reckless and depraved professional perjurers they were! "And the men of Belial witnessed against him, even against Naboth, in the presence of the people, saying, Naboth did blaspheme God and the king" (I Kings 21:13).

Then strong hands jerked Naboth out of the seat of the accused. Doubtless muttering curses the while, they dragged him out from among the throngs of people, while children screamed and cried, while women shrieked in terror, while men moved in confusion and murmured in consternation. They dragged him roughly to a place outside the walls of the city and with stones they beat his body to the ground. Naboth fell to the ground as lily by hailstones beaten to earth, as stately cedar uprooted by furious storm. His head by stones is crushed, as eggs crushed by heel of giant. His legs are splintered! His arms are broken! His ribs are crushed. Bones stick out from the mass of human flesh as fingers of ivory from pots of red paint. Brains, emptied from his skull, are scattered about. Blood splatters like crimson rain. Naboth's eyes roll in sockets of blood. His tongue between broken jaws becomes still. His mauled body becomes—at last—still. His last gasp is a sigh. Naboth is dead—dead for cursing God and the king as many were led to believe!

And we learn from II Kings 9:26, that by the savage law of those days his innocent sons were involved in his overthrow. They, too, that they might not claim the inheritance, were slain. And Naboth's property, left without heirs, reverted to the crown.

Thus it came to pass that in an orderly fashion, in the name of religion and in the name of the king, they stoned Naboth and his kin to death. And Naboth really fell, not by the king's hand, but by the condemnation of his fellow citizens. Yes, the old-fashioned conservatism of Naboth was, in the judgment of many, sorely out of place in that "progressive" state of society. No doubt Naboth's righteous austerity had made him extremely unpopular in many ways in "progressive Jezreel." And since Jezebel carried out her purpose in a perfectly legal and orderly way and in a "wonderfully" democratic manner, we see a fine picture of autocracy working by democratic methods. And when these "loyally patriotic citizens" of Jezreel had left the bodies of Naboth and his sons to be devoured by the wild dogs which prowled after nightfall in and around the city, they sent and told Queen Jezebel that her bloody orders had been bloodily and completely obeyed! "Then they sent to Jezebel, saying, Naboth is stoned, and is dead" (I Kings 21:14).

I do not know where Jezebel was when she received the news of Naboth's death. Maybe she was out on the lawn watching the fountains splash. Maybe she was in the sun parlor, or somewhere listening to the musicians thrum on their instruments. But, if I judge this painted human viper by her nature, I say she received the tragic news with devilish delight, with jubilant merriment. What was it to her that yonder, over twenty miles away, sat a little woman who the night before had her husband but who now washes his crushed and ghastly face with her tears? What did it matter to her that in Jezreel only yesterday her sons ran to her at her call but today are mangled in death? What did it matter to her that outside the city walls the dogs licked the blood of a godly husband? What mattered it to her that Jehovah God had been defied, His commandments broken, His altars splattered with pagan mud, His holy Name profaned? What mattered it to her that the worship of God had been dishonored? What did she care if a wife, tragically widowed by murder, walked life's way in loneliness? What did she care that there was lamentation and grief and great mourning, "Rachel weeping for her childen because they were not"? What did she care if justice had been outraged just so she had gotten the little plot of land close by their palace, within which was evil girt with diadem? Nothing! Did pang grip her heart because innocent blood had been shed? Just as well ask if the ravenous lion mourns over the lamb it devours.

Trippingly, as a gay dancer, she hurried in to where Ahab sat. With profuse caresses and words glib with joy she told him the "good" news. She had about her the triumphant manner of one who has accomplished successfully what others had not dared attempt. Her "tryout" in getting the vineyard was a decided "triumph." She had "pulled the stunt." She had been "brave" and "wise"—and because of this her husband now could arise and hie him down to the vineyard and call it his own.

In her words and manner there was jubilant elation bordering on the satanic. "Arise!" she said, "Get thee down and take possession of the vineyard of Naboth! I *told* thee I would get his vineyard for thee. And I got for *nothing* what thou wast going to give a better vineyard for!"

> And it came to pass, when Jezebel heard that Naboth was stoned, and was dead, that Jezebel said to Ahab, Arise, take possession of the vineyard of Naboth the Jezreelite, which he refused to give thee for money: for Naboth is not alive, but dead (I Kings 21:15).

And it was the plot hatched in her own mind and it was her hand, her lily-white hand, her queen's hand, that wrote the letters that made this tragic statement true.

And the next scene in this tragedy of "pay day—some day" is

VI—THE VISIT TO THE VINEYARD—"Ahab rose up
to go down to the vineyard."

How Jezebel must have paraded with pride before Ahab when she went with tidings that the vineyard which he wanted to buy was now his for nothing! How keen must have been the sarcasm of her
attitude when she made it known by word and manner that she had succeeded where he failed—and
at less cost! How gloatingly victorious were the
remarks which she made which kept him warmly
reminded that she had kept her "sacred" promise!
What a lovely fabric, stained and dyed red with
Naboth's blood, she spread before him for his "comfort" from the loom of her evil machinations!

"And it came to pass, when Ahab heard that Naboth was dead, that Ahab rose up to go down to the
vineyard of Naboth the Jezreelite, to take possession
of it" (I Kings 21:16). Ahab rose up to go down—
from Samaria to Jezreel. He gave orders to his
royal wardrobe keeper to get out his king's clothes,
because he had a little "business" trip to make to
look over some property that had come to him by the
shrewdness of his wife in the real estate market!

Yes, Naboth, the good man who "feared the Lord,"
is dead; and Ahab expresses no condemnation of this
awful conspiracy, culminating in such a tragic horror. Though afraid or restrained by his conscience
from committing murder himself, he had no scruple
in availing himself of the results of such crime when
perpetrated by another. He flattered himself that,
by the splendid genius of his queen in bloody matters,
he, though having no part in the crime which did

Naboth to death, might, as well as another, "receive the benefit of his dying."

And you will notice just here that not one noble
or elder had divulged the terrible secret which had
given the semblance of legality to atrocious villainy.
And Ahab, rejoicing in the bloody garment woven on
the loom of his wife's evil machinations, gave orders
to those in charge of the livery stables to get ready
his royal chariot for an unexpected trip. Jehu and
Bidkar, the royal charioteers, make ready the great
horses such as kings had in those days. Jehu was
the speed-breaking driver of his day, known as the
one who drove furiously. The gilded chariot is drawn
forth. The fiery horses are harnessed and to the king's
chariot hitched. The outriders, in gorgeous garments
dressed, saddle their horses and make ready to
accompany the king in something of military state.
Then, amid the clatter of prancing hoofs and the
loud breathing of the chariot horses—eager-eyed,
alert, strong-muscled, bellows-lunged, stouthearted,
and agile of feet—Jehu drives the horses to the
chariot hitched up to the palace steps. Out from
the palace doors, Jezebel walking, almost strutting,
proudly and gaily at his side, comes Ahab. Down the
steps he goes while Jezebel, perhaps, waves a bejeweled hand to him or speaks a "sweet" good-bye.
Bidkar opens the chariot door. Ahab steps in. Then,
with the crack of his whip or a sharp command by
word of mouth, Jehu sends the great horses on their
way—away from the palace steps, away from the
palace grounds, away through the gates, away,
accompanied by the outriders, away down the road
to Jezreel!

Where is *God?* Where is God? Is He blind that He cannot see? Is He deaf that He cannot hear? Is He dumb that He cannot speak? Is He paralyzed that He cannot move? *Where is God?* Well, wait a minute, and we shall see.

Over there in the palace Jezebel said to Ahab, her husband: "Arise! Get thee down and take possession of the vineyard of Naboth." And over yonder in the wilderness way, out yonder where the tall cedars waved like green plumes against a silver shield against the moon blossoming in its fulness like a great jonquil in the garden of the patient stars, out yonder where the only music of the night was the weird call of whippoorwill and the cough of coyote and the howl of wolf, out yonder God had an eagle-eyed, hairy, stouthearted prophet, a great physical and spiritual athlete, Elijah. "And the Word of the Lord came to Elijah." And God said to Elijah: "Arise, go down."

Over here, in the palace, Jezebel said to Ahab: "Arise, get thee down!" And out there, near Carmel, God said to Elijah: "Arise!" I am so glad that I live in a universe where, when the devil has his Ahab to whom he can say, "Arise," God has His Elijah to whom *He* can say, "Arise!"

> And the Word of the Lord came to Elijah the Tishbite, saying, Arise, go down to meet Ahab king of Israel, which is in Samaria: behold, he is in the vineyard of Naboth, whither he is gone down to possess it. And thou shalt speak unto him, saying, Thus saith the Lord, Hast thou killed, and also taken possession? And thou shalt speak unto him, saying, Thus saith the Lord, In the place where dogs

On the Steps of the Bellevue Baby Bungalow, Given to the Bellevue Baptist Church by Dr. and Mrs. Lee in 1947. With the Pastor and His Wife Are Nancy Outland, Daughter of Mr. and Mrs J. B. Outland, and Cloid Riley Kidd, Son of Mr. and Mrs. S. E. Kidd. Mr. Kidd is Superintendent of the Bellevue Sunday School

A Portion of the Throng at Crump Stadium, Memphis, for the Southern Baptist Cotvention, May, 1948

licked the blood of Naboth shall dogs lick thy
blood, even thine (I Kings 21: 17-19).

As Ahab goes down to Jezreel, the voice of Jehu,
as he restrains the fiery horses, or the lash of his
whip as he urges them on, attracts the attention
of the grazing cattle in adjacent pasture land. The
sound of clanking hoofs of cantering horses resounds
in every glen by the roadway. The gilded chariot
catches the light of the sun and reflects it brightly,
but he who rides therein is unmindful of the blood-
stains on the ground where Naboth died. Dust
clouds arise from the chariot's wheels and wild
winds blow them across the fields where the plowman
or the reaper wonders who goes so swiftly along the
highway. The neighing steeds announce to all that
Ahab's royal horses tire not in carrying him down
from Samaria to Jezreel. And soon many know that
the chariot carried the king who was going down to
possess what had reverted to the crown, even the
vineyard of Naboth, which Naboth refused to sell
to him. Would the "game" be worth the "candle"?
Would Ahab learn that sin buys pleasure at the price
of peace? We shall see—and that right soon!

And that brings us to the other scene in this
tragedy of "pay day—some day." It is—

VII—The Alarming Appearance—"The Word of the
Lord came to Elijah."

The journey of twenty-odd miles from Samaria to
Jezreel is over. Jehu brings the horses to a stop
outside the gate to the vineyard. The horses stretch
their necks trying to get slack on the reins. They
have stood well the furious pace at which they have

been driven. Around the rim of their harness is the foam of their sweat. On their flanks are, perhaps, the marks of Jehu's whip. They breathe as though their great lungs were a tireless bellows. The out-riders line up in something of military formation. The hands of ready servants open the gate to the vineyard. Bidkar opens the chariot door. And Ahab steps out into Naboth's vineyard. There, no doubt, he sees, in the soft soil, Naboth's footprints. Close by, doubtless, the smaller footprints of his wife he sees. Naboth is dead, and the coveted vineyard is now Ahab's through the "gentle scheming" of the queen of his house. Perhaps Ahab, as he walks into the vineyard, sees Naboth's pruning hook among the vines. Or he notices the fine trellis work which Naboth's hands had fastened together for the growing vines. Perhaps, in a corner of the vineyard is a seat where Naboth and his sons rested after the day's toil, or a well where sparkling waters refreshed the thirsty or furnished water for the vines in time of drouth.

Ahab walks around his newly-gotten vineyard. The rows of vines glisten in the sunlight. Maybe a breeze moves the leaves on the vines. Ahab admires trellis and cluster. As he walks, he plans how he will have the royal gardener to pull up those vines and plant cucumbers, squash, garlic, onions, cabbage, and other vegetables that he may have his "garden of herbs."

And while Ahab strolls among the vines that Na-both tended, what is it that appears? Snarling wild beasts? No. Black clouds full of threatening storm? No, not that. Flaming lightning which dazzles him?

No. War chariots of his ancient enemies rumbling
along the road? No. An oncoming flood sweeping
things before it? No; not a flood. A tornado goring
the earth? No. A huge serpent threatening to en-
circle him and crush his bones in its deadly coils?
No; not a serpent. What then? What alarmed Ahab
so? Let us follow him and see.

As Ahab goes walking through the rows of vines,
he begins to plan how he will have that vineyard
arranged by his royal gardener, how flowers will
be here and vegetables yonder and herbs there.
As he converses with himself, suddenly a shadow falls
across his path. Quick as a flash Ahab whirls on his
heels, and there, before him, stands Elijah, prophet
of the living God. Elijah's cheeks are swarthy; his
eye is keen and piercing; like coals of fire, his eyes
burn with righteous indignation in their sockets;
his bosom heaves; his head is held high. His only
weapon is a staff; his only robe a sheepskin, and
a leather girdle about his loins. Like an apparition
from the other world, like Banquo's ghost at Macbeth's feast, Elijah, with suddenness terrifying, stands
before Ahab. Ahab had not seen Elijah for five years.
Ahab thought Elijah had been cowed and silenced
by Jezebel, but now the prophet confronts him with
his death-warrant from the Lord God Almighty.

To Ahab there is an eternity of agony in the
few moments they stand thus, face to face, eye to eye,
soul to soul! His voice is hoarse, like the cry of
a hunted animal. He trembles like a hunted stag before the mouths of fierce hounds. Suddenly his face
goes white. His lips quiver. He had gone to take
possession of a vineyard, coveted for a garden of

herbs; and there he is face to face with righteousness, face to face with honor, face to face with judgment. The vineyard, with the sun shining upon it now, is as black as if it were part of the midnight which has gathered in judgment. Like Poe's raven "his soul from out that shadow shall be lifted—nevermore."

"And Ahab said to Elijah, Hast thou found me, O mine enemy?" (I Kings 21:20). And Elijah, without a tremor in his voice, his eyes burning their way into Ahab's guilty soul, answered: "I have found thee: because thou hast sold thyself to work evil in the sight of the Lord." Then, with every word a thunderbolt, and every sentence a withering denunciation, Elijah continued: "God told me to ask you this: Hast thou killed, and also taken possession? . . . Thus saith the Lord, In the place where dogs licked the blood of Naboth shall dogs lick thy blood, even thine . . . Behold, I will bring evil upon thee, and will take away thy posterity . . . And will make thine house like the house of Jeroboam the son of Nebat, and like the house of Baasha the son of Ahijah, for the provocation wherewith thou hast provoked Me to anger, and made Israel to sin!" And then, plying other words mercilessly like a terrible scourge to the cringing Ahab, Elijah said: "And of Jezebel also spake the Lord, saying, The dogs shall eat Jezebel by the wall of Jezreel. Him that dieth of Ahab in the city the dogs shall eat: and him that dieth in the field shall the fowls of the air eat."

And, with these words, making Ahab to cower as one cowers and recoils from a hissing adder, filling

Ahab's vineyard to be haunted with ghosts and the clusters thereof to be full of blood, Elijah went his way—as was his custom so suddenly to appear and so quickly to disappear. Ahab had sold himself for nought, as did Achan for a burial robe and a useless ingot, as did Judas for thirty pieces of silver which so burned his palms and so burned his conscience and so burned his soul until he found relief in the noose at the rope's end. And when Ahab got back in the chariot to go back to Jezebel— the vile toad who squatted upon the throne to be again with the beautiful adder coiled upon the throne—the hoofs of the horses pounding the road pounded into his guilty soul Elijah's words: "Some day—the dogs will lick thy blood! Some day the dogs will eat Jezebel—by the ramparts of Jezreel." God had spoken! Would it come to pass?

And that brings us to the last scene in this tragedy of "pay day—some day." It is—

VIII—PAY DAY—SOME DAY.

Does pay day come? As to Ahab and Jezebel, pay day comes as certainly as night follows day, because sin carries in itself the seed of its own fatal penalty. Dr. Mcyer says: "According to God's constitution of the world, the wrongdoer will be abundantly punished." The fathers sow the wind and the children reap the whirlwind. One generation labors to scatter tares, and the next generation reaps tares and retribution immeasurable. To the individual who goes not the direction God points, a terrible pay day comes. To the nation which forgets God, pay day will come in the awful realization of the truth that the "nations that forget God shall be turned into hell." When nations trample on the principles of the Almighty, the result is that the world is beaten with many stripes. We have seen nations slide into Gehenna—and the smoke of their torment has gone up before our eyes day and night.

To the home that has no room for the Christ, death and graveclothes are certain. "Ichabod" will be written about the church that soft-pedals on unpleasant truth or that stands not unwaveringly for "the faith once delivered"—and it will acknowledge its retribution in that it will become "a drifting sepulchre manned by a frozen crew."

A man can prostitute God's holy Name to profane lips if he will, but he is forewarned as to the pay day in the words: "The Lord will not hold him guiltless that taketh His Name in vain."

A man can, if he will, follow the way of some wicked woman; but God leaves him not without warning as to the pay day, in the words:

> He goeth after her straightway, as an ox goeth to the slaughter, or as a fool to the correction of the stocks; till a dart strike through his liver; as a bird hasteth to the snare, and knoweth not that it is for his life . . . For she hath cast down many wounded: yea, many strong men have been slain by her. Her house is the way to hell, going down to the chambers of death (Prov. 7:22,23; 26,27).

People can drink booze, if they will, and offer the damnable bottle to others, if they will, but the certainty of pay day—some day is read in the words: "No drunkard shall inherit the kingdom of God," and in the words: "At last it biteth like

a serpent, and stingeth like an adder." The certainty
of pay day—some day for all who regard not God
or man is set forth in the words of an unknown
poet:

> You'll pay. The knowledge of your acts will weigh
> Heavier on your mind each day,
> The more you climb, the more you gain,
> The more you'll feel the nagging strain.
> Success will cower at the threat
> Of retribution. Fear will fret
> Your peace and bleed you for the debt;
> Conscience collects from every crook
> More than the worth of what he took,
> You only thought you got away
> But in the night you'll pay and pay.

Churchill expressed the certainty of God's retributive justice when, speaking of Mussolini, he
said: "Mussolini is swept into the maelstrom of his
own making. The flames of war he kindled burn
himself. He and his people are taking the stinging
lash of the whip they applied to Ethiopia and
Albania. They pay for Fascist sins with defeat,
despair, death. Mussolini's promise of life like a
lion turns into existence of a beaten cur!"

All these statements are but verification of Bible
truth:

> Whoso diggeth a pit shall fall therein: and he
> that rolleth a stone, it will return upon him
> (Prov. 26:27).
> Therefore shall they eat of the fruit of their
> own way, and be filled with their own devices. For
> the turning away of the simple shall slay them, and
> the prosperity of fools shall destroy them (Prov.
> 1:31, 32).
> Even as I have seen, they that plow iniquity, and
> sow wickedness, reap the same (Job 4:8).

"The gods are just—and of our vices made instruments to scourge us."

When I was pastor of the First Baptist Church of New Orleans, all that I preached and taught was sent out over the radio. In my "fan mail" I received letters from a young man who called himself "Chief of the Kangaroo Court." Many nasty critical things he said. Sometimes he wrote a nice line—and a nice line was in all the vulgar things he wrote like a gardenia in a garbage can. One day. I received a telephone call from a nurse in the Charity Hospital of New Orleans. It was about this fellow who so often dipped his pen in slop, who seldom thrust his pen into nectar. She said: "Pastor, there is a young man down here whose name we do not know, who will not tell us his name. All he will tell us is that he is chief of the Kangaroo Court. He is going to die. He says that you are the only preacher he has ever heard—and he has never seen you. He wants to see you. Will you come down?" "Yes," I replied. And I quit what I was doing and hurried down to the hospital.

The young nurse met me at the entrance to the charity ward and took me in. Inside were several beds against the wall on one side and against the wall on the other side. And in a place by itself was another bed. To this bed, on which lay a young man about eighteen or nineteen years old, slender, hollow-eyed, nervous, the nurse led me. "This is the chief of the Kangaroo Court," she said simply.

I looked upon the young man. "Hello," I said kindly.

"Howdy do?" he answered, in a voice that was half a snarl.

"What can I do for you?" I asked, trying to make him see my willingness to help him.

"Not a thing! Nothin' 'tall" he said grouchily, "unless you throw my body to the buzzards when I am dead—if the buzzards will have it!"

A rather painful silence, in which I looked kindly at him and he wildly at me, ensued.

Then he spoke again. "I sent for you, sir, because I want you to tell these young fellows here something for me. I sent for you because I know you go up and down the land and talk to many young people. And I want you to tell 'em, and tell 'em every chance you get, that the devil pays only in counterfeit money."

This was in desperate earnestness, in his eyes and in his voice. I held his hand as he died. I saw his eyes glaze. I heard the last gurgle in his throat. I saw his chest heave like a bellows and then become quiet.

When he died, the little nurse called me to her, excitedly. "Come here!" she called.

"What do you want, child?" I asked.

"I want to wash your hands! It's dangerous to *touch* him."

Pay day had come!

But what about Ahab? Did pay day come for him? Yes. Consider how. Three years went by. Ahab is still king. And I dare say that during those three years Jezebel had reminded him that they were eating herbs out of Naboth's vineyard. I can hear her say something like this as they sat at the king's table: "Ahab, help yourself to these herbs. I thought Elijah said the dogs were going to lick your blood. I guess his dogs lost their noses and lost the trail."

But I think that during those three years, Ahab never heard a dog bark that he did not jump.

One day Jehoshaphat, king of Judah, visited Ahab. The Bible tells us what took place—what was said, what was done.

> And the king of Israel said unto his servants, Know ye that Ramoth in Gilead is our's, and we be still, and take it not out of the hand of the king of Syria? And he said unto Jehoshaphat, Wilt thou go with me to battle to Ramoth-gilead? And Jehoshaphat said to the king of Israel, I am as thou art, my people as thy people, my horses as thy horses (I Kings 22:3, 4).
>
> So the king of Israel and Jehoshaphat the king of Judah went up to Ramoth-gilead (I Kings 22:29).

Ahab, after Jehoshaphat had promised to go with him, in his heart was afraid, and had sad forebodings, dreadful premonitions, horrible fears. Remembering the withering words of Elijah three years before, he disguised himself—put armor on his body and covered this armor with ordinary citizen's clothes.

> And the king of Israel said unto Jehoshaphat, I will disguise myself, and enter into the battle; but put thou on thy robes. And the king of Israel disguised himself, and went into the battle (I Kings 22:30).

The Syrian general had given orders to slay only the king of Israel—Ahab.

> But the king of Syria commanded his thirty and two captains that had rule over his chariots, saying, Fight neither with small nor great, save only with the king of Israel (I Kings 22:31).

Jehoshaphat was not injured, although he wore his royal clothes.

> And it came to pass, when the captains of the chariots saw Jehoshaphat, that they said, Surely it is the king of Israel. And they turned aside to fight against him: and Jehoshaphat cried out. And it came to pass, when the captains of the chariots perceived that it was not the king of Israel, that they turned back from pursuing him (I Kings 22:32,33).

While war steeds neighed and war chariots rumbled and shields clashed on shields and arrows whizzed and spears were thrown and swords were wielded, a death-carrying arrow, shot by an aimless and nameless archer, found the crack in Ahab's armor.

> And a certain man drew a bow at a venture, and smote the king of Israel between the joints of the harness: wherefore he said unto the driver of his chariot, Turn thee thine hand, and carry me out of the host; for I am wounded. And the battle increased that day: and the king was stayed up in his chariot against the Syrians, and died at even: and the blood ran out of the wound into the midst of the chariot . . . And one washed the chariot in the pool of Samaria; and the dogs licked up his blood; and they washed his armour; *according unto the Word of the Lord which He spake* (I Kings 22:34, 35, 38).

But what about Jezebel? Did her pay day come? Yes—after twenty years. After Ahab's death, after the dogs had licked his blood, she virtually ruled the kingdom. But I think that she went into the temple of Baal on occasions and prayed her god Baal to protect her from Elijah's hounds.

Elijah had been taken home to Heaven without the touch of the deathdew upon his brow. Elisha had succeeded him.

And Elisha the prophet called one of the children of the prophets, and said unto him, Gird up thy loins, and take this box of oil in thine hand, and go to Ramoth-gilead: and when thou comest thither, look out there Jehu the son of Jehoshaphat the son of Nimshi, and go in, and make him arise up from among his brethren, and carry him to an inner chamber; then take the box of oil, and pour it on his head, and say, Thus saith the Lord, I have anointed thee king over Israel. Then open the door, and flee, and tarry not. So the young man, even the young man the prophet, went to Ramoth-gilead. And when he came, behold, the captains of the host were sitting; and he said, I have an errand to thee, O captain. And Jehu said, Unto which of all us? And he said, To thee, O captain. And he arose, and went into the house; and he poured the oil on his head, and said unto him, Thus saith the Lord God of Israel, I have anointed thee king over the people of the Lord, even over Israel. And thou shalt smite the house of Ahab thy master, that I may avenge the blood of My servants the prophets, and the blood of all the servants of the Lord, at the hand of Jezebel . . . And I will make the house of Ahab like the house of Jeroboam the son of Nebat, and like the house of Baasha the son of Ahijah: And the dogs shall eat Jezebel in the portion of Jezreel, and there shall be none to bury her. And he opened the door, and fled (II Kings 9:1-7, 9, 10).

Jehu was just the man for such an occasion—furious in his anger, rapid in his movements, unscrupulous, yet zealous to uphold the law of Moses.

Then Jehu came forth to the servants of his lord: and one said unto him, Is all well? wherefore came this mad fellow to thee? And he said unto them, Ye know the man, and his communication. And they said, It is false; tell us now. And he said, Thus and thus spake he to me, saying, Thus saith the Lord,

I have anointed thee king over Israel. Then they
hasted, and took every man his garment, and put
it under him on the top of the stairs, and blew with
trumpets, saying, Jehu is king (II Kings 9:11-13).

Mounting his chariot, commanding and taking
with him a company of his most reliable soldiers,
furiously did he drive nearly sixty miles to Jezreel.

So Jehu rode in a chariot, and went to Jezreel;
for Joram lay there. And Ahaziah king of Judah was
come down to see Joram. And there stood a watchman on the tower in Jezreel, and he spied the company of Jehu as he came, and said, I see a company.
And Joram said, Take an horseman, and send to
meet them, and let him say, Is it peace? So there
went one on horse back to meet him, and said, Thus
saith the king, Is it peace? And Jehu said, What
hast thou to do with peace? turn thee behind me.
And the watchman told, saying, The messenger
came to them, but he cometh not again. Then he
sent out a second on horseback, which came to
them, and said, Thus saith the king, Is it peace?
And Jehu answered, What hast thou to do with
peace? turn thee behind me. And the watchman
told, saying, He came even unto them, and cometh
not again: and the driving is like the driving of
Jehu the son of Nimshi; for he driveth furiously.
And Joram said, Make ready. And his chariot
was made ready. And Joram king of Israel and
Ahaziah king of Judah went out, each in his chariot,
and they went out against Jehu, and met him in the
portion of Naboth the Jezreelite. And it came to
pass, when Joram saw Jehu, that he said, Is it
peace, Jehu? And he answered, What peace, so long
as the whoredoms of thy mother Jezebel and her
witchcrafts are so many? And Joram turned his hands,
and fled, and said to Ahaziah, There is treachery, O
Ahaziah. And Jehu drew a bow with his full strength,
and smote Jehoram between his arms, and the

arrow went out at his heart, and he sunk down in his chariot. Then said Jehu to Bidkar his captain, Take up, and cast him in the portion of the field of Naboth the Jezreelite: for remember how that, when I and thou rode together after Ahab his father, the Lord laid this burden upon him; Surely I have seen yesterday the blood of Naboth, and the blood of his sons, saith the Lord; and I will requite thee in this plat, saith the Lord. Now therefore take and cast him into the plat of ground, according to the Word of the Lord (II Kings 9:16-26).

"And when Jehu was come to Jezreel, Jezebel heard of it." Pause! Who is Jehu? He is the one who, twenty years before the events of this chapter from which we quote, rode down with Ahab to take Naboth's vineyard, the one who throughout those twenty years never forgot those withering words of terrible denunciation which Elijah spoke. And who is Jezebel? Oh! The very same one who wrote the letters and had Naboth put to death. And what is Jezreel? The place where Naboth had his vineyard and where Naboth died, his life pounded out by stones in the hands of ruffians. "And when Jehu was come to Jezreel, Jezebel heard of it; and she painted her face, and tired her head, and looked out at a window. And as Jehu entered in at the gate, she said, Had Zimri peace, who slew his master?" Pause again just here. "Had Zimri peace, who slew his master?" No; "there is no peace, saith my God, to the wicked." "And he lifted up his face to the window, and said, Who is on my side? who? And there looked out to him two or three eunuchs. And he said, Throw her down" (II Kings 9:30-33).

These men put their strong men's fingers into her

soft feminine flesh and picked her up, tired head and all, painted face and all, bejeweled fingers and all, silken skirts and all—and threw her down. Her body hit the street and burst open. Some of her blood splattered on the legs of Jehu's horses, dishonoring them. Some of her blood splattered on the walls of the city, disgracing them.

And Jehu drove his horses and chariot over her. There she lies, twisting in death agony in the street. Her body is crushed by the chariot wheels. On her white bosom are the black crescent-shapes of horses' hoofs. She is hissing like an adder in the fire.

> And when he was come in, he did eat and drink, and said, Go, see now this cursed woman, and bury her: for she is a king's daughter. And they went to bury her: but they found no more of her than the skull, and the feet, and the palms of her hands (II Kings 9:34-35).

God Almighty saw to it that the hungry dogs despised the brains that conceived the plot that took Naboth's life. God Almighty saw to it that the mangy lean dogs of the back alleys despised the hands that wrote the plot that took Naboth's life. God Almighty saw to it that the lousy dogs which ate carrion despised the feet that walked in Baal's courts and then in Naboth's vineyard.

These soldiers of Jehu went back to Jehu and said: "We went to bury her, O king," but the dogs had eaten her.

And Jehu replied: "This is the Word of the Lord, which He spake by His servant Elijah the Tishbite, saying, In the portion of Jezreel shall dogs eat the flesh of Jezebel."

> And the carcase of Jezebel shall be as dung upon
> the face of the field in the portion of Jezreel; so
> that they shall not say, This is Jezebel (II Kings
> 9:37).

Thus perished a female demon, the most infamous queen that ever wore a royal diadem.

Pay day—some day! God said it—and it was done! Yes, and from this we learn the power and certainty of God in carrying out His own retributive providence, that men might know that His justice slumbereth not. Even though the mill of God grinds slowly, it grinds to powder; "and though His judgments have leaden heels, they have iron hands."

And when I see Ahab fall in his chariot and when I see the dogs eating Jezebel by the walls of Jezreel, I say, as the Scripture saith: "O that thou hadst hearkened to My commandments; then had thy peace been as a river, and thy righteousness as the waves of the sea!" And as I remember that the gains of ungodliness are weighted with the curse of God, I ask you: "Wherefore do ye spend money for that which is not bread? and your labour for that which satisfieth not?"

And the only way I know for any man or woman on earth to escape the sinner's pay day on earth and the sinner's hell beyond—making sure of the Christian's pay day on earth and the Christian's Heaven beyond the Christian's pay day—is through Christ Jesus, who took the sinner's place upon the Cross, becoming for all sinners all that God must judge, that sinners through faith in Christ Jesus might become all that God cannot judge.

Chapter XVII

MINISTRY AT HOME

STRUGGLES AND ACCOMPLISHMENTS AT BELLEVUE

It is no less difficult to tell the story of Robert
G. Lee's struggles and accomplishments at the Bellevue Baptist Church in figures than it is to describe
the man himself, or his preaching, in type. For as
Lee cannot be typed, so the value of the ministry
at Bellevue cannot be figured. Where shall we begin?
Statistics in themselves are generally rather uninteresting, and so we must keep them at a minimum.
And as a matter of fact, whatever statistics may be
written today must change tomorrow; therefore, we
shall simply show tendencies rather than endeavor
to give accurate figures as of the date of the
publication of this volume.

The total membership of the Bellevue Baptist
Church on December 11, 1927, when Dr. Lee assumed
the pastorate, was 1,430, and of these, 254 could not
be located. The membership on December 11, 1947—
twenty years after Dr. Lee arrived in Memphis, was
7,500. It is larger than that today, totaling 7,800.

Additions to the church during the year prior to
Dr. Lee's assuming the ministry were 142 as against
more than 1,000 in the year 1948. The Sunday school
enrollment in 1927 was 1,171, compared with the

369

present enrollment of 4,200; and the Baptist Training Union membership in 1927 was 109, with 52 present at the first general assembly, as against a membership of more than 1,200 today. On one Sunday, when special effort was made, the attendance was 2,656, the largest in the history of the B.T.U. anywhere.

Gifts to the church in the year 1927 were $35,996.05, whereas in a recent year, chosen at random (1948), they reached the figure of $322,548.84.

The value of the church property in 1927 was $170,000.00. Today the church property is valued at more than $300,000.00.

The annual total additions to the membership of the church, some by baptism, and some by letter— all by confession of faith—have been as follows: first year, 600; second year, 644; third year, 430; fourth year, 612; fifth year, 559; sixth year, 426; seventh year, 537; eighth year, 522; ninth year, 564; tenth year, 529; eleventh year, 625; twelfth year, 618; thirteenth year, 662; fourteenth year, 694; fifteenth year, 767; sixteenth year, 795; seventeenth year, 769; eighteenth year, 839; nineteenth year, 1,000; twentieth year, 989; twenty-first year, 740; and twenty-second year, 807.

Donations for all causes during the twenty-one plus years of Dr. Lee's pastorate total more than $2,500,000, with nearly $750,000 having been given to missions.

In the nearly twenty-two years since Dr. Lee became pastor of the Bellevue Baptist Church, 14,267 people (as we write in August, 1949) have united with the church, the average being about 12.5 members per Sunday over all these years.

On April 16, 1939, the church calendar of the Belle-

vue Baptist Church shows an addition on that date of
78 new members—45 of them for baptism, and the
balance by letter. We believe that this is somewhat
of a record for this church or any other, although
there have been many Sundays throughout the two
decades of Lee's pastorship that have shown great
increase, and thus many new members have been
added to the mystical body of the Lord Jesus Christ.

More figures could be given, but we refrain, lest,
on account of a multitude of them, none will be
read. He who thoughtfully examines these that are
here published will see the astonishing growth of
Bellevue during the years that Dr. Lee has been the
shepherd of the Lord's flock there in Memphis.

It was during the "boom years" that Robert G.
Lee began his ministry in Memphis. And, indeed,
there was an immediate spiritual boom at Bellevue.
Attendances increased, but more important, souls
were saved, and the impassioned and loving ministry
of this servant of God was immediately felt, not
only in the church, but throughout the city.

There was no boom, however, in the financial
status of the church. The year ending December
31, 1927, showed a balance in the treasury of $30.49,
and a deficit of $1,519.61—this, with an actual mem-
bership of 1,176!

The work of the servant of the Lord is a spiritual
ministry. He is not able to escape, however, entering
into the financial and business problems of the
church. And it is a very unspiritual thing when
a body of believers in the Lord Jesus Christ is, as
a body, without sufficient liberality, when there is

indebtedness or potential indebtedness through deficits. Consequently, Dr. Lee began immediately to work with the financial committee of the church toward increasing the contributions of the membership. It was necessary, as the minutes of the church show, to borrow certain sums to pay notes, as upon the organ of the church, and interest on the indebtedness on the church building. In spite of the difficulties of the times, Lee recommended the purchase of properties adjoining the church for enlargements which he foresaw would be necessary in the years to come, for within a year of his arrival the active membership had increased by approximately 50 per cent. At the same time the pastor was urging upon his people, especially upon the officers of the church, that they take to heart the needs and tithe their incomes to increase their offerings to the Lord. Thus, on December 7, 1928 (four days less than one year after his first message there), the minutes of the Deacons' Meeting state:

> Dr. Lee made inspirational talk speaking of great progress of church during year. He laid special stress on spirituality, the only sure foundation upon which a church can grow. He also expressed hope that soon every deacon would be obedient in the bringing of the tithe into the church.

It will be remembered that the great financial crash came in 1929. Nevertheless, with faith abounding, the Building Committee, under impetus from the pastor, let contracts for the enlargement of the church auditorium and the erection of a new Sunday school building in an amount "not in excess of $225,000" on June 1, 1930. Ground was broken for the new educational building four days later, June 4, 1930.

The financial strain was being felt very severely in 1930, and many were the criticisms that Dr. Lee received at that time. One businessman said to the pastor: "I think you are a good man, but you're sunk. You'll never get that crowd of folks to pay that debt and other expenses of the church, too."

"You talk like God was dead," Dr. Lee replied.

Some said: "The preacher will do what he did in New Orleans—get the church in debt and leave." And others made such remarks as "Bellevue is on the downgrade"; "You can't pay that much interest"; "The bonds will be no good"; and "Folks will not join a church that is in debt."

One man, leaving the membership of the church, said: "I'm not going to be there when the crash comes." Another, now one of the finest deacons, was told, when he was ready to unite with the church at that time: "Bellevue is so loaded with debt, they will never pay out."

But Lee knew that God is not dead. Pressing on, with deep faith in God and in the efficacy of prayer, the pastor set his sights upon a goal that he believed had been set by the Lord, and brooked no discouragement or well-meaning interference. For he agrees with the statement of Dr. F. B. Meyer, which he quotes frequently, that we never test the resources of God until we attempt the impossible.

The first service in the new auditorium was held on November 23, 1930. It was filled to overflowing, so that, even with chairs put in the aisles, some were turned away. The token of God's approval upon this step of faith was evident in the fact that 47 people united with the church that Sunday. Soon after the opening of the new auditorium the educational building was also ready for use.

For the next two to three years the finances of the Bellevue Baptist Church presented a grievous problem. There were times when money had to be borrowed from the banks in order to pay the interest on bonds, and many of the people were quite uneasy; but it is evident, from the minutes, that the Finance Committee stood with the pastor shoulder to shoulder to carry the organization through these difficult times, trusting in God. Excerpts from the Minutes will reveal the serious problem that the finances presented at this time.

May 11th, 1930

Borrow $10,000 temporarily in order to take up and retire the present outstanding bonds.

October 21st, 1931

The meeting called for the purpose of borrowing up to $4,500 for retirement of $10,000 Second Mortgage Bonds on November 1st.

June 23rd, 1932

Special meeting of the Board of Directors called for the purpose of borrowing $7,500.

November 23rd, 1932

Mr. J. E. Dilworth made a motion, which was seconded by Mr. E. F. Green, that the Finance Committee be authorized to borrow $2,000 to pay current obligations subject to the approval of the church.

December 21st, 1932

Mr. Fuller made a motion, which was seconded by E. F. Green, that the Board go before the church and request authority to borrow approximately $6,000 to pay interest on First Mortgage Bonds due January 1st.

Two of the leading men of Bellevue came to Dr. Lee one day and asked him if he would consent to the church's not giving anything to missions, but rather to place whatever amount they might have given to missions in a fund to pay off the indebtedness. Without hesitancy, the pastor replied: "No."

When these two brethren began to argue with him, Lee dismissed them rather abruptly with this remark: "Please don't argue with me. You are barking up a tree where there never has been a possum."

Yet shortly thereafter, the editor of one of the Baptist publications, writing to a member of the Bellevue Church, advised him to take his letter away from Bellevue, since "the preacher does not believe in missions." Dr. Lee was informed of this remark, and was deeply grieved. To his informant he said: "If I don't believe in missions, the sun is an iceberg, and Jenny Lind has a beard."

One day one of the ladies of the church brought $3,000.00 worth of second mortgage bonds on the church buildings to Dr. Lee and offered them to him for $1,500.00 for she was fearful that she might lose her full investment. The pastor told her to stop listening to bankers and financiers and to give ear to a Baptist preacher. He then advised her to take her bonds home, assuring her that the interest would be paid, and the principal also when the bonds would come due. He added: "You cannot get 7 per cent interest anywhere else in the world today."

As a matter of fact, when these second mortgage bonds had been sold originally, some of the men of the church, even members of the Finance Committee, would not take them, for they were seven-year bonds.

It was said that one-year bonds would be all right, and one man said that he would take a $1,000.00 bond, but with the thought that he might just as well "throw it in a rat hole." Lee himself borrowed $2,000.00 on his life insurance and purchased some of the bonds, for he never wavered in conviction that his program was of the Lord, and that therefore it could not fail.

Perhaps the most difficult period that the church had, financially, was between December, 1931, and June, 1932, as already intimated in the citations of certain minutes of the Finance Committee. A report from the minutes of the Deacons' Meeting of December, 1931, which includes mention of the operating figures for the fiscal year, contains a report on Dr. Lee's attitude at that time:

> Dr. Lee said he was counting on the deacons to see the [annual] canvass through, as he wanted certain information from each of them. He also said there were a number of outside women censuring Bellevue for not giving more to missions. However, records show that Bellevue is giving more to missions now than ever before. Dr. Lee said some women row with one-year oars instead of ten or twelve-year oars, and that ten years from now some leading Baptist churches would look like a wheelbarrow in an automobile parade, compared with Bellevue, and that criticism does not mean anything if we stand unified and pull together for the Lord.

> *February,* 1932 (Deacons' Meeting):

> Bro. West stated that they were concerned about the finances of the church and had cut every possible general expense, and were still unable to balance the budget. He stated that Dr. Lee had called a special

meeting and voluntarily asked that his salary be reduced 20 per cent. The general opinion was that this was too much of a reduction. After much discussion it was decided that the Finance Committee would see Dr. Lee before bringing the question before the church at regular business meeting.

February, 1932 (Church Meeting):

Mr. Fuller stated further that our pastor, Dr. Lee, had requested on numerous occasions that his salary be reduced, but the Committee has never seen fit to accept Dr. Lee's proposal until recently, when Dr. Lee demanded that his salary be reduced $1,000.00 for the year 1932 only, and that, after very careful consideration and the full understanding of Dr. Lee's repeated requests for this reduction, he recommended to the church that the reduction be approved.

June, 1932:

Bro. F. Fuller, Chairman of the Finance Committee, said finances doing remarkably well. Estimated pledges for the year, $54,000 . . . Taking all into consideration, he thought Bellevue was doing exceedingly well financially.

It seems that Dr. Lee was remarkably correct in his prophecy that "some women row with one-year oars instead of ten-year oars," for the records show that ten years and eight months after this statement, a glorious day came to the Bellevue Baptist Church.

September 9, 1942 (Minutes):

That the church have a day of celebration on the payment of our church debt. The day designated being the third Sunday of October, which is the 18th. A week of visitation for the church to be held the week before this celebration.

On October 18, 1942, at the morning service of the church, the mortgage on the building was burned by Messrs. C. G. Carter, J. E. Dilworth, and W. A.

Gaylor, with fitting ceremonies. From that time forward the gifts to and through Bellevue have increased annually, and today missions are receiving $100,000 or more a year through the donations of God's people in this spiritually directed church.

We have spoken more than once of the love that Dr. Lee bears to the Bellevue Baptist Church, his pastorate, and its people. Just how deep is that love? It is easy enough to record some of the things that a man says and some of the things that a man does. It is not so easy to know, as has been suggested by more than one student of human nature, what a man is. Phillip Guedella, the eminent biographer of the Duke of Wellington, said something of this kind when giving an address on the art of biography. He offered as an example his own problem when he wrote the life-story of Wellington. He asked himself: "What would be trustworthy evidence of the kind of man Wellington actually was?"— and added that he found that which he considered unimpeachable evidence when he came across the stubs of Wellington's checkbook.

We have not been through Dr. Lee's checkbooks, but because of his meticulous care in keeping records, and his very enlightening habit of retaining everything that he lays his hands on, we have a fair idea of his generosity. Dr. Lee does not intentionally let his left hand know what his right hand is doing, but long before this biography was under consideration, his own personal scrapbooks knew what his right hand was doing, and we risk the hazard of his ire by attesting certain things that

we have learned. For a man who would keep for
forty-two years a record such as this—

> Borrowed from Frank today the sum of
> twenty five dollars..................................$25.00
> Borrowed before this.................................3.00
> October 5, 1907...................Total $28.00

> Interest on $28.00 for four months at 8 per
> cent is forty cents. Will owe Frank on February
> first, 1908, the sum of $29.00
>
> (Signed) Robert Greene Lee
> October 5, 1907

will assuredly maintain records in later years, and
it is from these that we have discovered what Robert
Greene Lee's right hand is doing, without his knowledge that we have done so.

Some years ago the church wanted to buy the
property on the north side of the building, owned by
two wealthy ladies. A committee, appointed by the
church, entered negotiations for this purchase but
was unable to accomplish anything. So Dr. Lee called
on these ladies. With him, as with the committee,
they were adamant in refusing to sell. But the
pastor prayed about it—for he makes almost everything an object of prayer—and after a period of
time they reconsidered and consented to sell all of
the property. Lee explained to them that the church
was not able to finance all of it at that time, for
the need was actually for only a portion of the
property. But these ladies were not in want, and so
they suggested that the preacher himself buy notes
for a long period of time, to be paid at $30.00 a
month, without any interest, the payments to conclude in the year 1952. This Dr. Lee did. Later he

sold to the church at what it cost him, that portion of property that it could not afford earlier.

The Bellevue Baptist Church owns a bus that seats around thirty people, which is used to pick up those living at some distance from the church and unable to get there in any other way, and also in connection with the Bellevue Mission in another part of the city, and for conventions, and so forth. In the matter of the purchase of this bus, there is a "stub" for $500.00 in Lee's records. The same is true for the purchase of a 16 mm. motion-picture projector used in the showing of educational films.

Recently the classrooms and departments in the educational building were redecorated, but no allowance was made for the church offices. By his personal check, beautiful new draperies were purchased, made, and hung at the windows of the offices.

When Nelson Reagan came to Bellevue as the Director of Intermediate Activities, he did a fine work in organizing and training an Intermediate Glee Club of nearly a hundred voices. Mr. Reagan wanted robes for the Glee Club, but the budget for the Intermediate Department was already exhausted. Dr. Lee voluntarily gave his personal check for $1,000.00 to pay for the gowns. He is tremendously interested in the young people, loving them dearly, and wants them to feel that their pastor is one with them in their Christian service.

Later, because of the work that the Glee Club did, they were invited to sing before the Southern Baptist Convention in St. Louis in 1947. They accepted and were the recipients of high commendation for their contribution to the general program.

More recently, on June 4, 1947, Dr. and Mrs. Lee donated $10,000.00 to the Bellevue Baptist Church for the purpose of converting a cottage, which Lee had earlier given, into Bellevue Baby Bungalow. The money was to be used as follows: for construction, $5,000.00; and for furnishings, $5,000.00. The purpose of this bungalow is to provide a place for children while their parents are attending church services, and also to give them a regular program of study.

The cottage is a frame structure, painted white, and has six rooms. One is for children from birth to about one year old; another for toddlers just learning to walk; another for one-year-olds; another for children of two years; and another for three-year-olds. The classrooms are painted in pastel shades —mist blue, jonquil yellow, light orchid, pale pink, green, and peach. White child-size furniture is used throughout. There are drinking fountains, toilet facilities, and the building is equipped with bacterial lamps such as those used in hospitals.

In addition to a personal letter that was sent to Dr. and Mrs. Lee to thank them for this loving gift, a resolution was adopted at the Business Meeting of the church, reading as follows:

> At the Business Meeting of the church Wednesday night, June 4, 1947, all present were filled with joy upon hearing a letter from Dr. and Mrs. Lee read, giving to the Baby Building of Bellevue Baptist Church ten thousand dollars.
>
> We, the committee selected by the church to express appreciation in suitable resolutions, present the following:
>
> Because of the love of Dr. and Mrs. Lee for the mem-

bers of Bellevue and their families, this gift was made. The kinship of our pastor and his wife to Jesus Christ who said "Suffer little children, and forbid them not, to come unto me: for of such is the kingdom of heaven" has prompted this love gift.

Of their acceptance of the Bible as the Word of God, of their passion for teaching the Bible, of their emphasis upon the Christian home, this gift is noble evidence.

Because of their fidelity to the preaching of salvation by grace through faith in the shed blood of their Lord and Saviour, Jesus Christ, and because they are faithful stewards of the manifold grace of God, they administer their earthly possessions in keeping with the teachings of the Bible, and have been led by the Spirit of God to give this ten thousand dollars which increases the total gifts from our pastor and his wife to twenty-thousand dollars since November 1, 1946, in addition to their regular giving of tithes and offerings on each Lord's Day.

Be it therefore resolved by the members of the Bellevue Baptist Church, assembled on June 15, 1947, for morning worship—

First: We thank God for sending Dr. and Mrs. Lee to us in 1927, for their unselfish and never-ending labors among us; for their high Christian standards of living held before us in their teaching and practice, and for their unquestioning faith in the power of Christ to make men new creatures.

Second: We thank them for this generous gift, thus making possible one of the greatest buildings for the proper care and training of babies in any church of the Southern Baptist Convention.

Third: We thank them for all they have meant to our church during these busy, happy years together; for all they have meant to Memphis and the world beyond.

Fourth: That a copy of this expression of love and gratitude be spread upon the church record, copies sent to Dr. and Mrs. Lee and other members of their family, and to the denominational and secular press.

Signed by the Committee of Bellevue Baptist Church:

George J. Burnett

George E. Rusch

Charles A. Pinson

A friend asked Dr. Lee whether, in view of these wonderful gifts, he had a lot of money. To this he replied: "No, that is the last." And it was "the last" to that time. Subsequently, however, we observe that donations of $1,000.00 each have been made to a new Baptist educational institution, Grand Canyon College in Arizona, and to the Florida Baptist Bible Institute in Lakeland. So that it is evident that the purse strings of this servant of God are readily loosed for needs in His work.

If check stubs prove what a man is, then Dr. Lee's love for Bellevue is assuredly genuine—and so it is. And so also is Bellevue's love for Lee real, ardent, and operative, as exemplified in one letter chosen from many, and which we leave unsigned, since it contains the sentiments of a multitude:

My dear Dr. Lee:

I have never known a sweeter pastor than you are making for Bellevue Church. I appreciate your good wishes and kind words on my birthday more than you will ever know. So few big men realize what the little things in life mean to some people. You have been everything to me and my family that we could ask, and we are for you 100 per cent. I want again to assure you that you never go into your pulpit without my prayers and you have been a great blessing to us in your messages. Thanking you for your thoughtfulness, and asking God's richest blessing upon you and yours, I am,

Sincerely,

It seem to us that no one knows how much
Robert G. Lee loves the Bellevue Baptist Church.
A mother could not bear more love to her child
than he for this place and its people. Says Mrs.
Lee concerning her husband's devotion to his church:
"I believe, were it necessary, Dr. Lee would be
crucified for Bellevue." More than once he has
said something like this: "If Jesus were to walk down
these aisles and say to me, 'Come on, let us go home
to Heaven, as Enoch walked with God,' I would
reply with reverent courtesy, 'No, thank You, Lord
Jesus; what do I want to go to Heaven for now? I
love to preach, and I would not have any chance
to preach there. In Heaven I would have no chance
to comfort, for there is no sadness there. In Heaven,
no chance to help and strengthen my people at the
graves of their loved ones, as there is no death there.
In Heaven, no chance to visit the sick, for there is
no sickness there.'

"One day I buried a little girl who died of polio.
When I went to the home after the funeral, the
mother said to me: 'Oh, Dr. Lee, I don't see how we
could have gotten through today without you.' What
do I want to go to Heaven for—now?

"One Sunday morning I felt the Holy Spirit sweep
over the congregation. Hankerchiefs were brought out
and used, as people saw the Cross. Why should I want
to go to Heaven now, and miss the opportunity to
preach to such a congregation?

"One day an old woman whom I visited put two
wrinkled hands on my cheeks and kissed me, saying:
'You brought me light today.' Why should I want to
go to Heaven now?"

Dr. Louis B. Newton, Retiring President of the Southern Baptist Convention, Presenting the Newly Elected President of the Convention, Dr. Robert G. Lee, May, 1948

Dr. Robert G. Lee, President of the Southern Baptist Convention, Congratulates Dr. E. W. Perry, Vice-President-at-Large of the National Baptist Convention, U.S.A., at the S.B.C. in Oklahoma City, Okla., May, 1949

Not long ago some of the deacons began to urge upon the membership that which Dr. Lee has felt the church has needed for some time—a new auditorium that will seat a larger audience than the present one, which is totally inadequate for the size of the membership. As one of the deacons, George J. Burnett, wrote to Dr. Lee: "Why should not seven thousand Bellevue Baptists have an auditorium to seat five thousand to hear a man of God preach as their pastor preaches Jesus Christ and Him crucified?" Plans have developed very well for this purpose, and a very beautiful new auditorium is in the making. It will seat a minimum of 3,500 people, having two balconies, indirect lighting, a fine heating system, and will be air conditioned. It is to be carpeted from wall to wall and even up the edges of the base board, so as to eliminate noise as fully as possible. And, like the present auditorium, it will have a very beautiful baptismal pool, similar to that now in use in that it will be high above the choir, constructed half of plate glass, so that the congregation can view the candidate as his body is lowered into the baptismal waters.

The present auditorium will be converted into a memorial chapel in honor of the young people of Bellevue who served in the Second World War, and additional young people's departments of the Sunday school are to be installed there, the present departments being overcrowded with the rapid growth of the church. A great deal of the money for the new building is already in the bank, some having been contributed by those who are interested, and definite amounts being set aside from the offerings each

.nonth for this building fund. A special offering of
$56,000.00 was made by the membership on Thanks-
giving Day, 1948, for the new building.

The purpose of this auditorium and every thought
behind its planning are that it shall be used for the
winning of lost souls to the Lord Jesus Christ, and
for building up God's people in Christ and sending
them out for Him, to the glory of God the Father.

Who can tell, in a few pages, the accomplishments that have been wrought by God through this
servant of His at Bellevue during the last twenty and
more years? Not merely a few things, but most of
them must of necessity be omitted in a chronicle of
this kind. Assuredly God has done mighty works
through His servant in Memphis, because this servant
has given himself in prayer, love, and labors to his
calling and to the place of his appointment. A quotation from a communication from Dr. John Jeter Hurt,
President Emeritus of Union University, Jackson,
Tennessee, expresses, better than any words that we
could say, what Lee has accomplished, under God,
at Bellevue:

> Sir Christopher Wren was the architect of St. Paul's
> Cathedral, in London, and is buried there. On a tablet
> commemorating his work is this inscription: *Si monu-
> mentum requires, circumspice* (If you seek a monument,
> look around you). Bellevue and Lee; Lee and Bellevue.
> They have made and are still making, each other.

Chapter XVIII

MINISTRY ABROAD

Outside Activities and Miscellany

"If our hearts are not 25,000 miles in circumference, they are too small. If our arms do not embrace the whole world, they are too short." So spoke Robert G. Lee at the Georgia State Convention in Atlanta, in November, 1948. And that is the theme of this chapter, for the ministry of a man with the pulpit gifts that God has given to Robert G. Lee cannot be confined to one pulpit: it must reach abroad to many pulpits. Thus, as busy as Pastor Lee is in Memphis, he is no less busy outside of his own church—witnessing to the Lord both in Memphis, and in all Tennessee, and unto the uttermost part of the earth. So far his platform ministry has not carried him out of the North American Continent, although he has been invited to other places. But there is more than sufficient for him to do in his own country at the present time, and so he has never felt impelled to cross the seas for a preaching tour of any other land.

George Goodwin, Pulitzer-prize-winning reporter of the *Atlanta Journal*, writing in Morgan Blake's col- in the *Journal*, says of the meeting in Atlanta referred to above, addressing Mr. Blake:*

---

*Used with the kind permission of the Editor of the **Atlanta Journal**.

Robert G. Lee

I know now what you Baptists mean by powerful preaching. You mean the kind of preaching the Rev. Robert G. Lee, President of the Southern Baptist Convention, produced when he climaxed the Georgia Baptist Convention in the Baptist Tabernacle Thursday.

You should have been there. It would have done your heart—and your soul—great good.

He was the last thing on the three-day program. It is just as well, because after that sermon anything else was unnecessary.

There was something magnetic about the splendid white-haired man and something far more magnetic about what he had to say.

His voice lifted to a shout and fell to a whisper as he preached against sin—not sin as something general, but sin as something personal—something everyone has.

He thundered about the church men who spend their Sunday mornings on the golf course. He got a lot of "Amens" from the crowd when he preached against liquor.

He preached about the Church's duty to fight sin everywhere in the world and particularly at home.

"If our hearts are not 25,000 miles in circumference, they are too small," he said. "If our arms do not embrace the whole world, they are too short."

It was that sort of preaching, Mr. Blake. Powerful, moving, thrilling.

There was poetry, too. Several times his sentences took on a metrical quality, and his powerful words began to rhyme with each other.

He hit us where we live. Rearing back and making great gestures, he shouted against the "white-faced millions of Americans who translate freedom of religion into freedom from religion."

He roared out against the men and women who raise their children between their family arguments.

"We are living in a day when a lot of homes are dying in houses," he said.

He remembered the great Dr. Len G. Broughton, who made the old Baptist Tabernacle famous. I'm telling you,

Dr. Broughton would have been proud indeed to hear this man's sermon ringing through the high rafters of the temple he built.

There were touches of humor, too—not many, just enough to help him sweep the crowd to his will.

As the minutes sped on, he told the folks not to get restless.

"At Bellevue I preach until I run down," he said. "I never run out."

He did not have to worry about the people getting restless. He was capturing everybody. There was the polished up-and-coming Dr. Jim Middleton, of Atlanta's First Baptist Church, leaning forward to catch every word. Druid Hill's Dr. Louie Newton—who is something of a spellbinder in his own right—looked as moved as the newest seminary graduate.

He was preaching to preachers, but he treated them as though they were just a gang of backsliders at a tent meeting.

Brother Blake, he had it. He tramped on my own Presbyterian toes when he said he had no use for those who would modify the Gospel with reason, but he had me, too.

He ended with a short prayer—not a prayer that was just an excuse for more preaching—but a real talk with God. I'm pretty sure God heard him, because I've an idea that another Baptist, named John, used to preach that way a couple thousand years ago.

It was a wonderful experience. I'm still a Presbyterian deacon, but I know what you Baptists mean by powerful preaching.

GEORGE GOODWIN

The "outside ministry" begins right in Memphis. First of all, Dr. Lee broadcasts over the air at his regular morning service on Sundays. In addition he has had a radio program on Saturday mornings at 10:15, for fifteen minutes over station WHBQ. Occasionally he takes another Sunday morning broadcast that is presented by various pastors of the city of Memphis. Here, in these messages every week, is sufficient to keep the average man fairly busy.* But this is hardly a beginning!

Functions are held where Dr. Lee is the guest speaker. Many of the Negro churches invite him for special occasions, as do businessmen's groups, Rotary Clubs, etc.

In 1947 the Gideons made a presentation of 625 Bibles to the Peabody Hotel, where the Gideons International were having their midwinter cabinet meeting and mid-South rally. Dr. Lee was the speaker of the occasion, delivering the dedicatory message for these Bibles, and the lobby and mezzanine were crowded with about 1,000 people to hear him speak on that Sunday afternoon. He addressed the group on the subject, "God's Matchless Word, the Holy Bible." Throughout every corner of the first floor and mezzanine of that beautiful hotel, Lee's voice could be heard. The crowd did not become quiet and attentive immediately, for there were some who were not interested in a religious service; but after the preacher had gotten under way, a great change took place and it was not long before every noise except the sound of the preacher's voice had died out. People even got up from the dining room and came out into the lobby to hear what this man had to say. Some of them, appearing cynical at first, changed their expressions after a few moments. The

---

*As we go to press we are informed that the Radio Commission of the Southern Baptist Convention has contracted with the American Broadcasting Company for a year-round program on Sunday afternoons, to begin October 2, 1949. Dr. Lee, as President of the S. B. C., is the speaker for the first three months.

elevator boys stopped their cars at the mezzanine floor, refusing to take them all of the way down to the lobby for fear of interrupting the message; and the bellboys stood around open-mouthed and wide-eyed, as they saw this unusual demonstration in the lobby of a busy hotel. One who was there says that, while there was no public profession of Christ after the message, it is impossible that unsaved people could have gone away without having been stirred in their hearts by the Spirit of the living God.

Under the leadership of Dr. Lee, the Bellevue Baptist Church reaches out a helping hand to other groups of Christians in and about the city. For example, Bellevue has its own mission, on Adams Street, in a rather congested section of the city. It has a young preacher, sound in the faith, and the Sunday school superintendent is one of the deacons at Bellevue.

On the minutes of a deacons' meeting of Bellevue, under date of February 20, 1929, we find the following notation:

> The pastor stated that for almost a year Greenland Heights Baptist Church had been worshipping in a building without a floor, their building having been damaged by a storm last spring. Their pastor, Bro. Couch, now trying to raise money to at least replace the floor of their building.
>
> Mr. John L. West made a motion that $100.00 of mission money be designated for this purpose and that our State Sec'y, Dr. Bryan, be instructed to forward to Greenland Heights Baptist Church check for this amount.

Again, a few years later, this same church, located in Shelby County, was struggling with a debt that it seemed impossible for it to handle. Members ap-

pealed to Bellevue to take over the notes, and to let
them work under Bellevue as a mission. The Deacons
and Finance Committee recommended that Bellevue
do this, which it did. Fifteen hundred dollars was
advanced to free this little Shelby County church
from its bondage. Shortly thereafter the name was
changed to the Galilee Baptist Church, and Bellevue
released it as a mission, so that it is an independent
church at this time.

In another community, where quite a number of
Baptists lived without a local church, a group of
them asked permission of the Methodist officials to
repair an abandoned Methodist chapel in their lo-
cality. Permission was granted and repairs were
made, but after a few years the Methodists decided
to take the building back again. This small group of
Baptists, challenged by their unexpected predicament,
went to Dr. Lee and begged him to come to their
community and to preach for a week under a
brush-arbor. This he did, and many were won to
the Lord Jesus Christ. The hearts of the believers
were fired also, to a point of sacrificial giving, and
they raised sufficient money to buy land and build
their own church. Dr. Lee was a liberal donor to this
project, and today the Oaklawn Baptist Church is
a monument to the faith, enthusiasm, and initiative
of this group of people and to Dr. Lee's help at
a critical hour.

Bellevue also opens its heart to the needs of other
Christian works in various places, as will be amply
demonstrated by donations such as these on its
records: to Tabernacle Baptist Church, Memphis—
$1,400; to Southern Baptist Seminary, Louisville, Ken-

tucky—$5,000; and to Blue Mountain College, Blue Mountain, Tennessee—$25,000.

A rather unique experience was had by Dr. Lee some few years ago when he dedicated, in one day, seven Baptist churches, one in Tennessee, and six in Mississippi. The first dedicatory service was in Mississippi, at Grove, in Alcorn County, and the service was at 6:30 a. m. The second church was at the North Cross Road Baptist Church, in Tishomingo County, twenty miles from Juka, Mississippi. The service was held at 8 a. m. Following this, Lee and his associates drove seventy miles to the Philadelphia Baptist Church, near Waynesboro, Tennessee, where Lee spoke at 11 o'clock At 2:30 in the afternoon, the party—Mr. Percy Ray, who led in the building of these churches; Dr. J. B. Lawrence, Secretary of the Baptist Home Mission Board, Atlanta; Hugh Latimer, Associate Secretary of the Southwide Baptist Brotherhood; Dr. Lawrence Lowrey, President of the Blue Mountain College; the Rev. A. L. Goodrich, Editor of *The Baptist Record*, Jackson, Mississippi; and the Rev. J. P. Kirkland, pastor of the Walnut Baptist Church—went to Tiplersville, Mississippi, to the Tiplersville Baptist Church. Following this, they conducted dedicatory services at the Valley Grove Baptist Church, Tupelo, Mississippi, at 6 o'clock; the Tula Baptist Church, Tula, Mississippi, at 8 o'clock, and at the Buckhannon Baptist Church, six miles outside of Ecru, Mississippi, at 10:30 p. m.

More recently, in June, 1949, and with the same Mr. Percy Ray in charge, Dr. Lee dedicated eight debt-free churches—six in Tennessee and two in Mississippi. After breakfast in New Albany at 3

a. m., the party went first to a service at 4:30 a. m. at
the Mt. Tabor Baptist Church, near Pittsboro, and
seventy miles distant from New Albany. Not more
than a few miles from Mt. Tabor, near Bruce, the
second dedication was held, at the Calvary Baptist
Church at 6 a. m. From there to the third service
was a distance of about 145 miles, at Pocahontas,
Tennessee. This was held at 9:30 a. m. At Hornsby,
Tennessee, the Hatchie Baptist Church was dedicated
at 11 a. m. After dinner, the party moved to Mt.
Gilead, near Selmer, for a 1 p. m. service; then to
Luttes, Tennessee, for a 3:30 meeting; to Clear Creek
for a 6:30 meeting; and finally to the Olive Hill
Church, near Savannah, for a 9:30 dedication. Dr.
Lee preached a different sermon for each church, so
that the members of the twelve-car convoy would not
be bored with hearing the same thing over again, and
so that each congregation might have a fresh message
especially for its own circumstances.

Ministry that reaches out to many places originates
in Lee's office at the church, for there he turns out
a tremendous number of letters on all sorts of
subjects—recommending men for pulpits; saying a
good word for this organization or that man; corresponding regarding Bible and spiritual problems;
acknowledging kindnesses and doing many of them.

We find a letter from Mrs. Herman H. Beusse,
dated August 19, 1947, reading:

Dear Dr. Lee:
Our son, Lee Hulton Beusse, was born last Friday
August 15. He was only six pounds big but a fine little
fellow. We are so proud and happy and so very thankful
for him.

We are hoping that as he grows we will be able to see in him some measure of at least some of the fine qualities of the pastor for whom we named him. And I want him to be like his daddy whose second name he bears.

Sincerely,
MARJORIE BEUSSE

Lee would respond to such a letter, of course. But not only babies are named for this much beloved pastor. There is a horse in Costa Rica named "Dr. Lee"! Hearing about a missionary in Costa Rica who needed a horse, the Bellevue pastor sent some money to this missionary for this purpose, and now the servant of the Lord in Costa Rica travels three times as far as he formerly could without the help of the horse. In honor of the donor, his steed is called "Dr. Lee." Such is fame!

As a member of the editorial staff of the Sword of the Lord Book Club, Dr. Lee receives books every week which must be reviewed. He also is the recipient of innumerable requests for sermon outlines, and he obliges the inquiring pastors whenever he can, so that some of his sermons are preached in many places. We wonder if he would recognize all of them should he hear them! There was an occasion when the widely-known evangelist, Mel Trotter, delivered a message from notes and an outline that Dr. G. Campbell Morgan had given him. As Trotter was speaking he observed Dr. Morgan come into the church and take a seat in the audience. So, after the service, Mel went to Dr. Morgan and said: "That was your message I used tonight."

"Don't blame that thing on me!" Morgan replied—

and it might be that Dr. Lee would have to say the same in some instances.

Practically every time Lee quotes a poem in a sermon, he receives requests for copies of the lines, and it is no light task to respond to all such requests when a man preaches as frequently as he does.

Still, in his office the Bellevue pastor takes time to write letters of good wishes on anniversaries of ministers whom he knows, for special occasions at different churches that he has visited, and for a multitude of other things. No act of kindness to him goes without response from him. A letter came from Mr. James C. Grist, a member of the family that published the *Yorkville Inquirer,* to which Bob Lee, as a young man, sold his early stories. Mr. Grist was in the hospital and sent a note to Dr. Lee, congratulating him upon his election to the presidency of the Southern Baptist Convention. In reply, Lee wrote a typical letter, the kind that he sends to so many people, evidencing that deep sense of sentiment that has never left the one who began as a poor boy in the hills of South Carolina.

August 7, 1948

Dear Bro. Grist:

Your letter of July 25 came to me at a late date because I have been on a preaching tour in California. I preached two and three times a day under the auspices of our Convention. It is a wonderful state and our Southern Baptist people are doing a wonderful work.

I do not know when I received a letter which stirred me as to Memory Lane more than your letter. I was just fifteen or sixteen, or thereabouts, when I was writing stories—and you were a lad of twelve setting the type. Your letter brought me unusually sweet and sad memories of the "dear, dead days beyond recall." During these years,

I have received fair sums of money for writing, but I can truly say that the first money I got from the "Yorkville Inquirer" for writing gave me more joy than any I have ever received. Those were days when dollars were as scarce with me as were duck's teeth in a hen's mouth.

I shall ever be grateful to the Grist family for what they did for me in this line.

I am so sorry to know that you are in the hospital. I shall continue to pray that you will get completely well. Please write me again as to just how you are getting along.

With grateful heart, I received your earnest words of congratulation as to my being elected President of our great Southern Baptist Convention. For a friend, whose friendship I value greatly, to take time to write me cheers my heart greatly and gives me added strength for all the new duties which are mine.

With every good wish,

Yours sincerely,
ROBERT G. LEE

Just sitting at his desk doing nothing—which, by the way, he *never* does—Lee could be assured that his service for the Lord was continuing day in and day out. For such reports as this come to him with striking regularity. The Rev. Brooks Ramsey, once the young pastor of the Bellevue Mission in Memphis, but now a minister in Waco, Texas, through Dr. Lee's intercession, wrote to Dr. Lee and told him of certain incidents which he thought would be of interest to his former pastor. This is one of them:

In a class in a large seminary the professor was lecturing on the book of Jonah. He presented the two important views concerning the book—one, that it presents a historical fact; the other, that it is merely allegorical. It was easy to see on which side of the question the lecturer stood, for he had given great prominence to the liberal idea of allegorizing the book and had only briefly glossed over the fact of literal interpretation. When a certain student was called on to recite, he was asked about these two views. He replied in somewhat this manner: "Somewhere I have read that Dr. Lee said that if the book of Jonah is an allegory then you have an imaginary man going down to an imaginary city, getting on an imaginary boat, sailing on an imaginary sea, being swallowed by an imaginary fish who cast him up on an imaginary shore, going to an imaginary city and preaching to an imaginary people!" The answer immediately threw the class into an uproar, much to the delight of the students, and to the consternation of the "learned professor." Just another example of the fact that it's common sense to believe the Bible.

Without even leaving Memphis, then, Lee's outside ministry goes to places all over the continent. But Dr. Lee does leave Memphis. Here, for example, is a list of his speaking engagements during the year 1947—in forty different cities, for engagements that range from one meeting to ten or twelve, depending upon how long he stayed in each place. He gave approximately two hundred and fifty messages in fulfilling these engagements.

Outside Speaking Engagements—1947

January 14—Dallas, Texas, Evangelistic Conference.
January 21—Birmingham, Alabama, Associational S. S. Meeting.
January 24—Fort Worth, Texas, Brotherhood Meeting.
February 3-10—Miami, Florida, Revival Meeting.
February 4—Jackson, Mississippi (Banquet of Mississippi College.
February 20, 21—Birmingham, Alabama, Howard College.
February 25—Shawnee, Oklahoma, State-wide Evangelistic Conference.
March 4-6—Evansville, Indiana, Evansville Gospel Mission.

March 17, 18—Los Angeles, California, Bible Conference.
March 24-30—Roanoke, Virginia, Revival Meeting.
April 1—Knoxville, Tennessee, Bible Conference.
April 7-14—New Orleans, Louisiana, Revival Meeting.
April 21—Jackson, Tennessee, "Pay Day—Some Day" sermon.
April 26—Hattiesburg, Mississippi, "Pay Day—Some Day" sermon.
April 28—Winona, Mississippi, Dedication of Library.
May 1, 2—Chattanooga, Tennessee, Bible Conference.
May 5-10—St. Louis, Missouri, Southern Baptist Convention.
May 13—Akron, Ohio, Bible Conference.
June 2-8—Philadelphia, Mississippi, Revival Meeting.
June 16—Atlanta, Georgia, Brotherhood Meeting.
June 20—Mineral Wells, Texas, Training Union Convention.
June 26, 27—Ridgecrest, North Carolina, Southwide S. S. Conference.
July 1-4—Sandy Cove, Northeast, Maryland, Morning Cheer Bible Conference.
July 13—Farmersville, Louisiana, One Hundredth Anniversary Celebration.
July 23, 24—Winona Lake, Indiana, Bible Conference.
July 29-August 3—Pinebrook Bible Conference, East Stroudsburg, Pennsylvania.
August 4—Allentown, Pennsylvania, W. M. Farley.
August 6-18—Asheville, North Carolina, Revival Meeting.
August 25, 26—Brownwood, Texas, Men's Brotherhood.
September 15-19—Grenada, Mississippi, Revival Meeting.
October 6-13— Chickasha, Oklahoma, Revival Meeting.
October 19—Pensacola, Florida.
October 20—Little Rock, Arkansas, State S. S. Convention.
October 31—Meridian, Mississippi, State D. S. U. Convention.
November 3-5—Lebanon, Tennessee, Revival Meeting.
November 12—Winston-Salem, North Carolina, State Convention.
November 13—Kingsport, Tennessee, State Convention.

November 18—Orlando, Florida, State Convention.
December 1-8—Jacksonville, Florida, Revival Meeting.
December 10—Nashville, Tennessee, Meeting of Program
Committee for S. B. C.

During 1948 and 1949 Lee's appointments were about twice as many as in 1947.

At the same time, Dr. Lee declined, during the year 1947, 207 invitations which it was simply impossible for him to accept. They covered the following territory: Louisiana, Illinois, Mississippi, Georgia, Texas, North Carolina, South Carolina, California, Virginia, Ohio, Alabama, Tennessee, New Mexico, New York, West Virginia, Pennsylvania, Arkansas, Kentucky, Minnesota, Maryland, Connecticut, Indiana, Michigan, Florida, Kansas, Iowa, Oklahoma, Missouri, Massachusetts, Wisconsin, and Maine.

In the course of his travels to a majority of the states in the Union every year, Lee has had many interesting experiences. He is a great believer in prayer, of course, and so he often makes inquiry of those whom he meets on his journeys as to whether or not they pray. This gives him opportunity to witness for Christ. An experience that Lee had on a train from Houston to New Orleans some years ago will be of interest, as it is told by him in one of his sermons on prayer:

> Once—years ago—I went to San Angelo, Texas, and preached for nine days. On my return to Memphis via Houston and New Orleans, I added to my weariness occasioned by preaching, by reading a dry book someone had asked me to review. I had much weariness of flesh in reading, in looking out the windows, in watching the tumbleweeds roll across Texas plains, in hearing, in spite of my efforts not to do so, the small talk that was all

around, and in eating about as much sand as sugar in my grapefruit as we ran into a small sandstorm.

So, believing that rest is more of a change of activity than doing nothing, I decided I would ask all the passengers on the train if they had prayed that day. I started in the smoker. That was in the days before the women, slaves to the cigarette habit, made a smoker out of the whole train.

A big fat man with huge hands and heavy eyebrows, a cigar tilted upward in one corner of his mouth which drooped downward, was reading a newspaper. Politely I said to him: "Excuse me, sir, but have you prayed today?" "Huh?" he answered—with about as much surprise as a man has when thunder booms on a winter day, and with about as much courtesy as a bulldog uses in greeting a tramp. Then he answered my query by a scornful silence.

To a young man sitting beside him—a young man neatly dressed, having the personality of an intellectual, probably a college professor or a schoolteacher, slightly amused at what had taken place—I put the same question. Rapidly he began to talk. "Pray? Prayer!" he said. "Prayer is a mere subjective matter—potent and good only as it influences the subject. Prayer can have no objective. I insult God when I go to Him and ask Him to give me something—as one wheedles Santa Claus into giving a larger gift than I at first thought to obtain. Subjectively, prayer is good and—"

"Yes," I interrupted, "I have met your kind before. But I still believe that prayer can do, in helping people reach objectives worth while, what the steam in this oil-burning engine can do in helping the engine pull these cars into Houston."

Others I asked—some were young, some old. Some shook their heads. Some said, "No," with a bit of shamefaced apology in the tones of their voices. A few would not answer at all.

Presently as I went my way interviewing the passengers, I came to three young women—college girls, I think, judging from the college stickers on their suitcases. "Young

ladies," I said, "excuse me; but have you prayed today?"
All looked quickly at me as though I had thrown mud in
the bubbling brook of their chatter.

One looked at me about like an old maid greets a
burglar with a hat pin as he sneaks in the window. Her
look was the only answer I got. The fountain of her speech
froze quickly before the blizzard of my question about
prayer.

One informed me that she felt that my question was a
rude intrusion and intimated that I could be more pro-
fitably engaged in doing something else, even though she
smiled, her parted lips revealing beautiful teeth.

The third—more mild than the other two companions—
said: "Well, I believe in prayer and in being religious,
but I do not believe in parading one's religion in public or
in wearing one's heart on the sleeve or in advertising one's
piety."

After a few minutes, still having no affirmative answer
from anybody, I came to a little grandmotherish-looking
woman, with lovely white hair, a little old-fashioned bonnet
covering half her head, and with two ribbons tied in
a bow under her chin as a sort of anchor for the hat.
Her eyes beamed brightly as I approached her—as I
approached my sweetheart in courtship days—with affection
in my heart, with perfection in my manner, with confec-
tion in my pocket. "Grandmother," I said, "excuse me,
but have you prayed today?" To my utter amazement,
she sat upright in her seat, her eyes flashed, her lips
grew tight, her hands came together in a grasp in her lap
as she said, with some show of indignation: "My mother
taught me never to talk to strange men when I travel."

Somewhat taken aback or nonplussed, I stopped to ask
the same question of the next person across the aisle
from her—just a seat ahead. She leaned across the aisle and
loudly whispered in a little raucous voice: "He's crazy!"
and I think nearly everybody on the train thought I was
crazy. But the frigid hush with which I was greeted

or the disappointing replies or the mere shake of the
head did not deter me. I came at last to another big
fat man—my last hope. "Excuse me, sir," I said, rather
dolefully, "have you prayed today?" "Yes, sir," he said
loudly and gladly, even jubilantly, "God bless you, have
you?" He was a Methodist preacher. And I have loved
Methodist preachers a bit better since that day—because he
kept me from striking out completely every time I
went to bat—to use baseball language. I went to bat
thirty-six times that day and I got only one hit. Poor
batting average that—a mere twenty-eight.

Now if prayer is practiced by people, if prayer is a part
of their lives, why would they not talk about it? Why
did I get some answers I received? Why did I get no
answer—and nobody seemed happy to talk about prayer
except the young man I interviewed who had the erroneous
idea that prayer is good only as it influences the one who
prays. If prayer meant anything to those people interviewed, why did they consider me as a squawking crow
in the midst of a chorus of nightingales?

Concerning prayer I believe God will, if He sees fit,
send rain, make fields fruitful, stay famine, avert calamity,
stop pestilence, hush anarchy, raise suffering loved ones
to health. Then why should people be reticent about
talking about prayer?

Does God answer prayer for physical good? Yes. God
has not locked Himself out of His universe and thrown
the key away—has He? No. Is God a bellhop running up
and down the corridors of His world-hotel—having lost
the key to some of the doors? No. Has He made His own
laws which have unmade Him? No. Can not the Maker of
law adjust law according to His will—and so adjust it as
to make it the servant of the humblest individual on
earth? If the most insignificant individual asks God for
what he really needs, will not God, in return, marshal
all law in his behalf? Abraham on the summit of Mt.
Moriah, his trembling hand stayed by God as he lifts it
for the fatal stroke, would answer correctly all these ques-

tions. In answer to prayer, God will take Joseph languishing in the loathsome prison and set him on the throne of Egypt, the keys of the kingdom in his girdle. In answer to prayer, He will walk with Shadrach, Meschach, and Abednego into the fiery furnace and "ensheathe them with the fireproof garments of His divinity" so that the greedy flames will harm them no more than the clumsily gentle fingers of a man bring harm to his baby's head as the man plays with the curls on that head. In answer to prayer God will go down with Daniel into Darius' den of lions and make them lose their thirst for blood and food and give them lockjaw by His magic power so that His servant is harmed less by their teeth and jaws and paws than is a woman's cheeks by the falling of rose petals upon them while she sleeps. In answer to prayer, God will draw nigh to Elijah on Mt. Carmel and answer with fire from Heaven and then send clouds—clouds across skies that have been brass for years, above fields whose furrows have been iron for years—and cause them to pour rain upon the famine-stricken earth. In answer to prayer He will stop the funeral procession at Nain and take from the skeleton arms of death the widow's son and give him back to her joyful embrace. "The effectual fervent prayer of a righteous man availeth much" (Jas. 5:16).

Many honors have come to Lee through the years and during his travels, and it is right that they should have, in view of the fact that he has had a share in the dedication of buildings, chapels and churches, Bibles, and numerous other things. He is *always* ready to help others out, such as to bring the message at the dedication of a new building for the Baylor University College of Medicine, or to assist in the Convention of the United Dry Forces of Tennessee, Inc., by bringing his "Pay Day—Some Day" message to a joint session before the House and

Senate of Tennessee, and so forth. Among the honorary degrees that Lee has received since going to the Bellevue Baptist Church are:

Doctor of Divinity (D.D.) from Union University, Jackson, Tennessee, May 20, 1929.

Doctor of Laws (LL.D.) from Union University, Jackson, Tennessee, May 29, 1934.

Doctor of Divinity (D.D) from Furman University, Greenville, South Carolina, May 31, 1937.

Doctor of Letters (Litt. D.) from Bob Jones College, Cleveland, Tennessee, May 31, 1939.

Doctor of Divinity (D.D.) from Stetson University, De Land, Florida, June 1, 1948.

Governor James H. Davis, of Louisiana, who was tremendously influenced under Lee's preaching in New Orleans, appointed Dr. Lee an honorary Colonel on his Staff in the year of 1945. He was President of the Tennessee State Baptist Convention for four successive terms, 1932 to 1935, and was a Trustee of the Baptist Bible Institute, New Orleans, from 1923 to 1925, and on the Board of Greenville Women's College, Union University, and Bob Jones College. He is a member of the Home Missions Board of the Southern Baptist Convention. Elected an honorary member of the Alumni Association of the Southern Baptist Theological Seminary, Lee is the only man ever to have been thus honored.

"God is no respecter of persons." The soul of the highest monarch or the greatest scholar or the wealthiest philanthropist is of no more value in His sight than that of the humblest peasant, or the most illiterate pagan, or the poorest of the poor. Christ died for every man and woman who ever lived, whatever his or her position or condition, neither can any man receive forgiveness for his sins, life everlasting, and the assurance of eternal blessedness with the Lord in the Father's house of many mansions, apart from faith in the blood that was shed at Calvary to make atonement for our sins. "For *all* have sinned, and come short of the glory of God" (Rom. 3:23). Far from promising that special favor should be shown to those of high estate, or that multitudes in positions of leadership would believe on the Name of the only begotten of the Father, the Scripture tells us that "not many wise men after the flesh, not many mighty, not many noble, are called: but God hath chosen the foolish things of the world to confound the wise; and God hath chosen the weak things of the world to confound the things which are mighty; and base things of the world, and things which are despised, hath God chosen, yea, and things which are not, to bring to nought things that are: that no flesh should glory in His presence. But of Him are ye in Christ Jesus, who of God is made unto us wisdom, and righteousness, and sanctification, and redemption: that, according as it is written, He that glorieth, let him glory in the Lord" (I Cor. 1:26-31). Not *many* wise men after the flesh, not *many* mighty or *many* noble are called; but *some* are, else the adjective would have been "any" instead of "many."

In the providence of God, and by His grace, some of His chosen vessels are called to bear the Name of Christ before rulers. When the Lord commanded Ananias to visit the converted Saul of Tarsus in the house of Judas, on the street called Straight in the city of Damascus, He told the protesting Ananias that Saul was "a chosen vessel unto Me, to bear My name before the Gentiles, and kings, and the children of Israel: For I will shew him how great things he must suffer for My Name's sake" (Acts 9:15,16). Robert G. Lee appears to be another of the Lord's chosen vessels to bear His Name before those in high places, for he has had opportunity to witness to His saving grace to not a few political heads in this great land. How fruitful that witness has been is the responsibility of the Holy Spirit. Let the record speak for the faithfulness of the servant of the Lord.

The first governor with whom Bob Lee had any contact was ex-Governor Martin Ansell of South Carolina, who was, it will be recalled, one of the judges at the oratorical contest at Furman University, the contest which won a medal for Bob Lee from the University, and the first kiss from his girl, Bula Gentry. At that time Governor Ansell stated that he hoped that Lee's speech "would be read by future generations." That was in 1913.

It will also be recalled that, when the young pastor, Robert G. Lee, was the minister in Edgefield, South Carolina, a member of his congregation, who was also president of the bank at that time, was ex-Governor John C. Sheppard, of South Carolina. That was in the year 1918.

Another with whom Dr. Lee has had first hand contact during the years is Governor Cooper of South Carolina, who met him at the station in his official car and was Lee's host at breakfast, on one occasion. Governor Cooper's sister-in-law had been a member of the Baptist Church, of Princeton, South Carolina, when Bob Lee was pastor there.

In later years Governor Brough of Arkansas and Dr. Robert G. Lee appeared on a program together, at the dedication of a church at Tyronza, Arkansas.

Governor Horton, of Tennessee, spoke in the Bellevue Baptist Church at one time.

With others in places of leadership Lee has had even more intimate contact than with those already mentioned. Going through the files simply for the year 1947, we find the following letters:

The first is from the office of J. Strom Thurmond, Governor of the State of South Carolina, and is dated May 22, 1947. It will be remembered that Gov. Thurmond was a member of the First Baptist Church of Edgefield, South Carolina, of which Dr. Lee was pastor in 1918 and 1919.

Dear Dr. Lee:

Your kind letter of 19th instant has been received, and I was glad to hear from you. With regard to the case against—will say it has been my policy not to grant pardons or paroles until the same have been recommended by the Probation and Parole Board. I shall turn your letter over to Mr. Jake C. Todd, the Director of the Probation and Parole Board, and request that he consider it along with the other evidence in the case in making a determination with regard to this matter. I appreciate your writing me, and feel certain that the Probation and Parole Board will give great weight to your letter.

Any time that you are in Columbia, I want you to feel at home in the Mansion, so come right on out and take a meal or spend a night with us. I would like very much to see your family, as it has been many years since I saw them last.

Again expressing my pleasure at hearing from you, and with kindest regards and best wishes,

Very truly,

J. Strom Thurmond, Governor

On June 27, 1947, ex-Governor Pat M. Neff, former Governor of the State of Texas and now President of Baylor University, in Waco, Texas, wrote Dr. Lee:

Dear Dr. Lee:

For my daily letter of good wishes, I just want you to know that I cherish you very much as a friend, as a preacher, as a lecturer, and as a citizen.

Yours cordially,

Pat M. Neff

It will also be recalled that in 1927 Dr. Lee received a letter from Jimmie Davis, a member of the graduating class of Louisiana State University when Dr. Lee delivered the commencement address there. Twenty years later, Jimmie H. Davis became the Governor of the State of Louisiana, and under date of June 29, 1947, a letter came to Dr. Lee from the office of the Governor:

My dear Dr. Lee:

Many thanks for your letter of the 22nd. I am always delighted to hear from my favorite speaker and my good friend.

I was a member of the First Baptist Church in Pineville when I first heard you speak (at Louisiana College) and can say very frankly that your message was such an inspiration that I've never forgotten it. This one message did much toward the shaping of my career.

I hope to be in Memphis sometime this year, and in this event I shall give you a telephone call. With all good wishes, I am,

Sincerely,

Jimmy Davis, Governor

In the year 1925, Dr. Robert G. Lee spent two weeks in evangelistic effort at the First Baptist Church of Shreveport, Louisiana, of which Dr. M. E. Dodd is the gifted and beloved pastor. During the service one evening, Dr. Lee saw Huey Long in the audience, far back in the auditorium. Suppose we let Lee tell of a brief interview he had with Long during that stay in Shreveport:

> In my visitation which I did during the days of the meeting, I had an interview with Huey Long about the matter of his soul and the Christian life. With exuberant courtesy he received me. I told him I had come to talk with him about the Christian life and the church. He said: "If you have a double barrel, take good aim and pull both triggers at once."
>
> I asked him if he were a Christian. He said: "If I told you 'Yes,' many would think I am a big liar. But if believing that Jesus shed His blood for hell-bound sinners, like me and some church bigwigs are trustin' in, makes a Christian, then I am a Christian. Of course, there ain't many who think I am, but I have the best Christian mother any man can have."
>
> I said: "Well, if you are a Christian, you ought to show your colors and come and place your membership in the First Baptist Church and have a pastor." I had prayer with Huey. Whether he prayed, I do not know.

And whether Long ever put his heart's trust in the Lord Jesus Christ is a matter that only God knows.

It is inevitable that Dr. Lee should have had calls to numerous churches throughout America during the last twenty years. There are too many of them to mention in detail, nor is there any particular purpose in identifying the churches. Some of the calls, or preliminary interviews which might have led up to calls, were from the great "name" churches in the United States, in the North as well as in the South.

In the fall of 1931, Union University, Jackson, Tennessee, issued an invitation to Dr. Lee to become its president. He took the matter under consideration, but decided that that was not God's place for him, who had been called into the preaching ministry. The following year, Lee was invited to the presidency of the New Orleans Baptist Seminary. Dr. P. I. Lipsey, Chairman of the Board of Trustees, conferred with Lee on several occasions and exerted considerable pressure, for he felt that the Bellevue pastor was just the man for the job. It was while the two men were discussing the matter on a train ride out of New Orleans to their respective homes that Dr. Lee said suddenly: "Dr. Lipsey, I have made a mistake even to consider this invitation. If I should accept the presidency of the Institute, and try to keep my church, it will disparage the Seminary in the eyes of many people, knowing that the president is giving only half of his time to this work. Then, too, I cannot do at Bellevue what I ought to do if part of my energy is exercised on behalf of the New Orleans Bible Institute."

Thus, twice at least, the man who had been called to preach as a lad in South Carolina resisted the temptation to be diverted in the slightest degree from that concerning which he had had a heavenly vision and which he knew to be the will of God for him.

In the year 1934, Lee was the Chairman of the Committee on Order of Business for the Southern Baptist Convention, which met in May in Fort

Worth, Texas. As a chairman of one of the com-
mittees, he was not on the program as a speaker.
But on the final afternoon of the Convention, Sunday, something occurred which prohibited the ad-
vertised speaker, Dr. George W. Truett, from making
his appearance. The Convention voted unanimously
that Robert G. Lee should bring an address, and
he spoke that afternoon on "A Greater Than Solomon." It has now become one of his most famed
messages, although up to that time he had only
spoken on the subject sparingly. God was in the
message and many hearts were blessed. Dr. L. R.
Scarborough, who was President of the Southwestern Theological Seminary, Fort Worth, and once the
President of the Southern Baptist Convention, declared, after the message was over: "It is the greatest
sermon I have ever heard about Jesus."

During the last twenty years it has been Dr. Lee's
privilege to preach the baccalaureate sermon, or
deliver the commencement address, or conduct re-
vival meetings in fifty or more colleges, univer-
sities, and seminaries. Among these are the Univer-
sity of South Carolina; the University of Louisiana;
Texas State College; the Women's College of Denton,
Texas; Baylor-Belton College, Waco, Texas; Coker
College; Citadel Military College, of South Carolina;
Limestone College; Furman University; Greenville
Women's College; Winthrop College; Lander College;
Carson Newman College, Tennessee; Peabody College;
Tennessee Woman's College; Cumberland University;
Union University, of Tennessee; Southwestern
University; Memphis State College; Sophie Newcomb
College, of Louisiana; Tulane University; Louisiana

College, Pineville, Louisiana; Mississippi College, A
& M College; Mississippi Women's College; Baptist
University, of Oklahoma; Northwestern Seminary;
Louisville Seminary; Southwestern Seminary; New
Orleans Seminary; Bob Jones University, Greenville,
South Carolina; Berkley Divinity School; Wheaton
College, Illinois; Georgetown College, of Kentucky;
University of Florida; Stetson University; Woman's
College of Tallahassee, Florida; Howard College, Bir-
mingham, Alabama; Judson College, of Alabama; Blue
Mountain College; Shorter College, Rome, Georgia;
Oklahoma University; Georgia Military Academy;
Brennau College, Gainesville, Georgia; Kentucky
University, and Mercer University, of Georgia.

As an illustration of the value of this kind of
ministry, we review the influence of a week's revival meeting at Baylor-Belton College. At one of
the services, the President of the College said to
Dr. Lee: "Forget your watch. There are lots of lost
girls here. Hold the service as long as the Spirit
prompts you."

And so Lee, with all the ability that God has bestowed upon him, preached the Gospel to this
student body every day for a week. During the
series of meetings, 100 confessed their faith in the
Lord Jesus Christ, 56 of them coming forward in one
meeting. Among them was a little Jewish girl who
did not walk down the aisle, but literally ran, and,
as Dr. Lee took her hand, said: "What shall I do?
I believe in Jesus as my Saviour, but if I go home
and let my people know it, they will disinherit me.
What shall I do?"

"If you have trusted in Him as your Saviour,"

Lee replied, "you can trust Him in this matter, too."
And this the tearful, though joyful young Hebrew-
Christian did.

It is impossible to express the depths of feeling
and gratitude to God that Robert Lee experiences
every time he is invited to speak to college students.
In discussing the matter of these engagements, he
remarked: "Just to think that the boy who prayed
so much and worked so hard to go to college himself, has been permitted by God to take the Gospel
of Christ to all these colleges!"

Chapter IXX
HIGH HOURS

"A Vessel unto Honour, Sanctified,
and Meet for the Master's Use"

Every man has his high hours, his sublime experiences that stand out above all others of his life, and this is true even in a career that is drab and fruitless. Such lofty adventures may be confined to the not uncommon incidents that mankind knows—graduation from school or college, a home run with the bases full, the first job, an act of heroism, marriage, the birth of the first child, promotion in business, honor from one's fellows, the success of one's offspring, or retirement. There are loftier heights that are reached only by those whose whole manner and plane of living are more exalted than the average man's, experiences that tower above the commonplace as the soaring peaks of the Swiss Alps rise above the hills of Southern France. Nothing about Robert G. Lee, from his earliest recollections until the breath he draws today, has been commonplace. His has been an unordinary life, with a maximum of sacred and elevated experiences, but even so there have been high hours during which he has climbed to the summit and whose memory thrills him now even as it did when they struck. For it is a source of unceasing wonder and the ground of

415

continuous thanksgiving to God that He was pleased to take the underprivileged boy from the fields of South Carolina and, in answer to his prayers, place him in a position of power, in the Spirit, and usefulness in the things pertaining to His grace, kingdom, and glory.

Some of Lee's peaks have been recorded—the day when he left the farm to go to Panama, his entrance into Furman University, the prize and reward that he received for winning the oratorical contest in his Senior year at Furman, his first church, the great day of answered prayer in Edgefield in respect to the $14,000 offering, the birth of Bula G., her conversion and baptism, the calls to such churches as in New Orleans, Charleston, and Memphis, and the great day in Miami when he addressed the Southern Baptist Convention. The memory of these great days will ever recur to this servant of the Lord and he will praise God for these occasions, but we must remember that Dr. Lee is, above all else, a preacher and an orator, so it is the high hours in his preaching career, such as that experience at Miami, that must be given the supreme place as far as his personal experiences are concerned.

There was that hour in Waco, Texas, in November, 1924. It was with very solemn joy that Dr. Lee had accepted an invitation to address a state-wide Young People's Conference for his first sermon in the state of Texas, in the church where B. H. Carroll had once served God. Since he had been a lad, Robert Lee had heard of Dr. Carroll, called by some the greatest preacher with the greatest mind since the Apostle Paul, a great scholar, mighty in the Scriptures, be-

Dr. Lee in His Office at Bellevue, 1949

Bula G. Lee (Mrs. Edward R.) King and Commander King with Their Three Children, (L. to R.) Robbye Lee King, Edward Lee King, and Bettye Lee King, 1949

loved in Southern Baptist life, influential to the far corners of the earth, and founder of the Southwestern Baptist Theological Seminary of Fort Worth. Dr. J. M. Dawson was also pastor of the First Baptist Church of Waco for many years, and the city was known to Lee because it was the home of Baylor University.

When Lee knew that he was to try to preach Christ where that great giant, Dr. Carroll, once stood, he thought that he knew something of how Peter must have felt when, falling at the feet of the Lord Jesus, he said: "Depart from me, for I am a sinful man, O Lord." That the Lord should use him, the former country boy from the little log cabin and the red hills of South Carolina, to be His witness in such an hour and at such a place, almost overwhelmed him. It was not pride in his heart, but only gratitude, as he remembered the days of toil as he gazed between the ears of the white mule on the old farm, and the days of dreaming his dreams. He felt as if, had he one thousand tongues and could he talk one thousand hours or live one thousand years, he could not thank God enough for placing him in that pulpit to proclaim the unsearchable riches of Christ. So he wept as he awaited the moment he should ascend the rostrum.

The Holy Spirit was evidently present in great power that morning. The topic of the message was "Christ Crucified," and when the time came for the altar call, Lee asked the male quartette from the Southwestern Seminary to sing: "Shall I Crucify My Saviour?" As the quartette sang this Gospel song over and over again, Lee extended the invitation,

and three hundred young people came forward, some
in joy, many in tears and agony of soul, confessing
their sins and asking God to save them, or confessing
their backslidings and asking God for healing, while
others dedicated themselves anew, surrendering all
to the Lord Jesus. Memory of it still brings unspeakable gratitude to the heart of Dr. Lee, with
renewed vows to give God glory, and to give Him
all that he has until his days are done.

There was that hour in New Orleans in 1929. It
was the annual meeting of the Southern Baptist
Convention. A year earlier the Program Committee
had invited Dr. Lee to bring a message to the 1929
convention. It was the first time that he had been so
honored. When the preacher entered the vast auditorium, it was packed to the doors. People were
there from throughout all the states of the South.
Lee, feeling like an ambassador sent from Heaven to
deliver God's message to this gathering, ascended the
platform before the appointed time of the sermon,
as is his custom, dignified, outwardly calm, but within
strung high and ready to go.

The speaker preceding him went beyond his allotted time. The election of officers followed, an unusually long, drawn-out affair. One delay after a-
nother brought the time to fifty minutes past the
hour when Lee should have been introduced. No
one who has not had a somewhat similar experience
can have complete sympathy for the plight in which
Lee found himself, and no one who does not know
Robert G. Lee can possibly estimate the ordeal
through which he was passing. Dr. Lee is, and has
been through the years, exacting in respect to

promptness; he cannot bear anyone's being late for any kind of engagement, and has himself been meticulously careful to do an appointed task at the appointed hour. As he sat there, the minutes ticking by, he realized that he must shorten a sermon that he had prayed over and worked on for nearly a year. His heart was heavy and very fearful lest, because of these delays, he should prove inadequate as the mouthpiece of God.

When the time finally came for Lee to be introduced, and the chairman had finished his kind words, the speaker sprang like a cougar to the pulpit and began his message. It was the noon hour. Most of the people had been seated in the auditorium for from three to four hours. Many of them were hungry. Some of them were excited because of the balloting in connection with the election of the Convention president. Consequently there was considerable movement as numbers left their seats and others filled them, and a few minutes later as some who had departed came back again and sought advantageous standing space.

The preacher's text was I Corinthians 15:3-4: "For I delivered unto you first of all that which I also received, how that Christ died for our sins according to the Scriptures; and that He was buried, and that He rose again the third day according to the Scriptures." Speaking without notes, and beginning in his customary manner in a quiet voice, characteristically holding his Bible in his left hand and pressed against his heart, Lee proclaimed the message of God. The crowd, finally settled, listened like spellbound children for the full sermon. And as the

preacher spoke of the Lord Jesus Christ—of His
sacrificial death on the Cross, of His bodily resurrection from the grave, and of His exalted position
now at the right hand of the Throne of the Majesty
on high, his words were, as one of the audience said
later, quoting from the *Ancient Ballad* of Hindustan,
"as sweet as founts that murmur near to one who in
the deserts drear, with parched tongue, moves faint
and slow." The Spirit of God was behind that message, and souls were blessed and hearts made to
overflow with the joy of the Lord because of His
matchless sacrifice of Himself for sin and for sinners, and because of the privileges that belong to
those who have put their trust in Him, the living and
exalted Saviour.

There was that hour at Winona Lake, Indiana, in
1929, when, for the first time, Dr. Lee spoke in the
Billy Sunday Tabernacle to the 6,000 gathered there.
Again he spoke on the Lord Jesus, the title of his
sermon being "Jesus of Nazareth." So much had
he prayed for that message, so thoughtfully and
carefully had he prepared it and in such dependence
upon the Holy Spirit, that he was not amazed to see
the answer to his prayer in the response that the
vast audience, moved by the Spirit's wooing, offered.

There was that hour in Chicago in 1930. Dr. Lee
had been invited by Dr. James M. Gray, President
of Moody Bible Institute, to address, for the first
time, a large audience at the annual Founder's Week
Conference. This was one of Lee's first important
preaching trips to the North, one of the first times
that he was invited as the guest speaker outside of
his denomination. Dr. Gray had never heard Robert

G. Lee speak, but his fame had reached to Chicago,
and knowing Lee's sound doctrinal position, the
esteemed President of the Institute felt very sure of
his ground. In introducing the speaker, however,
Dr. Gray, careful not to place himself too fully
on record concerning a man whose message and
manner he was not familiar with, said: "Our brother,
Robert Lee, from the South will speak. I have never
heard him. You have the opportunity to judge for
yourself."

Burning within with a passion to proclaim Christ,
as always, and thrilled to the core to be standing
on hallowed ground, where the great D. L. Moody
had held forth the Word of Life, Lee was conscious
of the power of the Spirit behind his words. God
blessed the message, and at the conclusion, when
Dr. Gray gave an invitation, about threescore held
up their hands in response to the opportunity to
receive the Lord Jesus Christ as Saviour.

There was the hour in Dallas in 1935. Thousands
had come into the city for the annual Texas State
Baptist Training Union Convention, which was to
be held at the First Baptist Church, one of the
largest white Baptist churches in the world, if not
the largest. This was the pulpit that was brought
into prominence, and later became the outstanding
pulpit of the Southern Baptist Convention, because
it was where Dr. George W. Truett was the pastor
for some years, thrilling and blessing vast multitudes
by his eloquent preaching.

The opportunity to preach to this group of young
people was a glorious experience for Robert Lee. He
was very conscious of the high privilege that was

his in being the herald of the Lord to these young
men and women. Beginning very slowly and quietly,
as he usually does, the preacher was in a few moments extolling Jesus as the only begotten Son
of the Father. He marshaled one after another the
names of men of eminence in every realm of
thought and deed, and showed the consummate and
majestic supremacy of the One above all others, the
One bearing the Name that is above every name,
Jesus, the Son of God. The climax of the address
brought before the audience the beauty and the
glory of the Christ who is our Saviour, and the appeal
was made by the preacher that He should be, in
truth, Lord of all—Lord of all who sat within the
sound of the preacher's voice, and Lord of all
within the heart of every individual gathered there.

Years later, Dr. Floyd B. Chaffin, pastor of the
Polytechnic Baptist Church of Ft. Worth, wrote to
Dr. Lee and said, concerning that message: "I shall
never forget the great service in the First Baptist
Church of Dallas a few years ago when you preached
. . . on Jesus Christ, the Son of the living God, and
how that great congregation of some 4,000 people,
just in one accord, spontaneously broke out in a
resounding applause all over that great auditorium
as the Holy Spirit flooded our souls with His presence. I believe that was one of the greatest hours
I have ever been in or observed on an occasion such
as that."

There was that other great hour in Chicago in
1937. Twelve thousand people were gathered in the
Coliseum. A choir of 2,000 voices was led by Talmadge
Bittikofer. Lee's message on that occasion was on

"The Name of Jesus." It was another time when he felt an especial unction of the Holy Spirit. Following the benediction, there was a multitude of commendatory expressions from those who had heard the address, and Lee's heart was rewarded because these had not so much to do with the speaker as with the Christ whom the speaker portrayed as being beyond all words to describe.

There was that second hour in Dallas, this time 1947. Again Lee was to speak from the pulpit that Truett had made famous, on this occasion for the annual Evangelistic Conference. Lee preached twice, and the general aftermath of these messages was that this, as it fell from the lips of many, was "the greatest thing of its kind we have ever experienced." With power, with earnestness, and with effectiveness, the God-gifted speaker challenged the thousands from all over the state of Texas and nearby territories as they had never been challenged before, and when he spoke on "Jesus Above All," souls were blessed and a deep impression for Christ was made. Among the numerous prominent Baptist preachers and leaders who told Dr. Lee of their thankfulness to God for these inspired sermons we find the names of Dr. T. C. Gardner, Director of the Baptist Training Union Convention of Texas; Dr. Kyle M. Yates, Pastor of the Second Baptist Church of Houston; Dr. C. E. Matthews, Superintendent of Evangelism of the Southern Baptist Convention; Dr. Porter M. Bailes, Pastor of the First Baptist Church of Tyler, Texas; the Rev. B. W. Mantooth, Pastor of the First Baptist Church of Crystal City, Texas; the Rev. W. Fred Swank, Pastor of the Sagamore Hill Bap-

tist Church of Ft. Worth; and Marcellus Watkins, of
Dallas. Words such as these were heard on every
side: "If it had cost me five hundred dollars to come
here for this conference, it would have been worth
it"; "The power the preacher had proves the reality
of the Holy Spirit"; "I wish God would let Dr.
Lee live one hundred more years"; and "The days of
Spurgeon settled upon Dallas today."

Other high hours were experienced in various
places, such as Ocean Grove, New Jersey, where
Dr. Lee has preached more than twenty times in the
great auditorium that seats some 8,000 people. We
cannot mention all these lofty experiences, nor need
we do so. But there were others. For example, Lee
brought the Friday night address at the Southern
Baptist Convention of 1947, held in St. Louis, Missouri, following which he received scores of letters
from Baptist pastors throughout the South, with
such comments as: "I take heart from the ministry
of men like yourself," and "Jesus becomes more
precious when I hear you proclaim Him as you do,"
and "You have touched the hearts of more young
preachers than any man in our generation."

Highest hour struck in Lee's home city, Memphis,
Tennessee, in May, 1948, at the 91st Annual Southern
Baptist Convention. Two years before at Miami, Flor-
ida, Dr. Lee had been nominated for the presidency
of the S. B. C., but after the vote was counted
a second time, it developed that he was defeated.
But in 1948 Lee was elected by an overwhelming
majority, to become the President of the Southern
Baptist Convention, with its over 6,000,000 members.
In a day when denominational organizations as a

whole are falling away from leadership by men known to be fundamentalists, in this, one of the largest denominations, the newly chosen president was a cover-to-cover believer in the Bible—in the virgin birth, deity, bodily resurrection, and coming again of our Lord Jesus Christ, and that His return will be premillennial. Rarely do we see a man outstandingly conservative voted into high office, for it is some of these things which the liberals have scoffed at or renounced.

This highest honor that the Southern Baptist Convention can bestow upon any man is one that was fittingly given to Robert Greene Lee. For more than a decade he has been the outstanding pulpiteer of the Convention, ranking with T. deWitt Talmadge and Dr. George W. Truett as an orator, and being in demand and extremely popular both east and west of the Mississippi, not only on account of his oratorical ability but also because of his gracious manner and humble attitude.

When Dr. Lee was introduced to the Convention by the retiring President, Dr. Louie D. Newton, Pastor of Druid Hills Baptist Church, Atlanta, Lee said: "We Baptists are many, and all of us want to be much. We want to measure thirty-six inches to the yard for God, to weigh sixteen ounces to the pound on God's scales, and strike twelve for God on His clock. We want to be right—not somewhat right, not ten per cent right, but altogether and exactly right for God. With gratitude to God, and thankful for the confidence the Convention has placed in me, we shall go forward."

The announcement of Dr. Lee's election was publicized far and wide, as all such elections are. But nowhere was the event more cheerfully announced than in *The Fort Mill Times,* the newspaper of the little town in South Carolina where Bob Lee grew up. We quote in part from the article in this publication:

> Fort Mill received a double honor last week when two of its native sons were named top officials of the Southern Baptist Convention in its annual meeting at Memphis. Dr. Robert G. Lee, born and reared on a farm three miles southeast of Fort Mill, was elected the convention's president on the first ballot. A boyhood chum and lifelong friend, the Rev. Porter Bailes, was elected to the convention's first vice-presidency. Rev. Bailes was born and reared in the Gold Hill community, several miles northwest of town.
>
> Both are distinguished ministers of the Southern Baptist Church. . .

On the closing day of the Convention, the newly-elected president spoke at the evangelistic service in the Crump Stadium, where nearly 30,000 people were gathered, on "God's Inevitable Alternative." His text was John 3:36: "He that believeth on the Son hath everlasting life: and he that believeth not the Son shall not see life; but the wrath of God abideth on him." It was the largest assembly that had ever come together at any session of a Southern Baptist Convention. With all the fervor and ability which God has given him and in a Spirit-empowered message, backed by many days of prayer, Lee declared that:

> God's alternatives are open to all—eternal life or the wrath of God. They confront everyone today and a choice must be made. Any man who values his soul will surely

say, "Give me eternal life." . . . We must either meet Christ bearing our sins, or we must find someone else to bear our sins for us . . . I charge you, men and women, rest not until you have Him as your precious Redeemer. If you die without Him, or if you are unsaved when He comes, you must be shut out of His bright presence forever. Come to Him as He is, and now. Come to Him as you are—now.

There was a very wonderful response to the Gospel invitation, a great number coming forward to confess Jesus Christ as Saviour and Lord, and literally thousands re-dedicating themselves to Him.

A few days later, Lee received a letter from Robert C. Cannon, pastor of the Merton Ave. Baptist Church, Memphis, who was Chairman of the General Committee of the Evangelistic Service of the Convention.

Dear Dr. Lee:

I haven't words to express my gratitude to you and to God for the contribution made to the most remarkable evangelistic service that I have ever seen. Truly, God was in this undertaking from the very beginning and to Him be the honor and the glory for all that was accomplished.

You will be interested to know that 353 people signed cards and an undetermined number came forward who did not sign cards during the invitation, which you extended to them. That was a marvelous sight to behold. A splendid offering was received, which amounted to $6,480.37, the exact count of the committee in charge.

Thanks again for the very vital part you played and the splendid contribution made on your behalf.

With every kind wish always, I am

Fraternally yours,
ROBERT C. CANNON

Out of literally hundreds of congratulatory letters
in Dr. Lee's files, from Southern Baptists, Baptists
elsewhere, and others in places of leadership in the
evangelical faith, we have chosen a handful so as to
show the enthusiasm with which the new president's
election was received:

> Really I feel much better about our affairs generally
> when a man of your consecration, self-effacement, and
> genuine ability is called upon to lead us.
>
> JOHN L. HILL
> Editor, Broadman Press,
> Nashville, Tennessee

> My own heart is singing a song of thanksgiving. I am
> so happy that we have you as our leader. I do not know
> anybody in the entire Convention to whom this assignment
> could more appropriately be given.
>
> KYLE M. YATES
> Pastor, Second Baptist Church,
> Houston, Texas

> I am especially grateful because associations with you
> in the past have given me opportunities to know that
> not only are you a great preacher who glories in pro-
> claiming the inspired Word of God, but that you also are
> a wise leader, knowing how to find the will of God in
> the complex affairs of denominational responsibility.
>
> DUKE K. McCALL
> Exec. Sec., Southern Baptist Convention
> Executive Committee, Nashville, Tenn.

> This is to congratulate you on the marvelous victory
> which was yours recently at the Southern Baptist Con-
> vention when you were elected to its presidency. It was
> not unexpected to us, your many friends and admirers, be-
> cause we have looked forward to this time when you

would be elected to this high place of great responsibility and opportunity.

> PORTER M. BAILES
> Pastor, First Baptist Church,
> Tyler, Texas

I am taking this occasion to offer my sincere congratulations to you on your election as president of our Convention. I use the word "congratulations" with due attention to its meaning. Your election as president carries the personal confidence of tens of thousands of Southern Baptists. I am sure that you are primarily conscious of the responsibility which the position involves, but your many friends and supporters are conscious of their confidence in you.

> M. T. RANKIN
> Executive Secretary of the Foreign
> Mission Board,
> Richmond, Virginia

Our warmest congratulations on your recent election. We rejoice in the soundness in the faith of the Southern Baptist Convention. It is a real testimony that a man who holds all the truths that you do should be elected as president.

> WILLIAM CULBERTSON
> President, Moody Bible Institute,
> Chicago, Illinois

I love you better than I ever did . . . I have rejoiced in every step of progress that you have made in your great ministry. I rejoice in the new heights that you have just reached. I have felt for a long time that somebody ought to come into our midst to take the place of George Truett. He had heart-power. He wielded a tremendous influence over all groups in the denomination. I know of no man better fitted to do this than you.

> ELLIS A. FULLER
> President, Southern Baptist
> Theological Seminary
> Louisville, Kentucky

Beyond any question you are the man for the place, and it is a most worthy recognition of your remarkable services and abilities—though to me it was a recognition tardily expressed. You should have been accorded this honor years ago.

LAWRENCE T. LOWREY
President, Blue Mountain College,
Blue Mountain, Mississippi

I get a thrill every time I think about your election as president of the Convention, and the great victory which was won for democratic procedure and fundamental Christianity in your election.

W. HERSCHEL FORD
Pastor, First Baptist Church,
El Paso, Texas

Because of our intimate fellowship through the years, I wish to join your host of friends with a word of warmest congratulations, prayers, and best wishes for your administration as president of the Southern Baptist Convention.

May God give grace, guidance, and glory, strength, wisdom, and power for your many arduous duties.

M. E. DODD
Pastor, First Baptist Church,
Shreveport, Louisiana

Let me say that it is with deep appreciation that I send you my congratulations on being elected to the presidency of the Southern Baptist Convention. It is to me an answer to prayer.

JOHN W. BRADBURY
Editor, *The Watchman-Examiner,*
New York City

May the Lord continue to bless you and use you mightily. May He give you physical endurance and impart to you grace and wisdom for the tremendous responsibility under

which you labor as you lead on in the advancement of
the kingdom of God for the glory of our Master.

FRANK H. LEAVALL
Secretary, Department of Southern
Baptist Student Work,
Nashville, Tennessee

In response to these gracious, loving, and challenging communications, Dr. Lee replied, telling
his friends of the very deep gratitude abiding in
his heart because of their thoughtfulness in writing
him as they did. To all of them he brought one
common request:

Humbly do I beg of you to pray for me that I may
have the wisdom which is from above and that Christ
may be glorified in millions of Southern Baptists in
thousands of our Baptist churches even as the sun is
glorified in fragrant flowers.

Calling upon all Southern Baptists to pray as
never before and to reach out with the Gospel in
widening arc, President Lee set himself to the
task of fulfilling the position to which he was called
with indefatigable energy. This meant that he must
work harder than ever at Bellevue in order to do
a dutiful work and fulfil God's principal call to
him, in less hours than he had at his disposal hereto-
fore. The deacons and membership of the church,
conscious of the high honor paid to their pastor,
were enthusiastic in their co-operative spirit and
desire for Dr. Lee to work a good work for the
Convention. But the conscientious heart of the pastor
of Bellevue would not permit him to neglect God's
people under his care. Thus he drove himself tire-
lessly for them; at the same time, he carried on a

tremendous correspondence in connection with his office as President of the S. B. C., attended committee meetings pertaining to the office at various points in the South; and traveled from the Atlantic to the Pacific speaking as the Convention's Chief Executive. Within twelve months he had addressed thirty audiences on the Convention's behalf.

Was Lee's highest hour in Memphis in 1948? Yes, but that hour extended into a second hour when the Convention met in Oklahoma City in May, 1949.

In his presidential address, Lee straddled no fences in affirming his own convictions as to the efficacy of the blood of Christ. Said he:

> This body [the Southern Baptist Convention] is called upon to do great work for God, to endure hardness as a good soldier of Jesus Christ. Therefore, it must be forever free from pernicious anaemia—lack of blood in its theology, preaching, teaching, and its fight with sin. Plenty of healthy blood this body must have in a world that has a leprosy worse than that of Uzziah and Naaman, a palsy worse than that of the man borne of four, a fever worse than that of Peter's wife's mother, a blindness worse than that of Bartimaeus, an insanity worse than that of Gadara's wild man.
>
> Every bloodless prescription, we must reject. No bloodless surgery we must attempt—lest evangelization give way to emaciation. A Gospel stripped of the red blood stream "drawn from Immanuel's veins" may be a gospel of culture, of morality, of civilization, but it is not the Gospel of Christ.

Baptist Convention is concerned, took place on

> Not to preach Christ crucified is to rob life's sky of the sun by day and of the stars by night. To preach this Christ must be our delight, our most daring duty.

A history-making event, as far as the Southern

Saturday morning, when the Convention was addressed by a Negro, Dr. E. W. Perry, minister of the Tabernacle Baptist Church, Oklahoma City, and vice-president-at-large of the National Baptist Convention, U.S.A.

Dr. Perry, knowing of Dr. Lee's love for the colored people and his interest in them, a matter that has been publicized to some extent by the newspapers through Lee's advocacy of the addition of Negroes to the Memphis Police Force, turned to Lee just before he gave his address and said: "Mr. President, I've been more than sixty years coming from the log cabin where I was born to this high and exalted position to which my people have elected me, and knowing that you are a stickler for time, I'm asking you in advance—please don't ring me down."

Dr. Lee arose, and amid laughter among many, promised not to do so.

When Dr. Perry concluded his sermon and had seated himself, President Lee arose, and said: "Dr. Perry, I want you to come here and stand by me and take my hand. I want this Convention to witness a parable in black and white, written in red. You said that over sixty years ago you were born in a log cabin in Mississippi, and that now you have been lifted up to the high position to which your people have placed you. I, too, was born in a log cabin— in South Carolina; and my Southern Baptist people have honored me by placing me in my position. You and I both have been placed there by the vote of confidence of our people, but the same Christ who saved you is the same Christ who saved me, and both of us have been washed white in the precious blood of the Lamb. This is the parable in black and white, written in red."

Commenting upon the incident, Dr. O. W. Taylor, editor of the *Baptist and Reflector,* said: "That accomplished more for good race relations than all the academic theorizing in the world. There were few dry eyes in the audience."

Lee's ability as presiding officer showed itself in many ways, and perhaps never more than when a motion was made which threatened to divide the Convention in half. This was on Thursday morning. Dr. E. P. Alldredge moved an amendment to the Constitution, as follows:

> No one who belongs to or affiliates with any state or local Council of Churches which is connected with or sponsored by the Intercouncil Field Department of the Federal Council or anyone or more of its six affiliated Councils shall be eligible to serve on any board, agency, or institution of this Convention—either as an official, employee, or board member.

The motion, as it was made, was rather a popular one, and it seemed clear that it might pass immediately, in view of the fact that the very high majority of Southern Baptists disapprove of the Federal Council of Churches. Dr. Lee himself is strongly against the Federal Council, and only the night before this motion was introduced, in his President's address, stated in no uncertain terms his stand in this matter. He felt, however, that the motion was a grave mistake and that it might divide the Convention in half. Six men rose to their feet and spoke against the motion, only one of them being known as a Federal Council man. Then, very dramatically, Dr. Lee handed the gavel to Vice-President Porter M. Bailes and himself took the floor and stated to the audience at large: "Everybody knows my position as to the Federal Council of Churches, but we cannot afford to take a stand about which we will have to be defending ourselves for months and months to come. From our earliest history we have repudiated any coercive power over the consciences of men as to their religious actions. I do not walk with the presumptuous step of a "know-it-all," but, brethren, this motion is a mistake; therefore, I make a motion that it be tabled."

Immediately the Convention was swung over to his judgment. The motion made by Dr. Alldredge did not pass, and what Dr. Lee felt might be sure disaster, was averted.

The *Western Recorder,* issue of June 16, 1949, has a leading editorial entitled "One Man's Influence":

> The tremendous influence which one man can exercise over the masses was clearly demonstrated at the recent Oklahoma City Convention by President R. G. Lee.
>
> E. P. Alldredge had introduced a motion which, unquestionably, would have carried by a heavy majority. Though there was heavy opposition to it from the platform its passage seemed certain.
>
> President Lee, as a last resort (so far as we know he had not previously announced preference either way), turned the gavel over to the second officer and came to the microphone and said, quietly: "Brethren, this motion is a mistake; it ought not to pass. I move that the whole matter be tabled." He did not argue the point, he offered no reason for his opinion, he merely stated his belief. But that simple statement of belief was enough to turn the Convention in another direction. The second officer put

Dr. Lee's motion to table and the Convention passed it
overwhelmingly.

Only on one other occasion, so far as our memory goes,
has there been a like display of influence. There was a
trying moment in the Convention which met in New
Orleans in 1917. A leader had made a statement relative to the First World War, then in progress, which
precipitated heavy division. There was a dangerous spirit,
and confusion reigned. The fellowship of the Convention
was in jeopardy. Dr. George W. Truett moved quickly
to the platform, and, in quiet manner and voice but
with conviction as pointed as a steel blade, called on his
brethren to exercise caution lest their spirit do grave harm
to the cause of Christ. They listened to one man.

It will be a grievous day for Southern Baptists if the
day ever comes when there is not a man among them
whose voice and influence carries on out to the masses
and on to the last man on the outskirts of the denomination.

The young men of our day do well to see to it, moment by moment and in all their dealing private and
public, that their influence with the sheep of God's
pasture is kept wholesome and strong. Not only does every
man owe it to himself to be worthy; he owes it to the
cause of Christ. No matter how gifted, or how potentially
strong; a man's reach for good is no greater than the confidence of the masses in him personally and in his
leadership. Then, when the public discovers, once in a
while, and it will, that such good men have erred in
judgment, confidence lives on.

The Baptist Messenger, in its issue of May 26,
1949, commenting upon the Alldredge amendment
and the action that took place, states:

. . . The Convention, however, did not vote the issue.
It voted Dr. Lee's integrity. The question remains: Was
Dr. Lee right? Most people believe that time will prove
that he was. The second time the Convention appeared

moored to his integrity was in connection with the Chicago question.

This Chicago question has to do with vote of the S. B. C. to have its 1950 meeting in Chicago. Some were for this and some were against it. It was suggested that perhaps the S. B. C. was trying to woo the Northern Baptist Convention. Commenting again on Dr. Lee's integrity in saving the situation, this same publication states:

> . . . He [Lee] made a statement woven with unquestioned humility denying any ulterior motive. It is as follows:
> (1) "I acknowledge that the vote on next year's Convention may be misinterpreted—and may be labeled as 'religious imperialism.'
> (2) "We may be accused of seeking invasion into Northern Convention territory. We are not going there to make any effort to win any Northern Baptist Convention churches to affiliation with our Southern Baptist Convention.
> (3) "We go there by vote of this Convention after the minority reports to substitute Chicago were accepted.
> (4) "This Southern Baptist Convention is not meeting in Chicago to flirt with any Northern Baptist Convention church or Baptist body with purpose to get their affiliation with Southern Baptist Convention. We go to do our work without effort to rule or win Northern churches to join our Convention. We go only to do our work and glorify the Lord Jesus Christ and so to live that He may be glorified in us."

Returning to the Alldredge motion for a moment, this question will still need to be faced by the Convention. The motion was not defeated but tabled. By the end of another year, however, the mind of the Convention may be settled on a matter where hasty judgment might have been regretted.

During the first year that Dr. Lee held office as president, and during the Convention up to the night of the election, Dr. Lee's ministry was, as granted by many, "outstandingly and winsomely performed, [giving] the Convention a spiritual leadership and an evangelistic inspiration which meet the heart-hunger of millions of Southern Baptists." Thus it was that, when the time for election came and Dr. Porter M. Bailes placed the name of Dr. Lee in nomination to succeed himself, the messengers, ten thousand strong, "with unsurpassed unanimity" rose and re-elected him enthusiastically, thus declaring their approval of his first year's service. This, surely, was a prolongation of that highest hour that began one year earlier.

Following the Convention, once again a myriad of commendatory letters arrived at Dr. Lee's office. We cannot begin to quote from all of them, but we do cite excerpts from some—to show how God ruled in the act of Presiding Officer Lee as He has ruled so many times in the words of Preacher Robert G. Lee:

> "Thou art come to the kingdom for such a time as this." I don't know of another man in the Southern Baptist Convention that could have led the people, when they were battling between two opinions, as you did. I thank God for you, and may God keep you in His love is my prayer.
>
> A. M. VOLLMER
> Executive Secretary and Treasurer,
> Kentucky Baptist Foundation,
> Louisville, Kentucky

I am so grateful to the Lord that He has given you to us for just such days as these. I felt that you demonstrated wisdom that could come only from God in the way that you handled some of the problems that were presented during the Convention.

J. A. Pennington
Secretary, Brotherhood and Evangelism,
Oklahoma City, Oklahoma

I think we have never had a president during my attendance upon the Convention who was more respresentative of what I believe Christ would have in the president of our Convention than I saw in you.

S. F. Lowe
Director, The Radio Commission,
Southern Baptist Convention,
Atlanta, Georgia

Allow me to congratulate you for the wonderful way in which you presided during the meeting of the recent Convention . . . Your emphasis on prayer was a needed one, and will be, as we go forward in the work of the Lord Jesus Christ.

H. J. Rushing
Pastor, West Laurel Baptist Church,
Laurel, Mississippi

The dignity, consideration, and fairness with which you officiated deeply impressed all of us. God certainly brought you to this high and exalted position for just such a day as this.

Harwell Davis
President, Howard College,
Birmingham, Alabama

Your generous and gracious consideration of my illness and consequent absence from the Convention, and your prayers and the message have warmed my heart very deeply. Thank you, my dear friend, and God bless you always! I have read all the reports on the Convention that I could get my hands on and have seen some of the brethren who

attended, and from every source there come expressions
of highest appreciation for the magnificent manner in
which you presided and for the deep undertone of
spirituality which you created.

M. E. DODD
Pastor, First Baptist Church,
Shreveport, Louisiana

Dr. John W. Bradbury, Editor, *The Watchman-
Examiner,* New York City, in a letter addressed to
C. E. Bryant, Chairman of Publicity of the Con-
vention, stated:

> His leadership of the Convention was admirable and
> exemplary in the highest Christian sense. There was not
> one moment when he was in the chair but that we felt
> we were all in the presence of the divine Spirit under
> the faithfulness of Dr. Lee's spiritual purpose.

These, then, have been Robert G. Lee's high hours.
But of what value the praise of men, of what purpose
high hours, if there be not praise from God and
if such experiences do not draw one into closer
fellowship with the All Highest? With some men
the praise of their fellows is disastrous, for it turns
their thoughts upon themselves and their own prominence, and away from God. With other men, such
praise only casts them down before the feet of the
Lord and issues in an even deeper dependence upon
Him as their strength—for he who lives in the Book,
who spends much time in the Throne Room upon his
knees, and who seeks to live in obedience to the
revealed will of God, is very conscious of the fact
that he is but a sinner saved by grace, worthy in
himself of nothing but eternal judgment, and even
though he has been redeemed through the precious

blood of Christ, is aware that his best service is imperfect and that all his strength and all his power are in Christ and in the Holy Spirit. Such a one is the former South Carolina share-cropper lad—not given to self-centered pride over what God has accomplished through him or because of the favor that God has given him with his fellows, but amazed and awed that the Lord could take one such as he and raise him to the place of leadership over millions of His people. If he can perform this ministry, not in his own strength but in that of the Almighty, and to the praise and the glory of his beloved Lord Jesus, this is his highest hour.

Conclusion
A CHOSEN VESSEL

If, upon laying aside this volume, the reader should exclaim: "What a great man is Lee!" we have utterly failed in our purpose. For the life-story of Robert G. Lee is a record of the greatness of our God and an example of what He can and will do through one who is obedient to His Word, surrendered to Him, and willing and prepared to be an instrument to His hand. Dr. Lee's preaching is in the Spirit's power, his shepherding is in the Saviour's compassion and love, and his leadership is under God's direction. That which has been wrought by Lee has, in reality, been wrought by God through faith, and whatever commendation or praise has been received by the worker from his fellow-men has been accepted in the consciousness that God alone is worthy of praise. Thus the servant of the Lord has not been spoiled by adulation or made proud. On the contrary, he lives in a sense of constant wonder at the way that the Lord has led him day by day and year by year.

The life-story of Robert G. Lee serves as a challenge to multitudes of young men and women. For, in taking this lad of poor and humble parentage, with little opportunity for early training and seemingly insurmountable obstacles in his path, and enduing him with power and bringing him to a posi-

442

tion of wide influence and established leadership in his denomination and in the Church at large, God proves again His faithfulness toward those wno will trust Him wholly and His promise to make His own to be fishers of men.

The secret of Robert G. Lee's success in his service for Christ is in the simplicity of his faith, the will to do God's will, and the steadfastness of his purpose. First of all, he has believed God. No matter how unpromising the beginning, no matter how difficult the tasks, no matter how great the obstacles, Lee has known of a surety that God can and will remove mountains—literal mountains if that be the need— and so he has gone forward. Second, he has not allowed anything to divert him from the call which he has been convinced, since the early days of his salvation, is his from God. There have been temptations to follow other paths, and at times the financial need was great, but he has never wavered from the unquenchable aspiration to be a preacher of the Gospel of the Lord Jesus Christ, because God chose him for that high office. And third, he has worked hard all along the way, not satisfied with mediocrity, never lazy but always striving to employ to perfection the gifts that God has given him. He has sought, with the Spirit's enablement, to be like the Christ whom he magnifies so gloriously in his speech. It has been his desire to live out the life that is in him as a believer, the very life of Christ, and this is the reason for his helpfulness in shepherding the flock. He has often been heard to declare: "I don't want it known of me on earth or recorded of me in Heaven, that I ever darkened a road, or made heavier a load for anybody, or got pleasure out of another's pain."

What God has done for and through Robert G. Lee He will do for and through others who are willing to pay the price. The history of Christianity is filled with those who have considered it life's greatest privilege so to do—the Apostle Paul, Chrysostom, and in later centuries, Luther, Knox, Calvin, Finney, Spurgeon, Moody, Sunday, Talmadge, Carroll, Torrey, Truett, Gaebelein, Ironside, Fuller, Lee, Appelman, and others yet to come, until the Lord Himself returns.

We trust that Dr. Lee will be spared on earth for many years. His ministry has been a full one; it can be even fuller in time. Multitudes are in darkness who may be turned to the light by hearing the Gospel of Christ poured forth from the lips of this powerful preacher. Throngs of God's people may yet be awakened to their full responsibilities as Christians and inspired toward a higher walk through the fervid exhortations of this servant of the Lord. Hosts may still be comforted by his acts of compassion and kindness. It is all in God's hands, who never makes a mistake.

This is the end of a book, but not the end of a life. Nor will the end of that life, when it comes, terminate its influence; for Robert G. Lee has held high the light of the Gospel of Christ for all to see, and his ministry will live after him. But before we bid adieu to this chosen vessel of the Lord, this Mr. Great-grace, champion of the King and friend to pilgrims, we pause to let one who knows him better than anyone else on earth, saving Mrs. Lee—

Bula G. Lee King, the apple of her father's eye—walk a moment in memory lane and pay tribute to her "Daddy":

Despite the fact that I must have spent the greater part of my childhood in the pew, my father has left almost no impression, on the younger years of my life, as a "preacher." He was simply my daddy. Even on the spring day at the age of nine when I walked down the aisle to make a public profession of my faith in Christ, the man who met me there below the pulpit was not "pastor" or "preacher" to me—just "Daddy." I do have a vague image of his slender strength in the pulpits of the various churches he pastored; but my child's mind tucked away no particular word or typical mannerism.

The first memory I have of my father—my own memory, not one of those oft-repeated, fond tales that seem to become memory—is that of him standing in mud! This mud lay in thickly-rutted red masses in the road that ran between our home and the church in Edgefield, South Carolina; and my daddy, with his white shirt sleeves pushed high, was ankle-deep in it putting double handfuls of the slimy stuff up on the sidewalk for my mud pies on a plank. Incidents like this, small but colorful, are the ones that enriched the young years of my life.

Just as he was generous with the mud so has he been with gifts, financial and otherwise, to me all my days. He did not have a lot of time to give, for truly he kept about his Father's business. But when there was time for relaxing my mother and I were always included. I remember well the stories he told while I propped myself in the crook of his crossed leg. My favorites were those of the little chicken who wouldn't stay beneath the cabbage leaf and of the lighthouse-keeper's daughter who kept the light burning all through the night of storm (with tallow made from ham fat!). He's telling those and additional ones to his grandchildren now.

When there was time for a trip he made it count. I remember Kentucky wheat in its golden beauty because once on the way to Chicago by car we stopped to ride a threshing machine. I remember, too, waiting hours in that fair city to see the Graf Zeppelin. They say I was only three when he carried me up the eight hundred and ninety steps of the Washington Monument. The many steps didn't compare (to me) with the minuteness of the people and cars that I saw way below when he held me out the window at the top of the monument.

He was generous with other things than money, too. I don't know how old I was when once I pertly refused to do his bidding. But I do know that I never refused again, and he claims it was the last physical punishment he had to give me. He was dressing at the time he made the request or gave the command, and was in the act of fastening a stiff collar to his shirt. The collar didn't cause me half the pain that the ordinary switching would have, but the clatter and confusion it made, wrapping itself around and around my legs, is a lesson I'll never forget. Then, too, the day my new bicycle arrived is a memorable one. It was on that day that he caught me in a lie. So the decree was that my new bike, all shiny new and red, should sit untouched and unridden in the front hall for three solid weeks. It did, too; there was no reprieve. And I'm sure he enjoyed asking my friends in to see it and in hearing my explanation of why it couldn't be ridden.

He was generous, he was firm; but he was not a "handy man around the house." He could chop wood for the fire, but I never knew him to fix an electric cord or to stop a leak. To have the Christmas tree sit evenly on its base Mother had to drive a nail. To me he had a lot of style about his clothes and seemed to keep them quite neatly. But about his books he was quite different. They have always seemed the greatest hodgepodge to me, although he knew his way around among them perfectly. He had an uncanny memory for the pages and lines of the quotations he wanted; and many a time he has telephoned from his office for a clipping to be found like this: "Third down from the top of the second pile of the seventh pigeonhole."

As a preacher I find my father a little hard to evaluate because the very things that make him great to me are the same things that I at one time or another have thought to be his faults . . . his weaknesses. His lack of business acumen in this world of profit and loss is really just his *faith* in God's will revealed to him regardless of times and finances. His gullibility about the goodness of people as a whole and individuals, too, is another example of his *faith* in human nature. At times I have thought him "wordy." But when I accosted him with that thought he simply said: "My Lord is worthy of the best language I possess."

I have never known him to be ill at ease in any pulpit or before any audience. But he has always been very sensitive to the attitude of his congregation and the atmosphere created for his message. Hence his particularity about the music of a service. If ritual is not conducive to evangelism he does not want it.

One of my friends once told me that she thought that when my dad died my God would die, too. My God will not leave me with the death of a human being; but I do know that when Robert Greene Lee goes Home to God I and many others will lose an ever present light on the path to the throne of God.

The End

APPENDIX

Titles of Books by Robert Greene Lee

Bothersome Families, 1912
From Feet to Fathoms, 1926
Lord, I Believe, 1927
Beds of Pearls, 1930
Whirlwinds of God, 1932
A Greater Than Solomon, 1935
A Grand Canyon of Resurrection Realities, 1935
One Plus God, 1936
Lee Lines, 1937
Pickings, 1938
The Blood of Jesus Christ, 1938
The Name Above Every Name, 1938
Glory Today for Conquest Tomorrow, 1941
This Critical Hour, 1942
Be Ye Also Ready, 1944
Buried and Alive, 1945
The Rose of Sharon, 1947
Bread from the Bellevue Oven, 1947
Pulpit Pleadings, 1948

Printed in the United States of America